Rethinking US-China Relations
Through Public Choice Theory

THE China DILEMMA

RYAN M. YONK
ETHAN YANG

AMERICAN INSTITUTE FOR ECONOMIC RESEARCH

The China Dilemma?

Rethinking US-China Relations Through Public Choice Theory

By Ryan M. Yonk and Ethan Yang

ISBN: 9781630694210

Design: Vanessa Mendozzi

Rethinking US-China Relations Through Public Choice Theory

THE China DILEMMA

RYAN M. YONK
ETHAN YANG

AIER | AMERICAN INSTITUTE for ECONOMIC RESEARCH

CONTENTS

1. Introduction: The US-China Dialogue

Every year, there seems to be a new book on China. The market for literature on the subject is crowded. Esteemed foreign policy authorities and acclaimed journalists have all weighed in. Given this, what can we add that will bolster the conversation and advance a better understanding of China and international relations? We answer: Despite all the high-quality examinations of China and the Chinese Communist Party (CCP), a public choice political-economy lens has not yet been clearly and concisely applied.

By assessing the rational incentives of individuals and groups, public choice theory explains political actions. In the case of China, we can apply public choice theory to analyze the decision-making of the CCP.[1] Public choice theory is therefore necessary for any comprehensive assessment of China's overall state of affairs.

The US-China Dialogue in a Nutshell

In late September 2021, in the aftermath of the US withdrawal from Afghanistan, Ethan (one of your authors) was attending a typical DC political reception. The speaker that night, a notable Republican Senator, provided an opportunity to illustrate the failure of the traditional (Washington DC) understanding of China and the CCP.

Our research for this book was dominating much of our thinking at the time. This led Ethan to inquire about the Senator's thoughts on the CCP. In particular, Ethan was interested in how the Senator thought the US

[1] At the outset we should clarify that, when we reference the CCP, we are often referring to the actions of named or unnamed individuals and factions within the Party, not an ideological monolith.

should respond to China's controversial economic practices. The Senator's response, typical of tough-talking DC politicians, was "Western businesses and financiers are selling the Chinese Communist Party the rope it will use to hang the United States." According to the Senator, we need to be a lot tougher on China than the Trump administration had been.

The response typifies a particular understanding common in DC. Like many others, the Senator appears to subscribe to a hyper-romanticized conception of US-China relations: Good versus evil; Capitalism versus Communism; China, the would-be-world-conqueror versus the United States, defender-of-the-free-world. This understanding of China is worryingly simplistic. It neglects to recognize both sides as rational actors and it fails to identify the players and interests in modern China. It is therefore unlikely to result in policymaking that will prove successful.

Unfortunately, the senator's pejoratives towards China are close to those of the majority of the US political establishment. Hostility towards China is one of the very few points of bipartisan consensus, and confronting Beijing may be a just goal. However, there seems to be a bipartisan misunderstanding of the incentives driving Chinese policies. Politicians across party lines justify futile trade wars and employ abrasive rhetoric that not only misses the mark on the real issues at hand but may also aid the CCP.

A better framework for addressing China must go further than political posturing. International relations and national security studies typically employ theories that view states as singular actors. They thereby strongly emphasize foreign policy and downplay domestic considerations. While these theories do often view entire countries as rational actors in the strategic sense, they stop short of understanding the incentives faced by the individuals and groups leading those countries. International relations, therefore, may tell us that China is becoming increasingly aggressive on the world stage, especially in areas like the South China Sea, but international relations tells us little about what motivates political leaders to posture, and how domestic events in China play a role.

The Need to Understand the CCP and Chinese Political Economy

The rise of the PRC has drawn the enduring attention of academics, journalists, and pundits across America. Many books explore Beijing's plans to overtake the United States as a global superpower or the various excesses and flaws in the Chinese Communist Party's authoritarian system (Pillsbury, 2015). Countless popular press articles discuss contemporary developments, from human rights abuses in Xinjiang to the drastic expansion of financial regulation, and the Chinese press is no different in the depictions of the United States.

While this book will address these important topics, our primary focus will be applying public choice theory to Chinese leadership's behavior, whether it be individuals like Xi Jinping himself, or organizations like the Politburo, the central government, or regional offices. Public choice theory leverages economics in areas traditionally dominated by political science and sociology (Shughart II, 2023). It argues that political actors, much like individuals in the private sector, make self-interested decisions. Therefore, public choice explores the incentive structures that drive political decision-making. Whether these be constitutional frameworks, electoral pressures, or institutional power. Rather than simply pointing out that China is becoming increasingly authoritarian and aggressive, we explain the factors driving the CCP's priorities.

Accordingly, our perspective on Chinese political behavior frames the CCP's policies through the lens of public and rational choice, not culture, ideology, or grand strategy. It is one thing to hold an encyclopedic knowledge of Chinese domestic and foreign policies, and it is something altogether different to understand the party's decision-making calculus at the level of individual policymaker. A public choice analysis addresses the misunderstandings in the current US-China dialogue.

Our public choice approach focuses on why stakeholders in the CCP view authoritarianism at home, and aggression abroad, as important for its interests. Perhaps China's leaders want to stir up nationalism in the face of growing geopolitical rivalry and slowing economic growth. Perhaps internal politics within the CCP have forced decision-makers to take a tougher stance against the West.[2] Could it be that the leaders in the CCP believe the regional balance of power has sufficiently shifted to where countries will reconsider resisting China's expansion? Our analysis leverages the observations made in international relations, and in general China-watching, to paint a picture of why Beijing acts the way it does.

Many China-focused book authors describe Chinese behavior from a strategic standpoint. They often lay out the CCP's "secret plan to overtake America" and describe its various policies and doctrines in great detail (Pillsbury, 2015). There is some value to these works. Many of the CCP's writings, statements, and behavior appear to support such an interpretation. Chinese officials do feel China is entitled to be the dominant country in global affairs. At one point in history, it was. Not surprisingly, therefore, the rulers of China have historically considered themselves to be the center of the world, "The Middle Kingdom" (Florek, 2020).

China-in-a-broad-sense has a proud past, dating back over 3,000 years. Its history is filled with invention, conquest, culture, and wealth. But excessive isolation and complacency eventually led the Qing dynasty, China's final imperial regime, to lose its once dominant status to the West and Japan. Ultimately it was itself to be dominated by those powers. In the 19th century, this stagnation led to humiliating military defeats and concessions to Western powers. This period, which the Chinese deem the Century of Humiliation, is why Beijing often speaks in narratives about restoring China's former glory and ensuring other countries don't "push China around" (Kaufman, 2011).

Although this story may inform outside observers about China's grand vision, it doesn't provide much in terms of explaining individual policies. This shortcoming emerged during a debate organized by the Center for Strategic and International Studies on China's foreign policy (Glaser, 2020). On one side, Hal Brands, a notable international relations professor at John Hopkins, laid out many of Beijing's ongoing strategies, which included establishing military dominance in Asia and broadcasting soft power. He suggested that this was part of China's grand strategy and argued that the US and China had entered a cold war. His opponent, Melvyn Leffler, a history

[2] Something like that happened during the tenure of the hardline Communist faction in the Hu Jintao regime (Blumenthal, 2020).

professor at the University of Virginia, pointed out that China's actions were not necessarily a nefarious cold war strategy. Instead, Beijing's policies were merely the rational objectives for a state in China's position. Beijing is primarily concerned with Western powers interfering in its hemisphere, much like how the US was concerned with the Europeans in North and South America during the early 19th century, resulting in the Monroe Doctrine (Office of the Historian, 2023).

Leffler noted that shoring up a sphere of influence and expanding outward is what the US did during its early history. Establishing a regional sphere of influence is what all aspiring global powers seek to do. China's behavior accomplishes core national security goals: It secures historic territory and claims and protects vital strategic points.

If Beijing views military expansion as in its interest, it will only continue to expand. The perception of such interests is affected by both international reception and internal factors, such as changes in executive leadership, shifts in political economy, and swings in popular sentiment.

In many respects, public choice is the most appropriate approach to explain Chinese political behavior. It provides greater insight than either those who view China as a single strategic actor or those who attempt to use a purely cultural lens to explain their actions. It is overly simplistic to say that the reason the CCP runs China in a highly regulated, authoritarian manner is because the Chinese culture is inherently collectivist. For example, some have wrongly argued that China's Confucian culture of order and peace and the tradition of Chinese Legalism guides the CCP's decision-making (Šimalčík, 2016) (Lin, 2017). Confucianism and the Legalist tradition may partially explain behavior on the margins, but this analysis fails to explain much of the CCP's behavior. Chinese militarism towards Taiwan, Xinjiang, Tibet, and the South China Sea is clearly at odds with the peaceful tenets of Confucianism and the rules-based order of Legalism. Instead, expansionism fulfills key goals pertaining to regional strategic dominance and territorial integrity. Thus, the rational actor model of public choice, not culture, better explains the CCP's behavior.

It is also not uncommon to hear defenders of the Chinese political model pose cultural and civilizational arguments that have an unproductive orientalist ethos and suggest that the basic assumptions of political economy don't apply to China (Magnarella, 2004). One does not need to look further than the successful liberal democratic reforms in Taiwan, South Korea, and Japan to see that nothing forbids East-Asian civilizations from creating free and democratic societies. Even more, China's market and social liberalization measures in 1978 support the idea that Chinese culture is compatible with markets and freedom.

The reason why the CCP limited its liberal capitalist reforms is not because Chinese culture or civilization development is incompatible with liberalism. It is because the Chinese leadership understood that market and social freedom, if such freedom was so limited as to still preserve the party's power, could facilitate much-needed economic growth and therefore be beneficial to the CCP. As a result, the country broke out of its self-imposed stagnation and impoverishment to become what it is today. The logic of economics and rational self-interest applies to Chinese governance as much as it does to its American counterparts.

The Chinese state is the epitome of pragmatism and self-interested behavior. As a regime that embraces state capitalism, the CCP exerts control over almost every aspect of life with few institutional constraints. Rather, the key incentive structures guiding the CCP are the broader macro-issues arising in Chinese society, such as income inequality, social unrest, migration, and environmental degradation. Internal party actions and politics also play a large role in influencing decision-making in the absence of other limiting institutions, like an independent court system or a privatized economy (Li, 2012).

An example of this reality comes from the decision of the Chinese government to invest so much in solar panels and other green energy initiatives (Bloomberg News, 2022). No, the CCP is not run by especially environmentally-minded communists. China invests in green energy because its leaders understand that the country has a substantial pollution problem and because doing so positions Beijing as an influential player in the clean energy market (Chiu, 2017). Likewise, the adamancy with which Xi Jinping implemented and continued the Zero Covid Policy of aggressive lockdowns, even as the rest of the world moved away from such policies, illustrates this focus on the interests of the regime. Asserting Xi is a devout authoritarian, or has a certain view about Covid policy, feels good, but is ultimately an unsatisfying explanation.

A better explanation would note Xi had a reappointment to secure in the latter part of 2022. Were he to admit failure, it would stimy his push for an unprecedented third term. By implementing and continuing lockdowns, Xi could both demonstrate his focus on a pressing issue, and assert greater daily control over society (Cunningham, 2022).

It might also be tempting for casual observers to overly rely on political ideology to analyze the CCP's behavior. Although doctrine sets the framework of policy making, political actors still make rational decisions within those boundaries. The CCP has several political factions that can potentially pull the party in a more liberal or authoritarian direction. Public officials do not operate on rails. China's Leninist system gives its leaders vast discretion to be pragmatic. For example, some would say that China's aggressive antitrust policies targeting its domestic technology companies is an economic blunder inherent to Socialist ideology (Yang, 2021). However, the Chinese have long proven themselves capable of understanding sound economics. The best answer for why China would crack down on their tech champions at the expense of billions of dollars of economic activity is political control and long-term stability.

Among the greatest political obstacles to exercising power in China is not its institutions, which are relatively weak compared to liberal democracies, but the party's internal politics and, by extension, public sentiment.

Many of the authoritarian practices under Xi Jinping began under his predecessor Hu Jintao (Blumenthal, 2020). Hu faced considerable political opposition from the hardline Communists in the party, which likely forced him to roll back many of the liberalization measures of his predecessors. Dan Blumenthal from the American Enterprise Institute explains that "Hu buckled under intense pressure from ideological opponents of "reform and opening" and rolled back key economic and legal reforms (Blumenthal, 2020). Thus, accounting for structural obstacles and assets to power within the party is essential for understanding how political actors pursue their interests.

The current political atmosphere of the CCP affects the decision-making calculus of Chinese leaders just as much as their core objectives. Unlike his predecessor, Xi is widely regarded as the most powerful Chinese leaders since Mao. This allows Xi to set policy largely unchallenged. He is so influential that there are school courses on "Xi Jinping Thought" and even a legal doctrine known as "Xi Jinping Thought on the Rule of Law" (BBC, 2021). His signature Belt and Road Initiative was added to the Chinese constitution in

2017 (Xinhua, 2017). His political capital is indeed so significant that the CCP has removed its presidential term limits, allowing him the possibility of serving for life (BBC, 2018). The drastic consolidation of power under a self-described Mao-like figure also suggests that the CCP feels that mounting internal problems may require drastic action. Although Xi will still need to deal with China's macro-political problems, such as balancing economic growth with social control, his decision-making follows a different incentive structure than his predecessor.

At the same time, a public choice analysis informs us that the consequences of Xi's unilateral policymaking will influence his decision-making. Dexter Roberts (2021), a Senior Fellow at the Atlantic Council, notes, "There is no doubt that powerful political families have been upset to see their wealth diminished by Xi's sweeping crackdown on corruption. Party cadres and intellectuals are unhappy with Xi's unprecedented power grab and decision to discard the rule-by-consensus norm." Xi has shown himself perfectly willing to purge his political opponents, which he accomplished through an aggressive anti-corruption campaign (BBC, 2017). Political resentment in the future may incentivize him to remain in power as long as possible to avoid potential persecution once other leadership replaces him. Concerns like these may lead to further purges of high-profile leaders with potentially destabilizing effects on Chinese society (Pai, 2022). These are the necessary calculations that Chinese leaders must make on top of their existing goals to balance economic growth and social stability.

We believe that viewing Chinese political behavior through the lens of public choice can significantly augment the ongoing discussion of US-China relations and Chinese domestic affairs. Public choice understands that the CCP is a rational state entity composed of individuals who respond to incentives. Using this framework of analysis, better understand the CCP's past, present, and to an extent, future behavior. Moreover, we assume that China is not immune or exempt from the basic lessons of economics or political science within the public choice framework. Many of the ongoing political-economic challenges arising in China are best understood by applying that framework to make predictions on where current policy initiatives will take the country, and how external forces may affect internal affairs.

A public choice analysis is politically neutral; it merely seeks to understand and predict the actions of political actors within the system that they operate. Introducing the logic of economics into a space dominated by political science and sociology is an important addition to the discussion. We believe that our observations can be used to make a wide variety of observations on China and US-China relations. Our main priority with this book is not to necessarily promote one agenda over the other but to set the table for a more sober and complete conversation regarding China.

Unproductive Ways to Approach China

The issue of China is one that is easily dramatized and politicized. Although sobriety and level-headed analysis is important in any policy discussion, it is perhaps most needed when approaching US-China relations. That isn't just because there are nuclear weapons involved, the fate of entire countries on the line, existential questions about human rights, and trillions of dollars' worth of economic activity. A nuanced and measured approach is essential because great power rivalries are precisely the types of problems that become exacerbated by overly simplistic perspectives and self-serving narratives.

To make productive and effective policy, understanding China and the CCP is essential. Oftentimes an analysis of China stops at merely listing Beijing's excesses and devious schemes. There is no denying that the CCP actively erodes human rights, that their mixed economy maintains several critical structural fault lines, and that they have a clear goal of changing the balance of power in the world. An entire book on the damage Beijing has wrought on civil liberties, whether it be the jailing of Nobel prize winners or the destruction of Hong Kong's democratic norms could and have been written (BBC, 2017). China's political-economic shortcomings due to its state-capitalist model and Maoist past are worthy of yet other volumes of work. Furthermore, there are countless national security threats posed by the modernization of the People's Liberation Army (PLA) and Beijing's massive economic footprint, both of which are part of a larger tool kit of coercive instruments (Tanner, 2007, p. 135). The narrative of a threatening China riddled with political-economic concerns is one that is quite common in the national security and human rights community. Although all of these problems are real, they are not the full picture.

On the other hand, the benefits of doing business with China are substantial, if not unavoidable (Ramli, 2021). Nobody can deny that US-China trade and engagement have produced countless benefits, and not just between the two countries but for the betterment of humanity overall. Annual US trade with China exceeds 600 billion dollars; collaboration and competition have increased innovation and efficiency on both sides (US Trade Representative, 2023). Academic and cultural exchanges have undoubtedly benefitted both sides while making the world a more vibrant place. China's rapid economic growth and poverty alleviation have introduced the productive energy of hundreds of millions of people to the world. Furthermore, openness and trade have contributed to the proliferation of positive norms such as individualism, aspiration, and business ethics in Chinese society (Zou & Cai, 2016). This romantic depiction is often espoused by the American business community and other members of the private sector that interact with China on a personal level. Again, these are all important realities of the US-China story, but when viewed in isolation, neglect important security geopolitical concerns.

It can be very tempting to get caught up in any one of these approaches. It is understandable that someone who is passionate about human rights will likely only see the morally outrageous violations occurring in China, and nothing else. Someone who focuses on national security may only appreciate the grand scheme of great power politics and perhaps brush over the benefits of engagement. A person concerned with free trade and economic prosperity may see the relevance of geopolitical rivalries as trivial compared to the tangible benefits of interdependence. The positive incentives created by markets to trade rather than fight, conduct commerce rather than conquest is also a core facet of Capitalist Peace Theory. That is not to say that one concern should take clear priority over the other. In fact, viewing these issues together produces not only a more complete representation of the China issue but perhaps an insight into how the CCP functions.

Beyond these polar opposites within the international relations world a competing narrative focuses on cultural-ideological explanations. Like the other explanations we've reviewed it to is an incomplete approach to understanding China. This approach views the CCP's decision-making strictly through the lens of Marxism, Confucianism, or a sort of orientalist-intersectional lens. The Marxist lens would apply the scholarly underpinnings of Marxism-Leninism to understanding China. Understanding the ideas of Marx, Lenin, and Mao is certainly important as they explain some of the CCP's behavior. For example, The Chinese People's Political Consultative

Conference is a classic Leninist organ that allows a deeper penetration of the CCP into private society (CPPCC, 2021). The conference allows leaders from the private sector to have some input into government policy and therefore allows the central party to maintain a larger presence in influencing civil society. Despite this focus much of what China does flies in the face of traditional Marxist thought. Marx envisioned an international worker's commune. The CCP is highly nationalist and Sino-centric.

Mao envisioned a society in constant revolution, which contributed to the horrors of the Cultural Revolution, a society-wide political cleansing campaign that killed millions. China today is not a society in constant revolution as the CCP is highly paranoid about any sort of change by mass mobilization (Schram, 1971, 221). Of course, it is also worth pointing out that Mao's Cultural Revolution, although congruent with his espoused ideology, also conveniently aligned with his basic power-maximizing interests. Mao launched the great multiyear purge following his disastrous Great Leap Forward, an ambitious Socialist economic reform campaign that saw tens of millions starve over the course of four years (Brown, 2012) (History, 2020). The damage of the Great Leap Forward to not only Mao's reputation but the legitimacy of the CCP undoubtedly necessitated a massive scapegoating campaign and reconsolidation of power. Mao framed the Cultural Revolution through the lens of ideology and stressed the need for society to constantly undergo a revolution in order to progress. Although this may have rationalized the chaos and violence that followed, it is also easily argued that Mao needed the revolution to stay in power.

The Cultural Revolution, although initially framed in an ideological lens, can be understood through a public choice lens in that it was instrumental in reclaiming power after the disaster of the Great Leap Forward. That is, although Mao's ideological framework certainly played a key role in stoking the Cultural Revolution, the pertinent political considerations of his day likely played a causal role in driving his actions.

Culture and Colonialism

If the ancient Chinese philosopher Confucius were alive today, he would hardly recognize the ideology of the CCP. Part of this stems from the fact that the CCP deliberately villainized Confucianism, especially during the Cultural Revolution, due to its association with the dynastic period (The Economist,

2021). Many aspects of Confucianism play an important cultural role not just in China but across East Asia (Csikszentmihalyi, 2020). Some key components of this philosophy included a commitment to family, country, honor, and hierarchy which are all important tenets of Chinese society to varying degrees. However, much like how elements of Christianity can only explain so much of American political behavior, the same goes for the ideas of Confucius. Some may try to link the success of China's authoritarian system as a byproduct of Confucian culture, however, the success of liberal democratic Confucian influenced societies such as Japan, South Korea, and Taiwan undermine this assertion. Culture and Confucianism have little to do with the CCP's highly pragmatic behavior on the world stage, blending economic cooperation with aggressive unilateral pressure and violations of international norms?

Adjacent to the cultural argument is the post-colonial-critical theory style of analysis. Viewing Chinese behavior through a postcolonial lens focuses on the role of imperialism and its political-economic legacy. It tells a story of oppressed societies attempting to make their way in a world where the very assumptions and expectations of what makes a good society are already defined by dominant powers, such as the West. Such a framework may explain why China blatantly violates international norms regarding human rights, economic policy, and governance. A post-colonial theorist might say that China continually threatens to invade Taiwan, makes impositions in the South China Sea, and oppresses its own people because the imperialist West imposed the status quo (Chih, 1998, p.125). China feels insecure about being subverted, whether it be by Western conceptions of universal norms, borders, or economic rules. Therefore, the CCP represents a historically exploited society clashing with boundaries drawn by its oppressors and its stubbornness can be understood through historical anxiety against future impositions.

Again, this perspective certainly offers some important insights but fails to fully capture the causal factors at play. For example, Chinese foreign policy often invokes the Century of Humiliation as a core reason for its goals. During this period, one imperial power after another invaded and ravaged China, taking territory, treasure, and lives. As a result, the CCP claims that it is reclaiming what is rightfully theirs and that it is extremely sensitive to the possibility of future imperialist aggression. However, basic international relations theory and public choice economics explain Beijing's behavior with more consistency. Although one should not discount the cultural importance of the post-colonial narrative, China's behavior on the world stage is better understood by public choice theory and realist international relations theory.

The CCP's aggressive disposition towards Taiwan, border conflicts with India, expansion in the South China Sea, and so on are all basic strategic necessities and domestic mandates. It is very likely China would have acted exactly the same regardless of its history because of the nature of great power behavior. Taiwan represents a critical strategic point in East Asia and no country wants to lose territory to other nations. Furthermore, the CCP's own credibility lies in maintaining and expanding its geopolitical position, protecting China's integrity from outside powers, and keeping the nation together. Although elements of post-colonial anxiety exist, Beijing's behavior represents the classic priorities of a rational, power-maximizing entity.

Another possible perspective to view Chinese political behavior is the moral economy school of thought popularized by E.P. Thompson's (1971) "The Moral Economy of the English Crowd in the Eighteenth Century" (Moreno-Tejada, 2020). His general thesis contended that peasants are inherently skeptical of capitalism and favor institutions that promote the common good, whatever that may mean. Scott (1977) applied this theory to the behavior of Vietnamese peasants leading up to the Communist revolution against the then French colonial government in his book *The Moral Economy of the Peasant*. Samuel Popkin (1979) famously wrote a critique of Scott's work in his work, *The Rational Peasant*, which argued that Vietnamese peasants are as rational and self-interested as any other member of society. Rather than engaging in moral behavior and aligning with groups like the Communists out of an inherent affinity, the Vietnamese peasants were simply making the most out of the situation within the societal constraints at the time. In their case, the Communists provided effective institutions for social organization and provided the best opportunity to ameliorate their living conditions.

In the context of China, a moral economy perspective might suggest that the CCP's behavior is based on an inherent resiliency against ideas such as Neoliberalism and imperialism (Popkin, 1979). Although there may be a certain aversion against these ideas due to the Marxist-Leninist ideology of the CCP, being a member of the Global South does not seem to provide an adequate explanation of Chinese political behavior. Although China's economic and geopolitical position may provide certain incentives and constraints on its behavior, that is about as much explanatory power one can derive. Chinese elites ultimately demonstrate rational, self-interested behavior within their institutional boundaries much like the peasants studied in Popkin's research. Some strong examples of such behavior domestically include Deng Xiaoping's reform and opening policies and contemporary Chinese antitrust policies.

Deng's reform policies not only broke from the standard Communist model by liberalizing the economy, but they were also highly self-serving. In an interview explaining his book *The Cultural Revolution: A People's History*, University of Hong Kong Professor Frank Dikotter (2016) explains that pro-market activity actually began prior to Deng's reform policies. According to recently declassified information, Chinese peasants began engaging in market-style activities after the Great Leap Forward, and the Cultural Revolution greatly undermined the CCP's authority and power. As a result, Deng's reform policies were not necessarily just a good policy to bolster the strength of the Chinese nation but also a reading of the political tea leaves and a necessary step to preserve the long-term rule of the Party. The recent retractions in economic freedom and the cautious nature of the CCP's approach to markets is also an indicator of the Party's anxiety to relinquish control rather than a moral aversion to markets. That is why Xi Jinping has often made contradictory statements regarding the importance of private-sector dynamism while also calling for greater allegiance to the party line (Zhou, 2021).

Antimonopoly policies under Xi are another telling indicator of the CCP's pragmatic, self-interested behavior. Until the summer of 2021, Chinese antitrust regulation had been relatively dormant, allowing for the birth of large megacorporations like Alibaba that served as economic ship-of-the-lines. However, this dramatically changed following criticism by Alibaba's CEO Jack Ma about the state banking system; other private companies were labeled with a number of other political concerns such as contributing to China's declining birth rate (Yang, 2021; Zhou, 2021). Suddenly, Chinese regulators sprung to life, issuing hefty fines, and targeting companies in a manner that made little economic sense, but satisfied political goals. In particular, the US Chamber of Commerce (2022) points out that Chinese antitrust policy doesn't conform itself to a single goal such as maximizing consumer welfare or promoting competition, but a plethora of state objectives such as industrial policy. This development looks little like an intrinsic moral aversion to markets but more the work of self-interested, power-maximizing individuals within the context of a Leninist system and a great power competition with the US.

Viewing the CCP's behavior through the lens of Leninism is a good start in the sense that the Chinese political system is based on this framework. Lenin's idea of a pragmatic, single-party state that acted as the vanguard of the revolution seems to be the best fit. However, it is clear the CCP is setting its own terms, much like American politicians act within our republican system. Reading Marxist-Leninist texts can only get you so far in understanding Chinese political behavior. Again, the real indicators lie in the salient political-economic issues in society, whether that be maintaining economic growth or national cohesion, and the institutional boundaries with which political actors must conform. Here again we return to public choice theory. Chinese political leaders make rational, self-interested decisions within the context of their own institutions, much like leaders in every system. That system is a pragmatic Chinese Leninist system that, much like our own American constitutional republic or any other form of government, sets the terms of engagement for free-thinking, power-maximizing individuals.

A better way to understand and respond to the behavior of the CCP can be enabled by taking a more analytical approach to understanding China. Such a framework should look past the narratives surrounding Chinese objectives and behavior. Sometimes all this requires is a more thorough reading of history, as in the case of Taiwan and the general sanctity of the Chinese nation.

Although the CCP would say that places like Taiwan are inseparable components of China, such an assertion is a recent nationalist ideal, proposed during the 20th century (van der Wees, 2020). The island of Taiwan has a complicated history. It changed hands numerous times between various imperial powers from the Japanese to the Dutch. In fact, the Kangxi Emperor, widely regarded as one of the most famous rulers of China, once remarked "Taiwan is outside our empire and of no great consequence" and even offered to have the Dutch buy it back (Hearn & Zelin, 2022). Going deeper, holding Taiwan certainly has a nationalist and emotional appeal, but there are also existential political reasons for the CCP to prioritize discussion of the recapture of Taiwan. The first is a geostrategic reason. The island represents a vital location for maintaining control of the Asia Pacific region. Much like the provinces Xinjiang and Tibet (both with radically different cultures and history to Han China), Taiwan is a key location to launch an invasion on China, or for Beijing to antagonize other countries (Yang, 2021). Second, Taiwan represents an important promise the CCP has made to its people since its inception. A failure to demonstrate a desire to, or to actually attempt and fail to accomplish this goal, will not only be a massive humiliation but will undermine the very legitimacy of the CCP in the eyes of the Chinese public.

By framing Chinese political behavior in this analytical public choice framework, one can not only get a clearer understanding of the CCP but also observe the core incentives at play. The disappearance of Alibaba CEO and Chinese billionaire Jack Ma in the Fall of 2020 is another example (Yang, 2021). Beijing's regulators abruptly stopped the much-anticipated IPO of Ant Group, a Chinese fintech company, sending shockwaves through the global financial sector. Jack Ma was called before CCP officials and disappeared soon after. Ant Group is then forced to restructure and Beijing proceeds to unleash a regulatory storm on its top companies like Didi, Tencent, and Baidu (Asia Society, 2021). Then, China's once-quiet antitrust apparatus makes global headlines by drastically increasing enforcement. All this occurred following Ma's well-founded criticism of the Chinese financial regulatory system.

A superficial analysis might suggest that all this is occurring because China is still a Communist country, that they love central planning, and the CCP enjoys exercising power, much like any dictatorship. Although these factors all play a part in the larger picture, a public choice analysis reveals the rational objectives of CCP and its elite leadership. Since 1978, the Chinese have been more than willing to accept free-market reforms, and the results speak for themselves. They clearly understand and accept the principles of economics. However, they also understand political realities, such as the danger of having powerful private companies in a Leninist, one-party state. Jack Ma was the equivalent of Elon Musk; he was popular amongst the masses and seemingly untouchable. Ma's status allowed him to make controversial statements about the CCP in a way that was interpreted as a threat to the long-term stability of the CCP's rule. Similarly Chinese mega-companies represent a comparable perceived threat to the long-term stability of the party.

Greg Ip (2021) of *The Wall Street Journal* comments on the sudden surge in antitrust action by explaining,

> What they do not want them becoming is large enough and independent enough that they become, in some sense, a separate power center that actually threatens the Communist Party's own management of the economy. And they also don't want some of the negative collateral damage that those companies are seen to create.

The CCP's sudden and aggressive antitrust policies, although highly disruptive, correspond with key objectives and align neatly with the party's power maximizing objectives. A debate held by CSIS (2021) on the economic ramifications of China's recent antitrust policies revealed that many segments of the economy remained undamaged. Although large national champions like Alibaba and certain sectors like private education received a devastating blow, investment in other areas remained strong. Of course, it is still to be seen whether such behavior will be sustainable in the long term. However, it is clear that Beijing made a calculated, precise, and rational decision based on clear priorities. It would be foolish to say that the CCP simply destroyed its own companies in an act motivated by brazen Socialist dogma or classic Communist economic miscalculation. In China's context, where certain well-connected super corporations achieve dominance in a relatively illiberal system, it actually might make sense to artificially level the playing field by targeting their largest companies. Regardless, it is clear that the CCP is operating in a highly rational and self-interested manner within the boundaries of its political-economic priorities.

2. Public Choice as a Frame

Public choice applies the logic of economics to areas traditionally reserved for political science. Public choice views the actions of state actors through the lens of rational choice and self-interest, much like one would view private entities (Shaw, 2002). Although James Buchannan won the Nobel Prize in 1986 for the development of public choice theory, the root idea is quite intuitive (Nobel Prize, 2022). Public actors behave in the same manner as any private actor would in the same context. Members of the CCP, much like their counterparts in the US political system, pursue self-interested, maximizing goals based on the incentives inherent to their system. For example, in 2019, Berne Sanders, the staunch antiwar, anti-corporatist senator from Vermont, brought the F-35 fighter jet program to his state, a clear example of the incentives he faced (CNBC, 2019).

This contradiction is classic public choice theory at work. Senator Sanders understood that the economic benefits of having the jets in Vermont, and the political support it brings, would far outweigh any sort of backlash, either from his antiwar constituents or from his own ideological conscience. Within the boundaries of being an antiwar advocate, Sanders made a rational decision that forwarded his interests, which included getting reelected. Having fighter jets made in Vermont would bring much-needed economic activity while only upsetting a small fraction of his voter base, and therefore it made sense to do so.

Public choice theory is often used to explain the behavior of bureaucrats who are not beholden to reelection while often possessing executive power and are therefore free to act more explicitly in their self-interest. Public sector unions are a good example of this dynamic in action. Unions exist primarily to increase the benefit of the workers they serve and will therefore place those concerns above others all things being equal. One interesting example is the resistance of police unions to policing reform during the Black Lives Matter protests and riots of 2020 (Barron-Lopez, 2019). Despite an apparent public interest in seeing greater discipline and systematic reform the concerns of the police unions and the officers they served to preserve the status quo while also protecting their members as much as possible were actively argued for. Expecting the unions or the police to act any differently as rational, self-interested individuals was at best wishful thinking. This is a classic public choice style problem highlighting the disconnect between what can be perceived as the public's desires and the self-interested goals of the people operating in the public sector.

At the root of public choice analysis is an understanding of the institutional incentives at play. For example, why does the Department of Motor Vehicles tend to be slow, unresponsive, and unenthusiastic towards customers? A large part of the reason comes from the lack of competition and the mandatory use of the agency's services. There is little incentive to provide better service because you are required to use their service if you want authorization to drive. Although DMV workers are "public servants," they act just as any other person would if they were in such an environment. There is little incentive to care about customer experience and little motivation to improve because no competition exists, and the risks of replacement are low.

Public choice informs us that public officials make rational, self-interested decisions within their respective institutional frameworks. This might explain why the United States, as a liberal democracy, has to make policy subject to popular sentiment. President Trump's sudden trade war with China and Franklin Roosevelt entering World War II later than he would have liked are two examples (Leuchtenburg, 2022). Trump understood that segments of the American population feel left behind as certain manufacturing jobs are outsourced or automated. Roosevelt had to contend with a standing policy of neutrality and a strong isolationist camp in American politics (Leuchtenburg, 2022). Perhaps, due to its autocratic system, Beijing can make decisions that may not make sense to the average citizen but advance the long-term interests of the central government. The CCP's willingness to work with the Taliban and Xi's highly ambitious global trade project, the Belt and Road Initiative, are clear examples, both of which have been altered as the needs of the party changed (Johnson, 2021). At the same time, a public choice approach explains not only why the CCP can sustain these policies but needs to enact these policies.

Working with the Taliban may be a political necessity because Beijing has a vested interest in maintaining stability in Afghanistan, which borders the province of Xinjiang, and needs their cooperation to ensure that outcome (Yang, 2021). Furthermore, China is vying for international influence and has framed itself as the champion of the developing world and although China may have a shared empathy for other developing countries, this image is a political necessity. Further it is clear that the CCP is fighting an uphill battle to become a dominant global power, and it needs every friend it can find, and acts to attract those who want to cultivate economic ties. Many developed countries are liberal democracies skeptical of China's authoritarian system and aligned with the US. As a result, developing countries are the easiest for China to influence and are more inclined to appease.

Beijing has cultivated these relationships with substantial development loans and infrastructure investments, all designed to tie recipients closer to China (AidData, 2023). The United States, due to its political model, engages in different, but still deliberate, strategies that focus more on private investment, open markets, and cultural exchange. Despite this, the Chinese still promote some level of cultural exchange, and the US extends billions in foreign aid. These priorities are also why the United States prefers an international order that encourages freedom of movement, trade, and human rights. The Chinese, on the other hand, have stated a desire for a world that is inclusive of all forms of government and only focuses on areas that benefit Chinese interests (Ministry of Foreign Affairs (China), 2015). Little analysis is necessary to understand that this global model is more inclusive of authoritarian governments. With this reality in mind, many of the CCP's foreign ambitions stem from domestic considerations for economic growth, rather than a concern for the state of the outside world.

This framework is essential to making sense of the Chinese political system and better predicting future behavior. The political incentive structure faced by the CCP is demonstrative. The party is a centralized, authoritarian, institution with few checks on its use of power. The Party itself is rooted in ideology and functions with a clear top-down structure

(US China Business Council, 2023). Its organization includes Xi Jinping at the top as General Secretary, then below him a council of 25 elites known as the Politburo. Of these 25 high-ranking officials, a fraction are selected to be members of the Standing Committee, which meets frequently to discuss the day-to-day policies and is the de facto rule making authority. According to the Chinese Constitution, members of the Politburo are elected by the lower rung of the Party, the Central Committee, which is composed of hundreds of delegates from across Chinese society (US-China Business Council). In practice, however, the selection process for the Politburo is in fact top down, with decisions likely being made by the members themselves and the general secretary rather than the electoral bodies.

At the lowest level of leadership is the National People's Congress. It functions as a rubber stamp parliament to the upper echelons of the organization and has thousands of delegates, including some, allegedly, from Taiwan and Hong Kong (Saich, 2015, 6). The vast majority of the laws voted on by them have already been vetted by various state agencies as well as the more elite decision-making bodies of the Party such as the Standing Committee, leaving them with little actual policy making authority and they instead ratify the decisions of those above them in the party hierarchy (Spegele, 2011).

Within the Chinese system the traditional notion of rule *of* law is virtually non-existent. The government exercises broad discretion over society in what the CCP calls instead "rule *by* law", albeit law unilaterally made by institutions fully controlled by the CCP itself. Even the court system itself is under the direct control of the CCP's party-state (Oud, 202). The court system typically adjudicates decisions in ways that could be described as using more traditional legal approaches when the stakes are low and, when the stakes are high and the state demands a certain outcome, acting unilaterally in favor of the state (Zhu, 2021). As a result, the formal institutional framework that influences the decision-making constraints of officials is a clear reflection of the CCP itself.

This is not to say that different systems will always produce radically different incentives. Promoting economic growth is generally one such example. In the US, the necessity of reelection and the local power state officials have over their respective jurisdictions promotes policy that is often focused on economic growth. Although China does not have democratic elections, they do have a party appointment system (Huang, 2017). Local leaders who wish to move up the chain of command and in the party to more prestigious postings are incentivized to perform well as managers of their communities, cities, and regions. As a result, there is tremendous policy innovation and competition amongst provinces despite a lack of a democratic feedback mechanism. In many ways, this resembles the meritocratic civil service system of imperial China, which was instrumental in making the bureaucracy so advanced for its time (Asia for Educators, 2022).

At the same time, an authoritarian system of this nature also has its unique drawbacks that can be readily seen. The handling and cover-up of the Covid-19 outbreak in Wuhan, China is a particularly clear, albeit not novel, example in the Chinese system (Yang, 2020). Hiding news of a virus outbreak and calling for transparency does not bode well in a system that punishes both. Bad news about the outbreaks containment and origin as well as calling for reforms to increase accountability both were areas where benefits of misbehavior in the form of concealment outweighed the benefits of reporting accurate information.

A public choice approach is not only useful for explaining past events, it is similarly useful for predicting likely future behavior. Explaining the CCP's recent tightening of economic and social controls after such freedoms allowed the country to prosper is an illustration of both. The first step is to identify what priorities CCP leaders have as rational, power maximizing individuals in a Leninist system. The short answer is, like in any system, staying in power. This analysis would then suggest that past and future actions of the CCP should be viewed through the lens not of what is good for China, but rather what will allow the CCP to maintain power.

The CCP maintains and indeed grows its power in two basic ways. By increasing control, and by providing benefits to citizens. The first is achieved by physically increasing its hold on society through increased surveillance, penetration into private life, bolstering the security state, and similar activities. Providing benefits designed to appeasing and satisfy its population are the second method and includes maintaining economic growth, delivering on promises to increase China's standing in the world, neutralizing possible threats to public safety, and similar activities.

Xi Jinping's rigid and personal leadership style marks a rapid and almost 180-degree departure from the "collective governance" fostered by his predecessor Hu Jintao (Palmer, 2020). In many ways, Xi seems to represent a logical answer to many of the problems associated with China's reform and opening since 1978. Although the economy has grown tremendously, along with the strength of the nation, the contradictions of the state-capitalist system are starting to emerge. Income inequality has skyrocketed in a country that purports to be Communist, and regularly criticizes the West for disparities of this sort. The private sector has become the main driver of economic growth, not the state, challenging notions of party control and necessity (Buchholz, 2021).

Trade and openness with the rest of the world has led some citizens to think about politically sensitive topics like human rights and democratic reform, neither of which necessarily reinforce CCP control. As the population grows richer, they start to care about things other than their next meal and begin to demand not just better living conditions, but increased freedoms and greater autonomy from the state. The result of these demands can be seen in the local protests that are now somewhat common in parts of China, in the Shanghai anti-lock down protests in 2022, and in the limited protests around the 2022 people's congress (Huludao, 2022; Hall, Horwitz, Pollard, 2022).

One clear explanation of why the CCP is tightening its grip over society that emerges from our public choice analysis is rooted in the potential loss of control from these and other potentially destabilizing factors. Indeed, in their book *Violence and Social Orders*, Douglas North, John Wallis, and Barry Weingast, suggest that modern Chinese politics resemble a governing model they term as a limited access society (2009, 253). In a limited access society, elites aim to construct political and financial institutions that limit competition and preserve power. Liberalization is only permitted to the extent it advances the interests of the elite, as in the event of economic collapse or political revolution.

These realities reveal existential flaws that have not been contained and will need to be resolved soon. It appears that in response, the CCP is willing to make short-term, necessary sacrifices to economic growth for stability of their rule.

There is a rationale and self-interested reason why these policies are being pursued. China's Leninist system forms the boundaries that CCP decision-makers work within. Pragmatic governance within these constraints, not pure ideology or culture, explains their actions. Vahabi provides a predictive framework that asserts that state actors will deploy power and resources in a way which strengthens the actors' power over assets or restricts the future mobility of assets (Vahabi 2016, 3). A clear proof of concept to his theory was the CCP's crackdown on Big Tech, which both strengthened its control over the economy while also bringing "misbehaving" private tech firms under its control.

Public choice can provide indications of what the CCP is likely to do in the future. The patriotic education program is particularly interesting because of its role in consolidating a common national identity (Zhao, 1998, 287). The Tiananmen Square protests in 1989, where millions of human rights protestors took to the streets nationwide, showed the CCP could not simply rely on Communist ideology to hold the country together. In response to these concerns, Beijing rolled out an official narrative of the Chinese national identity to bolster loyalty and cohesion amongst the population.

A state-controlled narrative of national identity is perhaps the only viable way for the CCP to stoke the flames of nationalism. Most of China's grand history is villainized by the CCP, so invoking the success of the imperial dynasties would create problematic contradictions. Because of these issues, the Chinese cannot easily rally around national heroes, long-standing institutions, or a royal family. The People's Republic of China is a country that has undergone continual change to both its political and economic system, despite attempts to prevent such change. Therefore, alterations to the official narrative surrounding modern China's history have similarly been necessary. As such, what it means to be a part of the Chinese nation is also undergoing constant revision. The efforts of current president Xi Jinping to actively rewrite Chinese history to fit the party's new narrative is one such process (Buckley, 2021). A major theme is the role the Party and Xi play in advancing the condition of China, while minimizing the role of past leaders that were seen to be less effective. All of this follows a clear, rational objective: Securing the long-term rule of the party, and Xi himself, through the means afforded by the constraints of a Leninist system.

Xi, however, can't run all of China and not everything that happens is completely his fault or success. Individuals at every level of government make rational, self-interested decisions based on the boundaries and incentives at hand. For example, Xi might have endorsed a repressive security state in the province of Xinjiang where over a million Uyghur Muslims are reportedly detained. However, the enthusiasm and vigor of China's repression is also due to how it rewards officials for coming up with ingenious methods of coercion. Chen Quanguo, who will be discussed in greater detail later, is but one example. His brutal policies in governing Tibet and Xinjiang would earn him a spot on the Politburo. However, his recent demotion might suggest that priorities are changing (Wang, 2022).

Public choice theory applies a similar level of analysis to diverse areas of Chinese political activity. A public choice perspective cuts past the narratives and superficial assumptions of merely relying on ideology and culture. The Chinese state is an attractive target for such analysis because of its highly centralized and pragmatic nature. Not only are CCP officials able to pursue their rational, power-maximizing objectives with few institutional constraints, but they are able to affect almost any aspect of Chinese society.

How Public Choice Can Aid Foreign Policy Discussions

American foreign policy is an area where robust public choice analysis of Chinese domestic affairs reaps tremendous benefits. We are not here to propose a radical new fusion of economics with international relations theory, necessarily. We are instead suggesting that understanding the incentives at play within a country can greatly aid in understanding how it acts on the world stage. There are two major strands of thought that apply to US-China relations, the realist, and the liberal school. Both these perspectives provide important insights and predictions regarding Chinese behavior. Public choice analysis shares some similarities with the realist school of thought in its approach, albeit with important deviations.

A key distinction between public choice and realism is that the former focuses on the incentives of the elites within a country whereas realism is focused on the country as a unitary actor. Realism views the world through the lens of state interests and pays less attention to the individuals and coalitions that run nations. A public choice perspective considers a nation's interest but goes further to inquire the motivations of the individuals making foreign policy decisions, be it internal politics, popular demands, or unique personal interests.

The realist tradition is one of the most influential schools of thought in the realm of international relations. Realism views the world through the lens of power dynamics and posits that all states act within their self-interest, a methodological assumption it shares with public choice (Korab-Karpowicz, 2017). Realism explains many of the conflicts associated with great power rivalries and the US-China relationship is no different. Although there is much intersection with public choice theory, realism refrains from analyzing the domestic factors pushing great power competition. One of the most infamous of the realist phenomena is the Thucydides Trap, the tendency for declining and rising powers to wage war with each other in an attempt to preserve or take power (Allison, 2017). In the US-China context, this refers to the rational and natural inclination for a rising state like China to challenge the regional status quo set by the perceived declining power, the US, and vice versa.

The typical story of the Thucydides trap would go as follows: As China grows stronger, it acquires the means to assert itself in areas like territorial sovereignty. The US begins to sense that it is losing control, and thus takes steps to reassert itself and contain the challenging power. This dynamic is likely exacerbated by China's starkly different set of values and priorities. These tendencies to assert and reassert power inevitably lead to conflict, such as the trade war, and, potentially in the future, a shooting war. This version of the China-US dynamic is attractive for its clear and clean nature, but public choice suggests that something more is likely going on at each step.

The most important critique public choice theory has for realists and their version of the foreseen future is the value of focusing on the internal dynamics of states, rather than just focusing on the balance of power. Realism often has a static, deterministic tone, which proves problematic for navigating great power politics. A public choice analysis asserts that the internal dynamics of a country play a large role in a state's outward behavior. Taiwan illustrates this idea well. The CCP has played an instrumental role in constructing a specific narrative about national integrity and sovereignty, and in this narrative Taiwan has certainly not been forgotten. Reunification with Taiwan is now viewed as an essential part of national identity and security, but this notion emerged wasn't regarded as very important during the last imperial dynasty (van der Wees, 2020). Taiwan's significance is a relatively recent idea spurred by the nationalist underpinnings of the post-dynastic period, which placed a heavy emphasis on China's humiliation at the hands of imperial powers (Ye, 2020).

Realism suggests that China will continually pursue Taiwan because it is an important geostrategic interest. However, a public choice perspective suggests that internal dynamics are important for understanding China's actions. For example, some have suggested that the CCP's authoritarian rule has actually played a moderating effect. That is because the CCP can exercise patience and nuance while suppressing rash, overly nationalistic segments of the population when it comes to foreign policy (Chen-Weiss, 2014). Perhaps if China was a democracy or if the CCP did not have as much control over its population, Chinese foreign policy may be far more aggressive and reckless. One could also take the opposite view, without the CCP's control over society, different ideas regarding China's place and priorities in the world may flourish and gain traction in the public discourse. Either way, it is clear that the institutional structure of the Chinese government and the political incentives at play hold considerable influence in potential policymaking.

This contrasts with the assertion, commonly put forward by the great realist international relations scholar John Mearsheimer, that internal politics have little effect on foreign policy (2005). According to those like Mearsheimer, the physics of state-to-state power relations are far too great for internal developments to have a substantial effect. Although there may be some truth to this argument, we do not believe that the evidence indicates that internal politics have no consequential effect on foreign policy, especially when it comes to China. The rise of Wolf Warrior Diplomacy, where Beijing's diplomats engage in highly assertive and abrasive confrontations, is a key extension of domestic politics and not a grand strategy (Martin, 2021).

Peter Martin, a Bloomberg defense reporter, explains to the National Bureau of Asian Research that the shift in Chinese diplomatic tactics stems primarily from internal affairs (Martin, 2021). The first factor is a rise in Chinese nationalism that demands greater deference from the rest of the world. Another factor is Beijing's unwillingness to apologize for its style of governance in the face of global criticism. Finally, there are political incentives, such as career mobility, for officials who aggressively advance China's interests and align with Xi Jinping's preference for assertiveness. Unsurprisingly, after the 20th Party Congress and with Xi's third term secured, Xi authorized a more friendly diplomatic stance as stoking tensions with other countries began to deteriorate the country's standing.

Although realism and public choice theory have much in common, realism is primarily focused on international relations and discounts the role of internal affairs. Internal politics is especially relevant today where diplomatic and economic influence plays more of a daily role than direct military or interstate confrontation. It is clear that many of Beijing's internal policies, such as investments in technology, neo-mercantilist initiatives like Dual Circulation, and drastic swings in economic regulation, affect the outside world. Self-interested observers in the West, it is tempting to think that the CCP makes decisions in an attempt to compete with the West; in reality, the main motivation is often to address internal issues and demands. More importantly for the foreign policy and security community, these internal developments tell a story about our substantial geopolitical rival. This story informs us about what Chinese elites are concerned about, what their priorities are, and how they seek to advance those priorities, all of which impacts the US-China dynamic.

Other Approaches from International Relations

Liberalism is another important strand of international relations theory that is often used in discussion of US-China relations (Meiser, 2018). Unlike realism, the liberal school of thought considers more than power relations and state interests. Liberals believe that states can be constrained by institutions and civil society, which is why they place more emphasis on diplomacy and economic integration over military balancing. Although a realist may see the world through a Machiavellian lens where might makes right, liberals assert that norms, international institutions, and trade all fundamentally alter state behavior. Like the realists, they notably discount individual incentives of leaders. The liberal scholar Andrew Moravscik (1997) outlines some of the key assumptions of liberalism: democratic peace theory, the danger of power disparities, cooperation by economic integration, and the importance of international institutions.

These tenets of liberal theory play a large role in contemporary international relations discourse. Liberalism informed many of the initial policies the US employed in engaging with Communist China. Democratic peace theory posits that democracy tends to reduce a state's tendency for conflict as citizens would have more of a say in foreign policy (Reiter, 2012). Liberals believe that disparities in power tend to invite conflict because those in power tend to try to cement their position through rent-seeking and, potentially, the use of force. The economic integration argument is especially relevant to China as liberals believe that engaging in trade and commerce with the outside world tends to necessitate cooperation. Liberal theory also posits that international institutions, like the World Trade Organization and the United Nations, play key roles in moderating state behavior. Foreign policy liberals would generally assert that engagement and cooperation with China has resulted in better results compared to the counter-factual than realist skeptics believe it has.

Liberal assumptions regarding the diffusion of democratic norms and values cannot alone explain the actions of the Chinese State. Liberals, like realists, neglect the self-interests and rational power-maximizing tendencies of the CCP. A public choice perspective reconciles the merits of engagement and economic growth with the contemporary realities of China's governance.

Liberals point to Beijing's entry into the WTO as a net positive, even though it has allowed China to grow more powerful and achieve more influence over other countries. That is because China adopted some best practices in order to participate in global commerce which in turn generated mutual benefits for everyone involved (Wang, 2013). Although realists might contend that China's entry into global institutions has only made Beijing stronger to the West's detriment, a liberal would argue that the counterfactual would be much worse. China would have likely still developed into a powerful country except it would be less dependent on foreign cooperation and far more adversarial to the norms of the liberal order (Allen, 2021).

Perhaps the most significant and controversial liberal argument is that engagement with China should have led to the adoption of liberal democracy (Griffiths, 2022). The basic thesis is that increased living standards would cause Chinese citizens to start caring about things beyond their next meal, like political rights and human dignity. Richer citizens would then become interested in the way their country is governed; they would have concerns over societal issues, and they would start to prefer more economic freedom because they would like to enjoy the fruits of their labor. Following engagement, it is clear that Beijing merely leveraged the economic resources and political clout gained from liberalization to bolster its authoritarian rule. However, one cannot deny that the ideas and inclination towards freedom have entered Chinese society. Wealth and globalization fundamentally changed the country. There are hundreds of protests in China every day centered around topics like environmental health, corruption, and living conditions (Fisher, 2012). Despite the common narrative that China is a political monolith, intellectual debates over various policies are actually quite common and robust (Ownby, Johnson, Auslin, 2021). All these developments are great improvements from the drastic political and economic repression emblematic of Mao's rule.

These developments support the liberal assertion that engagement and international norms have changed China. So where did the liberals go wrong, and what can public choice do to bridge the gap between liberalism's predictions and reality? The first point to consider is not necessarily a public choice observation, the liberals were far too ambitious. They believed that they could change China into a drastically different country with the tools of statecraft; they ultimately failed in their objective. The core public choice observation is that democratization would drastically undermine the power of the CCP and is, therefore, a non-starter. The CCP understands both the opportunities and threats of liberalization and has actively worked to minimize the challenges of economic growth while extracting maximum benefit.

A public choice analysis suggests that the CCP's ultimate intentions are to never allow for full liberalization of the sort international relations liberals expect. It further highlights the complications and difficulties that eventually accompanied China's attempt to leverage markets to bolster its authoritarian system. After Mao's death, Deng Xiaoping explicitly justified capitalist economic reforms on the grounds that they would boost China's power and progress Communism. He justified political reform, such as the decentralization of power, as a way to prevent a disastrous centralization of authority under one man, which at the time was Mao. Deng's famous metaphor for the introduction of gradual and controlled market reforms translates to "crossing the river by feeling the stones" (South China Morning Post, 2002). The CCP, as a rational power-maximizing entity, would not allow liberalization for liberalization's sake so it made pragmatic decisions to use economic and some civil freedoms to bolster its own power. Coupled with this strategic effort it is clear that state institutions whether in China or the West, have tremendous staying power.

State-owned enterprises (SOEs) are a clear example of the unproductive infrastructure that have tremendous staying power (Borst, 2021). Largely emergent from the Maoist past, SOEs have become a case of what regulatory economists call the Baptists and Bootleggers scenario, with a political entrepreneur pushing for the arrangement to continue (Simmons, Thomas, Yonk). The CCP understands that China needs private industry and the SOEs are inefficient and stagnant. However, there are tremendous political forces at play that block reform. On one hand, there are the true believers, the Baptist in this analogy, who genuinely believe in socialist economic policies and oppose reform. On the other hand, the Bootleggers are the entrenched interest groups that benefit from the SOE system. That list, from employees to officials to friends and family, is nothing short of massive. Pushing them together is the CCP itself, which is interested in both managing the communist hardliners, and those who benefit from the system as it currently exists, to benefit their own governing position.

Finally, it is worth mentioning a more minor school of international relations, constructivism, that has had some sway in discussions of the China-US relationship (Cruz, Brabazon, Halfhill, Ritzel, 2020). Constructivists stress the importance of norms in global politics, whether that be respecting individual sovereignty or offering to help refugees during times of crisis. Constructivism attempts to explain why states follow certain patterns of behavior that may not be immediately explainable from a raw cost-benefit perspective, but makes sense from a cultural perspective. This may explain why some countries prize peace like post-World War II Germany, and some are more activist in their foreign policy, like the United States. A constructivist perspective argues that the reason why the Chinese are averse to foreign interventionism, and consistently make assurances that they do not seek a large military presence around the world, is grounded in their view of the proper order (Ministry of Foreign Affairs (China), 2004).

However, a public choice analysis would critique constructivism much like a realist would. On the matter of China in particular, perhaps the reason why Beijing's foreign policy is relatively peaceful is that they physically lack the capability to be expansionist. Not only has China's military been weak for much of its modern existence, but the country is bordered by powerful competitors such as India, and Japan. Furthermore, in order to peacefully ascend to global influence without inspiring backlash, the CCP has no choice but to promise peace. For a rational leader in Beijing, embarking on aggressive foreign adventures would be a nonsensical move, until recently. Perhaps the greatest counterpoint to the constructivist idea that norms define China's foreign policy and not rational self-interests is the recent uptick in Chinese assertiveness on the world stage. Furthermore, Beijing has engaged in more subtle modes of expansion, be it through infrastructure projects such as the Belt and Road or exerting power through economic leverage.

Chinese diplomacy has been known to be highly belligerent, aggressive, and often intrusive, when a country shows weakness; much of this is due to China's increased power and the internal nationalism that comes with it (Zhai and Wong, 2021). Perhaps the most ominous sign of China's declining aversion to military adventurism is its quiet naval modernization, which will give it the capability to project power as far as the Mediterranean (Makichuk, 2019). While the CCP, in its early days, did not have much reason to have its military anywhere except at home, today it is much different, with growing Chinese interests from Africa to South America. As it becomes easier and more attractive for Beijing to use its military abroad, whether it is for energy security in the Middle East, protecting its investments in Africa, or supporting friends in Latin America, a more powerful China will likely mean a more aggressive China.

Whether one subscribes to the seeming pessimism of Realism or the optimism of Liberalism, public choice provides important insights that resolve many of the discrepancies between theory and practice. China represents a fascinating and clear case of political-economic statecraft. The CCP and the Chinese nation are not monolithic, unthinking entities simply responding to external stimuli like power imbalances or economic growth. China's domestic and foreign policy is made by individuals and those individuals pursue their own self-interests within the context of the system they occupy and the challenges they face. Understanding the role of individuals and personal interests within Chinese politics provides a more complete picture of how Beijing behaves internally and externally.

Countries Balancing Their Relationship with China

Before looking at the various competing interests and entrenched constituencies driving Chinese policymaking, it is useful to consider how public choice applies to how the outside world approaches China. The policymakers and interest groups running every country have two basic competing interests when it comes to dealing with Beijing: economic interests, and security interests. How one priority wins out over another varies from country to country based on the unique incentives at hand. For the sake of brevity, when we refer to a country below we are speaking about the ultimate decision of their collective leadership, not the country as a single entity.

Australia, for example, recently placed security above economic interests after years of economic integration with China (Wilson, 2019). From 2009-2019, Canberra tripled its exports to China. Many believed that Australia would be too dependent on Chinese commerce to oppose Beijing in any meaningful way. Although the Australians had significant differences with the Chinese over important issues like human rights and democracy, the benefits of trade outweighed those concerns until recently.

However, the Australians have now prioritized security with China becoming more assertive in Asia and more daring with its global power projection. Canberra's membership in two balancing coalitions, The Quad, consisting of India, Japan, the US, and Australia, and AUKUS, a security pact between Australia, the UK, and the US demonstrates rising concerns regarding China's strategic behavior (BBC, 2021). Furthermore, Australia demonstrated a willingness to directly confront Beijing by calling for an investigation into the origins of the coronavirus outbreak in Wuhan, China (Burgess, 2021). Beijing retaliated by imposing economic sanctions which ultimately failed to inflict sufficient damage, likely emboldening Australia's resolve (Xue, 2021). The drastic shift from a preference for cooperation to confrontation demonstrated a basic cost-benefit calculation in response to China's recent actions. At one point, it was possible and advantageous to sit on the sidelines of the US-China rivalry, however, now that Beijing's actions threaten Australian security it became more rational to transition to a more skeptical stance.

India is another emblematic example of a country that once prized not just its economic relationship with China but its historic policy of neutrality. Beijing's recent actions have not only shifted New Delhi's cost-benefit calculus over cooperation but also pushed India towards a partnership with the United States. On the one hand, trade between India and China expanded from 1.8 billion dollars in 2001 to 100 billion dollars in 2021 however, the milestone came with little celebration as the two nations engaged in a military standoff over a border dispute (PTI, 2022).

This predicament demonstrates the nuanced tension between economic cooperation, on the one hand, and national security on the other. Trade with China is a necessary and beneficial activity that must be reconciled with important geopolitical matters that have their roots in basic state-to-state relations. India's position as a major South Asian power along China's border predisposes the two nations to conflict. That is because both countries have interests in areas like the Himalayas and contrasting visions for the future of the Asian continent. As a result, national security concerns and great power politics will have more of an influence on India's relationship with China than they would on other countries.

Southeast Asia is a region with diverse views on the strategic threat of China. Countries like Cambodia, have warm ties with Beijing, in some cases being labeled an agent of Chinese foreign policy (Bong, 2019). What separates Cambodia's national interests from India's may lie in the former's smaller economy, Communist history, and the fact it is a small nation, not a regional power. Cambodia benefits tremendously from economic engagement with Beijing and is not powerful enough to enforce its own interests on other countries. In this case, there is little detriment to cooperating with Beijing's agenda and Cambodia's leaders likely have much to gain and little to lose when working with the CCP.

Vietnam, on the other hand, maintains a historic suspicion of China due to past wars and ongoing territorial disputes in the South China Sea (Torode & Ngyuen, 2018). Hanoi as a Southeast Asian economic and strategic power has its own concerns and vision which includes balancing China's power. At the same time, the Vietnamese are extremely careful when dealing with the Chinese because of their robust trade relationship and because the two countries share a border. As a result, the Vietnamese play a careful balancing game of engagement with both Beijing and Washington, trade on the one hand, and security on the other. It would not be absurd to believe that as China becomes more assertive and problematic for Vietnam's security, Hanoi will continue to seek deeper ties with the United States as it is already doing (Poling & Natalegawa, 2021). Of note, Vietnam has been holding consistent talks with the US on human rights, and recent progress on labor reforms may be a product of Hanoi's attempts to gain Washington's favor (Buckley, 2022).

The European Union is another interesting case study for balancing business and security. China is the EU's largest trading partner and the EU is China's second-largest partner next to the United States. Initially, many European countries like Germany were resistant to joining Washington in taking a more skeptical stance on China (European Commission, 2022). They valued their extensive economic relationship and did not see much threat from Beijing given that most European countries had little strategic interest in Asia. However, tones are changing across the continent as German leaders lament that the country has gotten too dependent on Chinese trade and that the CCP's human rights violations and aggressive industrial policies cannot be ignored (Rinke, 2017).

By sending two carrier strike groups to the Indo-Pacific region, the United Kingdom has gone even further with its stance against China (Patalano, 2017). There are a variety of unique incentives that prompt this decision. They range from Britain's deep connection with the United States and Australia to Britain's historic involvement in the Indo-Pacific region, most notably in Hong Kong. Furthermore, the post-Brexit UK has forged closer economic ties with many Asian states, including becoming a dialogue partner with ASEAN and petitioning to join the Comprehensive and Progressive Trans-Pacific Partnership (Strangio, 2021; UK Department for International Trade & Truss). As Britain attempts to reengage with markets in Asia, London will also see value in being able to project power and forward stability in the region. This includes a potential confrontation with Beijing in response to its aggressive behavior in the region.

The diverse and delayed responses of European states with Germany being more cautious and Britain more proactive reflect the unique incentives that face each country. Every nation has both a beneficial economic relationship with China and real concerns about the threat posed by the CCP's behavior. The willingness to respond to these threats, and thereby jeopardize relations with the Chinese, varies based on how each country's leaders view their priorities. Such incentives also explain why we should not expect European powers to play as significant of a role in confronting the Chinese as the United States, which has a much larger stake in the matter.

Washington is largely responsible for the current status quo in Asia and the world order generally. Since the end of World War II, the US military and diplomatic footprint played an integral role in shaping the landscape of the Asia-Pacific (Shapiro, 2015). Countries like Japan, South Korea, and Taiwan were all formed with direct guidance from the US. The status quo of valuing open movement, trade, human rights, and security are all large components of the American-led order. Around the world, the United States maintains varying military, diplomatic, and economic footprints and is largely viewed as the shining city on a hill (Omara, 2016). A rising China threatens all of this, which makes the US cost-benefit analysis on security vs business unique (Chang, 2021). No other country in the world has an interest in waging an intense competition for global superpower status, because there can only be one incumbent.

From an economic standpoint, the Chinese are Washington's largest trading partner; in 2020 two-way trade in goods and services reached an estimated $615 billion (US Trade Representative, 2022). Economic engagement with Beijing since the signing of the 1979 bilateral trade agreement has been nothing short of tremendous (Library of Congress, 2023). The societies of both countries have since become highly intertwined to the point where, if one ignored the great power competition, it would seem that the US and China were quite friendly towards one another. The connection between the two countries runs deep, whether it be the 123.88 billion American dollars invested in China in 2020 alone, or the more than 317,000 Chinese international students studying in the US. President Trump's trade war demonstrated in vivid detail how intertwined the two economies were as a Brookings report points out,

> A September 2019 study by Moody's Analytics found that the trade war had already cost the U.S. economy nearly 300,000 jobs and an estimated 0.3% of real GDP. Other studies put the cost to U.S. GDP at about 0.7%. A 2019 report from Bloomberg Economics estimated that the trade war would cost the U.S. economy $316 billion by the end of 2020, while more recent research from the Federal Reserve Bank of New York and Columbia University found that U.S. companies

lost at least $1.7 trillion in the price of their stocks as a result of U.S. tariffs imposed on imports from China. (US Mission China, 2021)

Contemporary economic understanding informs us that protectionist policies harm consumers and the economy with little benefit in return. Tariffs are, in effect, a tax on the domestic population and studies show that former President Trump's policies had little impact on American investment in China (Zhang & Vortherms, 2021). The biggest drivers of decoupling had little to do with tariff policies and more so to do with the increasing cost of labor in China, and political risk. This begs the question of why politicians in Washington have so enthusiastically embraced a more combative stance against Beijing on both the strategic and economic front? Furthermore, why has is it rare for politicians to advocate for the renormalization of business ties with China whereas more hawkish stances have bipartisan support?

The answer again lies in a public choice understanding of American politics not just towards China but domestically. A confrontational stance is understandable if not justified given the threat Beijing poses to the American lead international status quo. If China becomes the world's most dominant superpower or even just pushes the US out of East Asia, global affairs will change forever, perhaps not to Washington's benefit. However, that only explains why American politicians wish to be more competitive and confrontational, it does not necessarily explain why many support broad protectionist policies. Here we see another example of the bootleggers and baptists dilemma. On the one hand, there are some politicians who are concerned with confronting China, and they perhaps have constituents who want them to look tough on China. Furthermore, politicians are often concerned with political issues, such as calling out the CCP's human rights abuses and unfair economic practices. On the other hand, are the genuine protectionists that depend on the support of groups that benefit from more constrained trade with China. These include labor unions like the United Steelworkers union and the AFL-CIO which have all been historically supportive of protectionism, even if the net economic effects are negative (Isidore, 2018).

Many groups support renormalizing trade relations with China, such as retailers and other businesses that benefit from engagement (Zheng, 2021). However, such groups face an uphill battle in the context of the

US-China rivalry and the domestic political benefits inherent to a more confrontational stance. When it comes to weighing security and business, the security threat in Washington's eyes is almost existential given that America benefits greatly from the international order it created. From a public choice perspective, politicians, given their priorities and incentives, find more inspiration in confrontation rather than normalization. These incentives can shift over such as if public opinion worsens on China or if constituents start to demand a more nuanced approach that balances engagement with confrontation.

Every country, from China to the United States, maintains its own calculus on security and engagement. Some nations will see little security threat from Beijing and much economic benefit from cooperation. Countries like Nepal, for example, benefit greatly from Chinese investment and see little value or hope in confrontation given the vast power difference. This might explain why Kathmandu has cooperated with the CCP to monitor Tibetans refugees within its own borders whereas India is happy to play host to the Tibetan government in exile (Budhathoki & Dahal, 2021; New York Times, 1959). Small to medium-sized countries like Nepal, South Korea, and Vietnam have a greater incentive to perform a balancing act between Beijing and Washington. More powerful countries like India, Japan, and the United States are more willing to assert their own interests and confront China. Furthermore, within the context of the geopolitical balance of power are the inclinations of the individual leaders within the countries themselves. Individual policymakers calculate their stance towards China given the incentives at play in their domestic context. Understanding these incentives, whether it be appeasing labor unions on tariffs, looking tough on strategic competitors, or satisfying constituents who benefit from engagement with China allows for a greater understanding of a country's present and future orientation towards Beijing.

3. Modern China and the CCP's Leadership

To understand the CCP's decision-making today, one must understand the historical context and the incentives that stem from it. Although the current president, Xi Jinping, and the Chinese elite have significant discretion in deciding policy, they still need to address the circumstances created by the actions of previous leaders, good and bad. The most pivotal moment in modern Chinese history and the foundation for the country's rise to global power status began with Deng Xiaoping's market reforms in 1978. However, to understand Deng's economic policies, one must go back another two decades to the reign of Mao Zedong, undoubtedly one of the most consequential leaders in all of Chinese history, if not world history. Understanding Chinese history provides the necessary context and grounding to make a more complete public choice analysis about contemporary events.

Mao's Terror

When one thinks of Mao, two major campaigns should come to mind, The Great Leap Forward and the Cultural Revolution. In 1953, the young People's Republic of China embarked on its first Communist-style development initiative known as the First Five Year Plan, which improved on lessons imported from the Soviet Union (Central Intelligence Agency (US), 1959). With the help of Soviet advisors, the Chinese successfully implemented important socialist reforms, focusing on minimizing imports to boost domestic industry while exporting raw materials. The Chinese avoided some of the major failings of the initial Soviet plans by concentrating on increasing industrial output but not at the expense of agricultural productivity (Central Intelligence Agency (US), 1959). Whereas the first Soviet

Five-Year Plan attempted to convert agricultural workers into industrial ones at an unsustainable rate leading to famines, the Chinese avoided this by prioritizing both. Perhaps a large incentive for this correction stemmed not just from observing the Soviet failure but the presence of a large workforce and low living standards in China that necessitated a focus on agriculture (Central Intelligence Agency (US), 1959). The result was an early victory for the CCP fostering annual GDP growth rates around 8 percent (Central Intelligence Agency (US), 1959).

However, the second five-year plan in 1958, infamously known as the Great Leap Forward, resulted in one of the greatest manmade killings in history, with an estimated 45 million people starved, tortured, or murdered to death in just four years (Somin, 2016). The initiative sought to further collectivize Chinese society, particularly the countryside, by organizing society into self-sufficient communes (University of Maryland, 2022). Such measures included breaking up the nuclear family and holding each commune responsible for producing its resources, from agriculture to industrial materials. Rather than creating a Communist utopia, the project led to mass starvation, crippling misallocations of labor, and a tremendous waste of natural resources. A paper by the Hsiung-Shen Jung and Jui-Lung Chen (2019, 58) isolated three main contributors to the massive famine that characterized the Great Leap Forward: a public canteen system, prioritizing urban populations for food, and the use of "people's communes." Before the Great Leap Forward, Chinese society was organized into over 740,000 agricultural cooperatives, which allowed for a decent level of local governance rather than the catastrophic incompetence that resulted from their consolidation into just 23,284 "people's communes." These communes used a highly centralized, militaristic structure that ultimately triggered massive famines, devastated social relationships, and drastically undermined the Chinese economy.

A lack of constructive guidance and political factors aggravated the famine further. Following the success of the First Five Year Plan, Mao invited public criticism of the government in what was known as the Hundred Flowers Campaign, which simulated a sort of marketplace of ideas to improve Chinese society (Brown, 2012). However, shortly after international events such as Nikita Kruschev's denunciation of Stalin in the Soviet Union and a Hungarian revolt against Moscow in October of 1956 shocked

Mao into reversing his position on free speech (Brown, 2012). In October of 1957, the CCP began a systematic persecution of suspected anti-Communists in what would be dubbed the Anti-Rightist Campaign, effectively clearing out constructive criticism and suppressing dissent (Wilson Center, 2012). From this point on, Mao entered a spiral of paranoia and stubbornness, targeting all who disagreed with his platform and doubling down on bad ideas rather than reforming them.

This increased radicalism and suppression of dissent exacerbated the Great Leap Forward and even frayed ties with the Soviet Union, which voiced disapproval of the disastrous Chinese commune system. As a result of the utter failure of the Great Leap Forward during its first year, Mao stepped down as president in 1959, and more realistic policies saw implementation in 1961, placing China back onto a gradual growth trajectory (University of Maryland, 2023). However, these more moderate policies came at the expense of Mao's revolutionary ideas and diminished his influence within the Party.

In 1966, Mao kicked off what would become the Cultural Revolution, a systematic purging of supposed counterrevolutionaries throughout Chinese society to reaffirm his power (World Peace Foundation, 2016). This purge would go on until Mao's death in 1976 and drastically undermined the country's stability as student groups known as the Red Guard engaged in insurgent tactics, attacking those deemed to be "class enemies." The violence would ultimately spread across the nation as those sympathetic to Mao rebelled against the state and desecrated cultural institutions deemed to be "reactionary" (Song 2011). The CCP's efforts to quell the unrest only exacerbated the violence as local leaders used military force to put down rebellions, resulting in the mass killing of unarmed civilians. Ultimately the death toll of the Cultural Revolution is unknown due to the CCP's unwillingness to release information on the matter (Song, 2011). Still, some estimates place the number as high as 8 million (Song, 2011).

Deng's Reform and Opening

After Mao's death in 1976, the organizers of the Cultural Revolution, the Gang of Four, were arrested. This restored some sense of stability (Yergin and Stanislaw). However, Mao's named successor, Hua Guofeng, would soon lose his control over the Party to Deng Xiaoping in December 1978, during the Third Plenum of the 11th Congress (Yergin and Stanislaw). With Deng in control of the CCP, the foundation was laid for China's ascendancy to global power status through a series of liberalization measures known as Reform and Opening. Deng had always been a moderate. He was a reformer during the Mao era, most notably playing a role in the correction to the Great Leap Forward before the Cultural Revolution. His reformist attitudes led to his purging in 1967 (Phillips, 2016). With Deng now at its helm, China took a more pragmatic approach to economic development: "Socialism with Chinese Characteristics." Deng's explanation of "Socialism With Chinese Characteristics" emphasized that market mechanisms and state planning are not inherently Socialist or Capitalist (CGTN, 2023).[3] Deng asserted "The Chinese socialist system and state governance system did not drop out of the sky but emerged from Chinese soil through a long revolution, economic development, and reform."

Regardless of Deng's ultimate intentions, his economic reforms, decollectivizing industries, removing price controls, legalizing private property, and opening for global commerce, greatly improved living standards. By 1978, GDP per capita stood roughly around $156. It exceeded $10,000 by 2019 (CGTN, 2023). From living in desperate rural poverty, hundreds of millions of people were now elevated to modern cities, within a single lifetime. A poor, rural nation, barely able to support a stable government had been transformed into arguably the second most powerful country in the world. Today, Socialism with Chinese Characteristics plays an integral role in political-economic thought, because state control over private industry remains a core tenet of the Chinese system. Deng would also set the foundation for China's foreign policy known as Hide and Bide, where China would act as benign as possible, never showing assertiveness or leadership on the global stage to avoid drawing attention to itself (Kelly, 2023).

Hide and Bide proved fruitful for decades. China integrated with the international system and formed deep economic ties with countless nations. Deng's thinking on the matter stemmed from his observation of the great power politics and massive expenses of global hegemony exhibited by the United States (Kelly, 2023). Furthermore, he believed that China

---

[3] There is a worthy debate about whether the term is simply a cover word that allows the CCP to be as pragmatic as it wishes.

couldn't take on the West in a direct confrontation but instead, it could use engagement to gradually increase its power and influence. Overall, Deng's shrewd and pragmatic thinking would turn out to be successful as China ascended the ranks of global power while also strengthening the power of the CCP.

Deng's Bid to Stay in Power

Although Deng's policy track record of pragmatism and reform seems evident, recent scholarship suggests that his reform and opening policies were not just his ideas. His decision to embrace limited market reform to strengthen the Chinese economy and, by extension, boost the party's power fits neatly into a public choice framework. Furthermore, the fact that the CCP maintains significant control over vast swaths of the economy whether, through state ownership, regulation, or elite capture demonstrates that the entire point of these market reforms was to boost the Party's power, not liberalize for liberalization's sake.

However, University of Hong Kong Professor Frank Dikotter's book, *The Cultural Revolution: A People's History*, cites recently declassified documents suggesting that Chinese citizens were already demanding economic reform leading to Deng's ascendancy to power (2016). In particular, Dikotter argues that the CCP lost a significant amount of power after the Great Leap Forward and the Cultural Revolution, not just in legitimacy but also in its physical capacity to control the population. As a result, Chinese citizens began engaging in capitalist practices, be it privately amassing resources or voluntary trade, long before such behavior was legalized. Furthermore, Mao's Cultural Revolution instilled a fear of the masses into the party elite and likewise taught citizens the power of mass movements.

Dikotter's book provides numerous examples that skepticism of the party line pervaded the citizenry, and that ordinary people did not buy into Socialist orthodoxy. In particular, villages in the countryside preserved the older ways of life either through black markets or by bribing local officials to look the other way (Dikotter, 2016). Following the conclusion of the Cultural Revolution, the Party had such a trauma of mass uprisings that Deng believed that widespread economic reforms were necessary to prevent a full-scale rebellion. Therefore, by hopping in front of what was essentially an ongoing parade towards economic freedom, Deng was able to contain and harness the movement's energy to make China richer and place the CCP in charge. As a result, Deng preserved the legitimacy of the Party by appeasing the masses and bolstered the power of the state by reigning in the forces of liberalization and placing them under the control of the government.

One can see this dynamic alive today as the CCP pays close attention to its citizens' demands to prevent democratic-style uprisings and ensure the state remains the solution to many of society's concerns. For example, in 1978, Deng saw a popular demand for economic freedom and was wise enough to place the state in charge of administering it. Today, Chinese leaders play the same balancing game of catering to concerns with environmental protection, income inequality, or great power politics while also advancing the ultimate goals of the Party.

The Tenure of Jiang Zemin

Following the Tiananmen Square crackdown in 1989, Deng voluntarily stepped down. For supporting the student protestors, party secretary Zhao Ziyang was ousted. Zhao's replacement was Jiang Zemin (BBC, 2016). Although Jiang assumed the mantle of leadership in 1989, Deng's massive political influence played a role in Chinese politics until he died in 1997. Although competent and stable, Jiang's leadership is relatively unremarkable compared to other paramount leaders such as Deng, Mao, and now Xi. Handpicked by the previous leader himself, his administration primarily focused on continuing what Deng Xiaoping started: maintaining stability, fostering economic growth, growing China's private sector, and quietly advancing Beijing's power without causing alarm (Ma, 2016).

Jiang took office in China after it had been internationally isolated because of Beijing's violent response to the Tiananmen Square protests. By the end of his administration, the country would emerge more globalized and prosperous. The crowning achievement was China's entry into the World Trade Organization in December of 2001 (Council on Foreign Relations, 2023). Under Jiang's administration, the CCP maintained a steady course of gradual economic growth, continued market reforms, and a non-assertive foreign policy. An example of his commitment to the pragmatism promulgated by Deng would be his 8 Point Proposal for reunification with Taiwan (China Daily, 2011). The document stressed a one-China two systems approach where the self-governing island could keep its way of life, invited Taiwanese officials for peace talks, and called for economic engagement. This strategy emphasized the gradual and peaceful rise doctrine, which recognized China's place in the global order and its vulnerabilities.

The Jiang administration's temperance would be tested multiple times as growing Chinese nationalism, and US militarism clashed. In 1999, American bombers attacked the Chinese Embassy (accidentally or purposefully is widely disputed) in Belgrade during the NATO air campaign in Kosovo (BBC, 2019). The outrage from the Chinese public was understandably immense as they saw an incumbent superpower attacking the sovereign office of a rising nation, one that the West had humiliated before. The American explanation was that they aimed for a Yugoslavian building a few hundred meters down the street and made apologies, including a monetary payment. Jiang resisted the temptation to retaliate despite furious outcries from his citizens, keeping in mind that it hoped to continue profitable trade relationships, including convincing the US to advocate for China's acceptance to the WTO (Council on Foreign Relations, 2023).

Jiang's administration continued overseeing economic reforms and globalization on the domestic policy front. State-Owned Enterprise (SOE) reform took a significant priority during his presidency as China hoped to create a modern and dynamic corporate system (Kobayashi, Baobo & Sano, 1999). SOE reform remains a pressing issue because these companies provide the political and social control the CCP needs but damage the economy and efficiency. SOEs as publicly run entities cannot offer the same wages and dynamism offered by privately operated companies, contributing to rising income inequality (Kobayashi, Baobo & Sano, 1999). In 1965, SOEs composed over 90% of total output in China; by 1997, due to the advent of privately owned businesses, SOEs only contributed to about a quarter of total production (Kobayashi, Baobo & Sano, 1999). Furthermore, by this time, these state enterprises began accumulating massive losses and by 1997, profit loss ratios exceeded 200%.

This predicament presented a looming crisis for the CCP, not just in terms of economic efficiency but for social stability and control. In 1998, Zhu Rongji launched a three-year reform plan to ameliorate the inefficiency and underperformance of SOEs (Kobayashi, Baobo & Sano, 1999). These reforms included government supervision of larger companies and liberalization of conduct for smaller ones.

Jiang's tenure as paramount leader also saw the start of an unusual persecution campaign against the Falun Gong, a Chinese spiritual group drawing influence from Buddhism and Taoism with practitioners worldwide (J.Y., 2018). The religion involves performing meditative exercises, reading texts, and upholding general values of truthfulness, compassion, and tolerance. The group also tends to emphasize traditional Chinese values and culture. Before 1999, the Falun Gong maintained strong popularity in China, being the second most popular religion after Buddhism and possessing more practitioners than the CCP had members (Cook, 2017). Jiang's decision to call for the banning of the Falun Gong and the relentless persecution of its members shocked many, as some CCP officials were also adherents or at least sympathetic to the religion.

Perhaps the most plausible reason for the unexpected crackdown on the Falun Gong is precisely a public choice reason; they were far too prevalent and potentially challenged the authority of the CCP. The Falun Gong provided the most dangerous threat to a single-party state, another center of power. The CCP persecutes religious groups not because they hate organized religion in the traditional sense. They do not have a historic rivalry with Christians or Muslims or what have you, but because religion provides a higher authority than the state. The Falun Gong not only captured a large segment of the Chinese population and created their own civil society groups that provided benefits outside the control of the CCP, but they actively advocated for a return to certain traditional notions of Chinese culture (Cook, 2017). Notions of culture that the CCP actively tried to abolish. Such an entity is highly dangerous to an authoritarian, single-party state because the legitimacy and staying power of a Leninist regime are to control the opportunities and livelihoods of its population. This reality alone necessitates decisive action from any regime that wishes to preserve its power.

Another key point is Jiang's falling popularity and his relative weakness compared to the political giants of Deng and Mao (Cook, 2017). Stoking a campaign against the Falun Gong served not just as a rational move to knock off a potential rival to the CCP's rule but also to prop up Jiang's standing in society. He united the Party against a common enemy and also created a new government entity known as the 6-10 Office, which Jiang and his political allies would control (Falun Info, 2023). Today, the 6-10 Office still focuses on persecuting and eliminating the Falun Gong in China. Conveniently, creating such an entity would allow Jiang to remain influential in Chinese politics to this day, even though he has formally retired (Cook, 2017). And retain his power he did. Jiang's allies and proteges would stay in control and exert influence over the even weaker president, Hu Jintao, in a period that would be called "One Country, Two Coalitions," in which Jiang's establishment "Shanghai Coalition" provided a considerable opposition to Hu's populist wing (Huang, 2012). In fact, "Jiang's men continue to play core roles in the highest levels of Chinese politics, including the current president Xi Jingping.

Jiang's tenure is easily overshadowed by the leadership of Mao, Deng, and Xi, in terms of its overall influence on Chinese society. However, his policies as paramount leader demonstrates a crucial point about Chinese politics. That is that the most powerful individuals in the CCP act in rational, self-interested ways. Because of the necessity of economic development and the political clout of Deng, Jiang had to continue the economic reforms during his tenure. Because of China's place in the world as a rising power, not a dominant power, as well as Deng's articulated doctrine of Hide and Bide, Jiang's administration had to stomach the Hainan spy plane incident and the bombing of the Chinese embassy. Finally, because of the influence of the Falun Gong and his falling popularity as a leader, the unexpected persecution of that religious group represented a necessary move.

The Presidency of Hu Jintao

Compared to the commentary on other leaders, Hu Jintao's presidency is little remarked upon. Many Chinese even refer to his tenure as "The Lost Decade," marked by corruption, relatively unimpressive reforms, and weak political leadership (Kirchner & Bone, 2013). Despite this, Hu's administration nevertheless oversaw excellent economic growth, generally strong social stability, efforts to combat environmental degradation, and important reforms to the still-emerging Chinese welfare system (Howell & Duckett 2018). Hu even began some of the initial steps towards assertiveness on the world stage, which are typically instead associated with Xi Jinping. In essence, Hu's presidency dealt with the benefits and challenges of China's ascension to modernity and global power status. However, Hu either managed it poorly, or things were just out of his control to the point that it prompted the heavy-handed policies of the next president, Xi Jinping. In fact, many of the main issues that Xi is attempting to address began ripening during the Hu administration, whether that be rampant corruption, expanding income inequality, or environmental devastation (Kirchner & Bone, 2013).

Hu's presidency is emblematic of China's general dilemma of attempting to become a global power under authoritarian rule. On the one hand, globalization and market reforms created drastic increases in prosperity. On the other hand, China's state-capitalist system and geographic makeup created large concentrations of wealth in commercial-friendly areas such as the coastline but preserved poverty in more rural areas. Furthermore, a lack of democratic rights, unaccountable enforcement of regulations, and a desire for rapid growth at nearly all costs enabled massive degrees of environmental pollution (Wang & Carl Minzner, 2015, 339). At the same time, ethnic and religious separatism exacerbated unrest in the Western regions of China in Tibet and Xinjiang, leading to public spectacles of self-immolation and terrorist attacks. The Chinese government responded to these threats to social stability by drastically expanding the security state, which by the end of Hu's administration, contained more employees than the military (Kirchner & Bone, 2013).

Much of the expansion of the surveillance state was out of Hu's control and was instead a product of the Chinese system itself. For one, much of the Chinese media attributes the expansion of the security apparatus to a single member of the Politburo Standing Committee, Zhou Yongkang (BBC 2015). Still, the impetus to create such a pervasive police state goes back even further to the early 1990s after the Tiananmen Square democracy protests and the collapse of Communist regimes across the world (Wang & Carl Minzner, 2015, 339). These developments instilled tremendous anxiety in the CCP that still exists today about the ultimate objective of maintaining control and stability. At the same time, this priority would take precedence over and even stunt helpful political reforms such as creating an independent court system and limited political rights (Wang & Carl Minzner, 2015, 339).. Although suppressing these reforms may have been necessary to reassert the power of the Party and create a larger security state, it also removed the long-term mechanisms for Chinese citizens to peacefully resolve their grievances. This problem still exists today as the CCP relies primarily on heavy-handed political solutions to solve perceived societal issues rather than allowing the solution to arise from civil society organizations.

The creation of a new social welfare net involving the use of NGOs represents a classic public choice issue in China, where competing interests in security and development clashed. The Hu administration made strides in improving China's still lackluster welfare system in part because of pressure and assistance from NGOs such as the World Trade Organization. An essential component of improving the provision of welfare in the rural countryside rested on allowing non-profit organizations, often of international origin, to conduct charity work (Howell & Duckett 2018). This idea required a regulatory approval process that had yet to be fully fleshed out. Part of the holdup owed itself to the fundamental clash of interests between the Ministry of Civil Affairs, Health, and Education and the Ministry of Public Security (Howell & Duckett 2018).

The social policy bureaucrats emphasized the necessity of allowing foreign NGOs to provide charity services to China's poor, while the security state protested the idea because of the destabilizing effects of foreign actors. Furthermore, there were concerns about the limits of civil society organizing, which, much like the Falun Gong, might create a center of power that existed outside of the influence of the CCP. Eventually, the agencies bargained for a middle ground, but this instance demonstrates the fundamental dilemma in Chinese politics between balancing stability with prosperity. Furthermore, it highlights the fact that Chinese decision-makers are not all united in support of a common cause but are subject to special interest and factionalism just like public officials are in the US.

The presidency of Hu Jintao is particularly interesting not because of his sheer vision and strength but because of his lack of such attributes. Unlike Mao, Deng, and later Xi, Hu did not have the level of political power and clout to exert a dominant control of the party. Instead, past leaders like Jiang Zemin, who during his time felt the political yolk of the previous leader, Deng, exerted influence over the even weaker president. This competition between Hu and Jiang created factional infighting that jeopardized their pro-reform platform and created an opening for the conservatives to reassert themselves (Blumenthal, 2018). These conservatives, who opposed the liberalization of Deng's Reform and Opening, explain much of China's shift to the authoritarian left that is mainly associated with Xi Jinping but began during Hu's presidency. These Neo-Marxists advocated for more resources for state enterprises, not less, opposed judicial reforms, and placed heavier restrictions on the private sector (Blumenthal, 2018).

However, one cannot simply credit Hu's platform as entirely defined by factional infighting and lack of power. Hu presided over China in the 21st century, which had to contend with massive changes socially, economically, and geo-politically. The former president had titanic issues to deal with, such as addressing income inequality due to Beijing's growing state capitalist economy, environmental devastation, anxiety over the fall of other Communist states, a more restless population, and so on. Many, if not all, of these factors, are structural and still exist today. Although we shouldn't discount Hu's lack of institutional clout and vision, the challenges he faced are emblematic that even in China, the realities of economics and politics remain.

There is no better representation of these contemporary developments in Chinese political economy than the presidency of Xi Jinping. Decades after Deng Xiaoping's reform and opening policy, his tenure signaled a strong shift to the left and marked the end of Deng's 'hide and bide' strategy. Deng's leadership-initiated China's trajectory to becoming an increasingly rich and influential country. His guiding philosophy, hiding one's strength and biding one's time, was the mantra for the subsequent two presidents, Jiang Zemin, and Hu Jintao. However, Xi's assumption of power comes at a pivotal point in history as China reaches global economic superpower status and challenges the US in the realm of geopolitical hegemony.

Xi's presidency marks a new stage in China's development story, which demands that he address the consequences of Deng's liberalization measures. The Chinese economy is capitalistic; living standards skyrocketed, and it is clear that free markets allocate resources more efficiently than the Communist command economy model. However, political, and economic freedom enabled new forms of corruption, a more educated and activist populace, plurality of thought, and potentially destabilizing economic trends.

Chinese income inequality skyrocketed. Large companies, like Alibaba, now wield vast economic power with the ability to threaten the party's political authority (Tang, 2022). In acknowledgment of the consequences of rapid economic growth, in 2007 and 2011, former Chinese premier Wen Jiabao stated that the Chinese economy was "unstable, unbalanced, uncoordinated and ultimately unsustainable (Goldkorn, 2019)." China relied heavily on outside investments to drive growth. Foreign investment means exposure to foreign influence. Foreign influence can be weaponized by China's adversaries through the use of sanctions and other policies (Bloomenthal, 2022). We know Beijing understands this lesson acutely because it actively leverages foreign direct investment to coerce countries to support its interests (National Endowment for Democracy, 2019). At the same time, Xi is a well-trained and devoted Marxist, as are most of the CCP's leadership. China's existing bureaucracy maintains a strong interest in keeping the less efficient, state-run model, and these economic issues only strengthen the leadership's state-run stance.

In a single-party state, the Party must be unquestioned, and social unrest is incredibly dangerous to the long-term stability of the regime. To maintain legitimacy, the CCP must sustain economic prosperity but also address existential issues, like inequality, pollution, market monopolization, or foreign influences.

In ongoing debates, there are two methods to combat these problems. The first is what many optimists in the West believed he would do: Implement liberal reforms (Kristof, 2013) From the Western perspective, Xi's turbulent upbringing during the Cultural Revolution would push him to embrace more reform-minded economic policies and political plurality. However, this is a non-starter for the CCP as it would weaken the regime. The second method is shoring up the power of the state and resolving China's problems with the bureaucratic force now synonymous with the CCP. Xi, an ardent supporter of the CCP, unsurprisingly embraced the second option.

Today's policy developments are narrowly tailored towards reasserting the power of the state and using brute political force to achieve desired outcomes in the economy. According to the CCP, a competitive market will be created by attacking megacompanies, like Alibaba and Meituan, creating room for smaller companies to compete. Workplace woes, like the 996 schedule, are resolved with outright bans (Zhang, 2021). A declining birth rate, due in part because of rising costs of living, prompted a regulatory crackdown on private education companies, encouraging families to spend on more children, not the education of one child (Li, 2021). In 2021, China's once-dormant antitrust regulatory apparatus abruptly unleashed a firestorm of fines upon the economy, which amounted to billions of dollars, and prompted investors to pull billions out. Bloomberg Quint contributors De Wei Dexter Low and Hau Tung Olivia Tam provide an example:

> Tencent Holdings Ltd. and Netease Inc. shed more than $60 billion of value as investor fears grow that Chinese regulators are preparing to tighten their grip dramatically on the world's largest gaming industry (2021).

A free and market-based society is self-regulating and self-correcting. The CCP, with Xi Jinping at the helm, attempts to demonstrate that an authoritarian and technocratic regime can also manage a dynamic economy while also retaining the primacy of the state. Some investors and onlookers, like CNBC host Jim Cramer, look at the financial chaos of 2021 as "Stalinist" and an attack on western investors (Takala, 2021). However, a public choice analysis suggests that Xi is making a rational move to sacrifice short-term economic gains for long-term political stability, a core tenet of his Common Prosperity initiative (BBC 2022). The onslaught of regulation will only proceed as long as it achieves what the CCP deems to be a sustainable economy and political longevity.

Under Xi's leadership, the country underwent a radical shift in economic policy, severe degradation of human rights, and witnessed the drastic reorientation of political power around one man. From the outside, it may seem like the CCP is simply carrying out a grand scheme to uphold Chinese style Socialism and undermine Western values. However, a public choice analysis, coupled with a more intimate analysis of the facts on the ground, reveals a method to the madness not too different from our own political decision-making calculus. The People's Republic of China is a Leninist regime with the primary objective of maintaining and growing the power of the CCP.

Growing and maintaining the power of the Party requires appeasing the population where it can and subduing or co-opting when it must. Like a liberal democratic government, the CCP must also balance the forces of public approval, political maneuvering, and special interests. The only differences are the ideological bent of the Party and the structural constraints, or lack thereof, in an authoritarian system. Human rights travesties in regions, like Xinjiang, may demonstrate a disdain for organized religion, but the primary drivers are territorial integrity and domestic stability, not necessarily anti-Islam sentiments, although they certainly are present. Beijing's actions demonstrate an understanding that economic growth alone can't fix China's ethnic tensions (Leibold, 2021). Combine the political necessity to pacify separatists with a lack of institutional or ideological constraints on power, and you arrive at Western China's egregious policies.

The recent swing to the economic left may have some roots in the Party's Communist ideology, but it also represents a serious effort to respond to severe political-economic issues in society. These include: soaring inequality, concentrating market power, environmental degradation, a declining birth rate, souring relations with the West, rising debt, and rampant corruption. Most importantly, there is the daunting task of transitioning from a middle- to high-income country that is nevertheless still ruled by an authoritarian state. Combine these concerns with a great-power competition with the US, and the CCP rightly sees very little room for error, with many ways things could go wrong. In this context, there are two basic choices: Either give up and liberalize, a non-starter, or strap in for the long haul and take sweeping actions to shore up the Party's control, while trying to prepare the Chinese economy to compete in the 21st century. In short, the drastic swing to the left seen under Xi Jinping is a conscious recognition of potentially existential problems facing the CCP and an assertion that the regime is committed to fostering a dynamic and modern economy, stewarded by an authoritarian regime.

Contemporary political issues and developments in China are as fascinating as it is disheartening. There are unconscionable human rights abuses, from the Uyghur concentration camps in Xinjiang to the development of an unprecedented surveillance state (Maizland, 2022). On the economic front, Beijing is embarking on a fundamental overhaul of its macroeconomy. Its so-called 'Common Prosperity Agenda' and its 'Dual Circulation' initiative both promote the long-term growth of the Chinese economy while maintaining the party's power (Hass, 2021; Pettis, 2021). However, these policies entail large and often unprecedented interventions ranging from multibillion-dollar antitrust fines to the reinvigoration of State-Owned

Enterprises (Qu & Cao, 2022; Huifeng, 2021). Then there are rather odd developments, such as crackdowns on private education, video games, and effeminate men on TV (Watanabe, 2021) (BBC, 2021). Most importantly, China's constitutional structure has been substantially made more authoritarian, most notably when current president Xi Jinping abolished term limits, overhauled Hong Kong's autonomy, and established Xi Jinping Thought (Doubek, 2018) (Human Rights Watch, 2021) (Buckley, 2018).

Furthermore, nationalism is surging, and the Chinese are developing a sense of exceptionalism that is intolerant of external criticism of the CCP's priorities. A large reason for these modern nationalist trends is the Patriotic Education campaign enacted by the CCP in 1989 following the Tiananmen Square Massacre (Zhao, 1998). These developments demonstrate a number of important indicators of the CCP's primary concerns, such as separatism and national stability. They also demonstrate Xi's sheer political strength, as well as the Party leadership's endorsement of Xi's tenure. These developments are not necessarily just the will of an authoritarian dictatorship but the consequences of individuals attempting to maintain control over society with the broad powers afforded by a Leninist system.

A casual onlooker may look at these developments and see an unhinged Communist dictatorship or a perfectly orchestrated master plan one hundred years in the making. However, a closer analysis reveals that the CCP is making pragmatic, rational moves to address self-serving goals as well as concerns that arise within Chinese society. Furthermore, it can be argued that even the chaotic policies of Mao Zedong, such as the Cultural Revolution, look more calculated and rational after more thorough analysis as discussed later in the book. The drastic departure from the status quo occurring in Xi Jinping's China reflects important, if not existential, political-economic stress points for the CCP. Understanding the underlying incentives driving CCP decision-making, while considering the structural constraints, or lack thereof, will not only provide a better picture of Chinese affairs but also provide insight into predicting future developments.

Politics and Self-Interest Apply in China

At first glance, Chinese policymakers may seem alien, nefarious, and seemingly focused on world domination. However, a deeper analysis of the incentives that drive the CCP's decision-making reveal that China's leaders are subject to the same laws of political economy that we are. A Chinese president like Xi is still subject to political opposition from other elites as well as popular discontent from the general population. The manner in which such challenges are handled is more so determined by the structure of the government rather than an inherent inclination for authoritarian behavior. A Leninist system where the Party remains the most powerful political entity and National People's Congress functions more as a rubber stamp invites different behavior than a liberal democracy (Sweeney, 2022).

China does not act as a monolithic, evil entity on the world stage. Just like every other country, China is led by self-interested and rational individuals. These individuals make their decisions within the structural context they occupy. Chinese citizens are also rational, self-interested individuals. They too have basic human desires, such as economic growth, opportunity, and a secure living environment. Not surprisingly, therefore, the actions of the Chinese government are logically focused on domestic concerns first, and foreign affairs second. Furthermore, the CCP is primarily concerned with maintaining order and stability for its rule, which often requires making compromises to its own objectives and tailoring policy to appease its own people. Finally, Chinese politics are not a monolith. The individuals within the system are extremely important to the overall trajectory of the nation, whether that be the vision of one person, the compromise of factions, or the self-interested motives of entrenched constituencies. That means understanding and acknowledging the incentives that drive CCP decision-making means one cannot just predict where the Party is heading but also craft more effective policies to confront China.

4. China and the Rest of the World

It can be tempting to view China as an exotic and novel political system. Is it something we do not and cannot understand, something outside or contrary to conventional knowledge in social science? Whether exaggerating or downplaying the CCP's abilities and intentions, lopsided narratives are abundant. However, a closer look at China's contemporary domestic affairs and history reveals: Beijing is not exempt from the lessons of political science and economics. Public choice analysis lays bare the method to the madness. It provides nuanced insights into the challenges facing the CCP and its actions. The ruling elites in the CCP, from the top and down to the lowest level of officials, act in rational, self-interested ways. Staying in power matters, advancing in the system matters, political divisions matter, and contrasting goals matter. Furthermore, although the CCP possesses tremendous power to control its society, like every regime, it does not possess authority over the logical consequences of its policies. Just like Maoist China learned that crippling socialist economic policies have the expected effect of crippling the economy, today's China is not exempt from the effects, good and bad, of its initiatives.

If the decades leading up to 2020 were the time of an ascendant China, growing rapidly economically, militarily, and diplomatically, then the 2020s onward is surely the time of an embattled China. There are serious challenges, whether that is a declining birthrate due to a one-child policy, a rowdy digital tech sector that challenges the CCP's authority, an unstable banking sector due to decades of reckless lending, or the world attempting to form a balancing coalition against Beijing. All these forces explain why

Xi's China tightened controls over society so drastically and why one can even observe a steady increase leading into his term.

Good Turns to Bad

Much like every country, structural incentives encourage unique types of poor policy making and make coarse correction painful, if not impossible. For example, China's economy may have grown at a breakneck pace, but part of that growth was due to overzealous banking (Mendhell, 2021). The Evergrande examples demonstrates how the expectations of political economy still function in China. Rational stakeholders will attempt to extract as much personal benefit out of a broken system as the structural incentives will allow.

In 2021, the consequences of decades of lackluster supervision and corruption in the housing finance sector culminated in the near default of Evergrande, a multibillion-dollar company (Mendhell, 2021). According to the Wall Street Journal, the megacompany struggled to pay back its debt, sometimes resorting to substituting cash payments with property transfers (Mendhell, 2021). Protests began to erupt at the company headquarters, and the central government refused to issue a bailout.

Eventually, a state-owned bank stepped in to provide a liquidity transfusion by buying out one of Evergrande's holdings. Indeed, this near-death experience led observers to liken the crisis to the collapse of Lehman Brothers during the 2008 Financial Crisis, a crisis that the Chinese consistently bragged about avoiding (Wong, 2021). Although China's regulators are competent enough to prevent a market collapse, the debt problems throughout the banking sector are daunting, especially amongst the smaller institutions (The Economist, 2021).

In June of 2022, protestors swarmed around a regional bank in Zhengzhou, experiencing a bank run due to its poor lending practices, a mounting concern in the country's small to medium-sized institutions. However, to make matters worse, the government attempted to curtail the civil unrest by marking travelers Covid-19 positive to leverage the national Zero Covid Policy (Bloomberg News, 2022). The scandal made international headlines and only exacerbated the problem by turning a financial problem into an emblematic reason to distrust the CCP's authoritarian public health governance. At the same time, one could not help but notice that the debacle represented the logical consequences of the Party's authoritarian, state capitalist policies that encouraged reckless lending and abuse of power.

Contrast this chaos with the decade before. China was the first major economy to emerge from the 2008 Recession, and its economy played a role in keeping other countries afloat (Wong, 2011). Much of this feat is attributable to the fact that the Chinese were not well integrated with the global financial system at the time but still suffered a sizable hit to overseas consumption in the West (Dollar, 2018). Therefore, Beijing never got caught up in the domino effect of financial chaos that characterized the Financial Crisis. This success played a role in the CCP's ego boost and also marked an important shift in Sino-US relations, where anxiety in Washington over China's rise coincided with a declining perception of American power in Beijing (Dollar, 2018).

Due to China's insulation from speculative investments overseas in 2008, continued growth, the West's preoccupation with other threats, and the political chaos created by President Donald Trump's election in the US in 2016, Beijing fancied itself to be the inevitable global leader (Womack, 2017). For years, things seemed to go in China's favor. Social unrest in the United States and the relative apprehension of other countries to join Trump's crusade against China made it seem like the world would be complacent or even accepting of Beijing being in charge. It seemed that the CCP's strategy of economic integration and sharp power projection had whipped the West into compliance. The lack of real action over any of the widely publicized atrocities, such as the Xinjiang internment camps or the crackdown on the Hong Kong Protest in 2019, seemed to confirm this narrative. Then, when the Covid-19 outbreak began in Wuhan and spread throughout the world, people like Microsoft founder Bill Gates endorsed the use of Chinese-style lockdown policies and mass testing to control the virus (Duffy, 2020).

Although there were signs of growing trouble for Beijing leading up to the 2020s, such as growing inequality, environmental degradation, geopolitical tensions, and a loss of party centrality, the narrative skewed toward an ascendant China. Today, the story is flipped; some China experts are starting to believe that we have reached "peak Xi" or even peak China (Kempe, 2022). Xi was once the political juggernaut that abolished term limits, reasserted the CCP in society, and kicked off a number of ambitious state projects, including the Dual Circulation Strategy, an industrial policy scheme that hopes to create economic self-sufficiency while making the world dependent on Chinese consumers, and the Belt and Road initiative. Today, however, Xi's defining traits are presiding over a disastrous Zero Covid Policy, a slowing economy, an implicit endorsement of the Russian invasion of Ukraine, and faltering business confidence over Common Prosperity. Although this is not to say he will be challenged and replaced during his bid for a third term, his image as an infallible political leader is over. Instead of setting the terms of engagement and molding China to his will, the consequences of his own policies are starting to mold his own decision-making.

A Backlash Abroad

Financing for the Belt and Road project is dwindling. Countries worldwide are becoming suspicious of Chinese investment (Mingey and Kratz, 2021). The word Common Prosperity has all but faded from usage as the Party desperately attempts to save face in front of a corporate world that sees far too much political risk (Hass, 2021). Finally, the West is increasingly united against Beijing, as the Australians increasingly disregard their economic ties to China for a security-focused stance with America, most notably through AUKUS, a pact between the US, Australia, and the UK (The White House, 2022).

The Europeans, previously unwilling to take sides in the US-China rivalry, are increasing their pressure on Beijing; Germany is raising human rights concerns and France has reasserted its strategic presence in Asia (Ministere Des Armees, 2019). Nations that once saw the US-China feud as an economically destabilizing drama between two superpowers now notice potential problems with uncontained Chinese influence. Furthermore, many analysts have theorized that Beijing fears the Biden administration more than the previous administration (Tharoor, 2020). Not only does President Biden intend to continue to improve upon the competitive strategy of the Trump administration, but the current commander-in-chief is likely capable of winning more partners abroad. Although the rhetoric may be softer, the policies and diplomacy of the Biden administration lack the stigma of the former while likely being more nuanced.

Some of these developments are the natural effects of China's increasing power and weight in the world as an authoritarian nation with values drastically different from the West. However, much of the backlash stems from the deliberate policy decisions made by the CCP, whether that be implicitly supporting the Russians in Ukraine, promoting wolf warrior diplomacy, or drastically undermining business confidence with Common Prosperity. In fact, in June of 2022, Foreign Affairs noted that Xi dispatched a special envoy to Europe on a 3-week tour to clean up China's image. The Atlantic Council notes,

> *The Chinese want to change the tone of the story, to control the damage," said one European business leader who asked to remain anonymous due to his Chinese business interests. "They understand they have gone too far (Kempe, 2022).*

Public opinion in the West and around the world is actively souring for one reason or another. Elected leaders, whether they sympathize with the CCP or not, must contend with the growing antagonism towards the Chinese government. Although the Chinese may have the corporate community to vouch for friendlier relationships, those interests are easily overshadowed by the growing chorus of national security, political, and popular interests.

In Poland, Xi's diplomatic envoy struggled to even get a meeting with government officials (Barkin, 2022). In Africa, a continent where Beijing still remains strong, but increasingly less so, resentment is building towards the problems caused by the Belt and Road Initiative (Wu, 2019). Although African governments once scrambled to receive Chinese aid, and many still do, many people are starting to point out the disruptive effects of corrupt lending practices, high debt rates, and the importation of Chinese workers (Wu, 2019).

Furthermore, other global powers, like the EU, Japan, and the United States are starting to see the value in engagement with Africa and Southeast Asia (Wu, 2019). Although the CCP may have established a first-mover advantage by noticing the lack of Western involvement in the Global South, that exclusivity is over. The Biden Administration's 2022 Indo-Pacific Strategy mentioned the term, Southeast Asia, 14 times while only being about 15 pages of substantive writing. ASEAN, the regional equivalent of the European Union, is mentioned 19 times (The White House, 2022).

The document detailed ambitious plans for economic engagement, investment, diplomatic ties, and strategic cooperation. Japan, a key ally of the US, is increasingly leveraging its high status as an economic and diplomatic influencer in Southeast Asia to position itself as a regional player (Thu, 2022). The nations of ASEAN are perilously split between China and the United States. Some like Vietnam have to balance Beijing and Washington while also considering that they receive over 80% of their military equipment from Moscow (SIPRI, 2022). Tokyo's unique position in the region may give it leverage in leading these countries in constructive dialogues while also creating space for partners like South Korea, Australia, and the US to break through (Thu, 2022).

Beijing believed it could use economic integration and diplomacy to exert influence across the world in a manner that would be irresistible. However, that leverage and control is starting to fade and more rival powers are declaring their intentions to compete with China. In many ways, the evidence suggests that China's leverage varies drastically and is not as pervasive as it may seem at first glance (Russel et al., 2018). Furthermore, countries that the CCP believed they could easily turn into client states are starting to notice the negative side effects of working with the Chinese and are now being presented with alternative partners, be it the US, Japan, or Europe. Perhaps if the CCP stuck to the hide and bide strategy for another decade or so without announcing ambitious projects or starting territorial feuds, things might have been different. Perhaps if Xi kept his head down and continued in the tradition of Deng Xiaoping by not taking the lead and not causing a commotion on the world stage, Chinese influence would still be increasing without concern.

This counterfactual is certainly an interesting one and raises the question of whether hiding and biding as an emerging global superpower would even be possible. For one, there is the inherent temptation for leaders, inside and outside of China, to take note of power. Xi's China and Deng's China were fundamentally different countries in terms of standing in the world, economic development, and military strength. Although President Trump made the first, flashiest, and most determined calls to confront China, the Obama Administration actually started Washington's "Pivot to Asia" (Lieberthal, 2011)

Regardless of whether Beijing did anything to provoke America, any rational observer could see that the Asia-Pacific region would be a consequential area for the next few decades. This is not just because of the massive economic presence of the Asia-Pacific, which in 2008 contributed to around 40 percent of global growth (European Central Bank, 2008). North Korean missile testing, an alarming strategic threat, is one of the most explicit events that pushed Washington to set its sights on the region, often making demands that were against China's interest, such as pressuring Pyongyang to stop (Lieberthal, 2011). To make matters worse, the US began conducting naval exercises in the Yellow Sea, Beijing's front yard, to deter the North Koreans.

Furthermore, during a territorial dispute with Japan over the Senkaku/ Diaoyu islands, the US State Department explicitly supported Tokyo, Beijing's bitter rival (Lieberthal, 2011). Regardless of whether the CCP wanted to continue hiding and biding, these actions were against their strategic interests and nationally embarrassing. As an upcoming great power, Beijing faced considerable incentives to assert itself and stand up for its interests, which, as a revisionist, authoritarian power, stand contrary to Washington.

The American media saw the pivot to Asia as a China-focused policy, even though it was far more complicated (Lieberthal, 2011). Beijing's exponential growth and increasingly assertive behavior in the region made clear that China would become an important player in global affairs. Although the Obama administration noted Beijing's increasingly assertive behavior in the region, it is likely that the great power competition we now see today was inevitable. The CCP as a Leninist, nationalist regime cannot justify to its own national interests or its domestic population that standing by as the Americans exert dominance in their backyard is a good idea. The US, as the reigning global hegemon and liberal democracy, cannot stand to watch an authoritarian power exert negative influence across the world.

But the reports of human rights violations and allegedly unfair trade practices, especially in a country as important as China, attracted demands from voters to be more confrontational. During the 2008 Beijing Olympics, when the world gazed in awe at the magnitude of China's economic development, pro-Tibet banners flew in places like California's Golden Gate Bridge (Christie, 2008). Even stronger human rights protests, including calls to boycott the 2022 Winter Olympics in China, emerged as Beijing continued to rise in power and publicity (Human Rights Watch, 2022). When a country is posturing for global leadership, that country is justifiably held to higher expectations and given more publicity. In China's case, such pressure to reform its socio-economic policies and check its strategic ambitions is unacceptable, as well as potentially destabilizing. Therefore, one can posit that the CCP's increasing aggression is not a tactical blunder of the Hu and Xi administrations, but instead necessary to maintain power at home and abroad.

The Monumental Challenge of Doing

Today's China understands deeply the problems it faces, including a shrinking population, a great power competition with the West, the need to create a dynamic internal market while maintaining an authoritarian system at its core, among other issues. The CCP understands that it is attempting truly monumental tasks and proposes ambitious solutions, see Dual Circulation, the Belt and Road Initiative, the Common Prosperity Agenda, and so on.

As important and as tailored as these ideas are toward addressing China's problems, whether they are even functional is a different question. For example, attempting to create "10,000 little giants" with highly intrusive industrial policies and antitrust laws may be a rational response to the CCP's desire to create a highly innovative economy (US Chamber of Commerce, 2022). Whether or not this sort of central planning is even possible is highly suspect given how the use of state subsidies and antitrust fines have created massive market distortions and frightened private investors. Furthermore, SOE reform, as mentioned earlier, is essential, but seemingly impossible, as each president has tried, and failed, to confront the massive interest that is state-run companies. Not only does the CCP have an interest in using SOEs to centrally run the economy, but these companies represent a considerable political force. Comprehensive SOE reform would likely leave many public officials out of a job or at least with less power. These disgruntled officials and employees will create an angry faction that is willing to support a challenger to the brave but unfortunate leader that decides to take on SOE reform.

Furthermore, the Chinese model of massive infrastructure spending may project an image of strength, provide jobs, and raise GDP numbers but such expansive state spending has long-term consequences. A study at Oxford's Said Business School (2016) notes,

> 'From our sample, the evidence suggests that for over half of the infrastructure investments in China made in the last three decades the costs are larger than the benefits they generate, which means the projects destroy economic value instead of generating it,' comments Dr Ansar. 'Unless China shifts to fewer and higher-quality infrastructure investments the country is headed for an infrastructure-led national financial and economic crisis, which is likely to spread to the international economy,' he adds.

The private sector allocates resources in a manner that is typically far more efficient and less politically driven than the state. There is little cost-benefit analysis that occurs when the state is not operating on a profit-and-loss basis but more so from a political interest framework. Bullet trains and roads may give the CCP the image of modernity and progress that is desired but ultimately, wasted resources have consequences. Furthermore, much like SOE reform, reigning in wasteful infrastructure spending may prove to be difficult given that there is likely a strong vested interest in continuing to finance various projects and funneling money toward various regions.

While necessary institutional reforms are difficult, the CCP also needs to address problems that nobody seems to know the answer to. The most pressing one is a low birth rate that threatens to cut the population in half by the end of the century (Anderson, 2020). This predicament is particularly existential for Beijing as a lower population not only means less economic power but also a fundamental imbalance of working to retirement age citizens. The end result of such an imbalance, provided that China does not make massive leaps in productivity, would be an inability to adequately fund social programs. Furthermore, the frustration of an overtaxed younger generation that believes that the older segments of the population are sapping all the resources will lead to social upheaval.

The CCP understands this threat and is taking a number of efforts to attempt to combat this trend, most of which are not producing favorable results. Lifting the One Child Policy, restricting abortion access, and expanding resources for fertility, all seemed to produce marginal improvements with no substantial benefit (Qi, 2022). Part of the problem is almost irreversible such as a deficit of childbearing women due to the consequences of the One-Child Policy. Other roadblocks are inherent to China's economic development such as a shift in priorities as more women move to the cities to start careers and sentiments about women's rights and autonomy spread (Huifeng, 2022). Therefore, although the CCP will go to great lengths and creativity to resolve the existential question of the country getting old before getting rich, it remains to be seen whether Beijing can solve the problem without potentially destabilizing reforms.

Finally, Chinese economic growth for the foreseeable future is likely going to be slower and less stable than in years past (Wright, 2022). For one, Beijing is steadily approaching the time where catchup growth ends and where cutting-edge growth is necessary. Companies are starting to reorient their supply chains away from China, not just because labor is cheaper in other developing countries but because of the political risk of doing business (Ghosh, 2022). Part of that risk stems from the escalating great power competition between Beijing and Washington, and another part is because of the CCP's own policies. The Zero Covid policies are an acute example of how the Party's lack of concern for individual freedoms and overconfidence in state power not only makes China dangerous for investment today but for the next problem that arises in society.

Beijing's political alignment with states like Russia and overly reflexive regulatory policy-making, such as the Common Prosperity Campaign, are exacerbating capital flight. Whereas China may have been a growing center for financial activity, recent developments have thoroughly frightened investors about the chance of another corporate crackdown or geopolitical scandal (Wright, 2022). Furthermore, the property sector, which accounts for around a quarter of GDP, has been steadily declining after the CCP took steps to avoid a bubble in 2021 post Evergrande, which included a systematic deleveraging of the industry (Bloomberg News, 2022). Furthermore, the Zero Covid Policy combined with attempts to mitigate fossil fuel emissions has only worsened the drag on the country's most productive sector (Wright, 2022).

Any observer should likely conclude that the problems within China will either persist indefinitely, such as its politicized economy or get worse before they get better, such as the banking system or social repression. Large policy initiatives, whether they be the redistributionism of Common

Prosperity, or the central planning of the Dual Circulation Strategy, will likely produce more disruption regardless of whether they achieve their goals. As China approaches the middle-income trap and gears up for a tech competition with the US, it remains to be seen whether Beijing's ever-present hand in the economy can actually lead to cutting-edge growth. Pair this substantial challenge with the need to maintain domestic order and international standing and the CCP may have bit off more than it can chew.

Although this is not to gloss over all the things working in China's favor, there is no denying that the challenges the CCP faces are existential due to its political system. The People's Republic of China maintains a rigid, inflexible regime with little room for dissent and an obsession with domestic stability. The lack of checks and balances means that rash, self-serving decisions are encouraged and frequent, not rare and mitigated. These decisions, whether they be waging war against one's own tech companies, antagonizing investors, or over-the-top human rights abuses may forward internal control but ultimately undermine progress. China's political system can be highly useful when it is used correctly and tremendously wasteful to downright catastrophic when human nature rears its ugly head.

The question for Washington in the context of the US-China rivalry is not just understanding the ins and outs of Chinese policy making, but also ensuring America puts its best foot forward. Although China certainly has a number of important shortcomings and limitations because of the nature of its political system, so too does the US.

Contemporary China and US Policy

In the 21st century, developments in contemporary Chinese policy appear disorderly, contradictory, and perhaps inhumane. The CCP is at the helm of an increasingly advanced economy and is actively attempting to reshape the global balance of power, yet the CCP is an authoritarian government attempting to exert heavy-handed control over dynamic issues, like financial regulation, high-tech industrial organization, and policing 1.4 billion people. Some might proclaim that Chinese leaders, such as Hu Jintao and Xi Jinping, have made tactical blunders in rolling back decades of liberalization and aggravating the West. Although it is fair to say China has overestimated its capabilities, much of what we might see as poor policymaking was also beneficial or politically necessary for actors within the Chinese government.

Chinese regulators are likely aware of the complications that arise from intrusive government intervention, but the political realities necessitate the use of such policies. Such delicate matters are typically addressed with a light touch, which is why liberal democracies can facilitate incredibly prosperous and diverse societies. Excessive government regulations often inhibit the private sector's corrective responses, whether it be managing boom and bust cycles in the stock market or facilitating the development of cutting-edge industries.

Perhaps the most publicized and most sensationalized actions the Chinese government commits are its social policies. Although interventionist commercial regulations may be easily understood as economic statecraft aimed at achieving strategic goals, a casual onlooker may struggle to see the rationale behind Beijing's involvement in social life. It can often be tempting to write off the CCP's treatment of its citizens as merely a disregard for individual rights and enmity towards targeted groups.

Consider the ongoing human rights abuses in Xinjiang. Perhaps a million Uyghur Muslims are locked up in what the CCP euphemistically calls "vocational training camps." The province was once an independent nation known as East Turkestan and as the name suggests, is home to a minority group of Turkic Muslims rather than Han Chinese (World Uyghur Congress, 2022). The territory itself has a complicated history. The Qing Dynasty annexed it in 1759; it became an independently governed Soviet satellite state in the mid-1940s; then the Chinese Communists annexed it once again in 1949 (Hasanli, 2020). Like in Tibet, Xinjiang's indigenous people are considered an ethnic minority in China and there are strong separatist sentiments. Several groups engage in pro-independence advocacy. Some are peaceful, like the East Turkestan National Freedom Center (ETNFC) in Washington, DC. Others are violent, like the Eastern Turkestan Islamic Party of Allah (ETIPA) (Chung, 2002, 8).[4] The CCP alleges that many of these separatist groups have ties to terrorist organizations operating in Afghanistan. Uygur separatist groups have conducted brutal terrorist attacks over the years. Such attacks include the 1977 bus bombing in Beijing and the attack of Turkey's Chinese Consulate that same year (Chung, 2002, 8). There are also a number of cells engaging in guerilla warfare-style attacks

[4] China executed the leader of the ETIPA in 2001.

against Chinese assets in Xinjiang's Taklimakan Desert.

Despite the apparent tenacity of Xinjiang to be independent, the CCP is stalwart in its will to hold onto the region. The Uyghur people are culturally and historically distinct from Han China. The leadership recognizes that Xinjiang shares very little in common with traditional narratives of Chinese history. This is why the CCP is systematically dismantling the Uyghur identity. Beijing has invested billions of dollars into the construction of concentration camps that collectively occupy the equivalent of over 140 soccer fields (Maizland, 2022). These camps and, by extension, the security state allows the CCP to engage in industrial scale repression. Those unfortunate enough to be detained by the government are reportedly punished with abuses ranging from renouncing their religion, performing slave labor, undergoing indoctrination, to outright torture.

According to documents obtained by the *New York Times*, a secret 2014 speech by Xi Jinping called for showing "absolutely no mercy" and "using the organs of dictatorship" to combat religious extremism (Ramzy & Buckley, 2019). In 2016, a party official known for the repression tactics he implemented in Tibet, Chen Quanguo, assumed leadership in Xinjiang (Wong, 2019). In 2017, the local government passed a law banning wearing veils, growing beards, and other expressions of Islam (Maizland, 2022). By importing ethnic Han Chinese, the central government is actively diluting the demographic concentration of the region. An article in *The Diplomat* explains,

> The Communists thus encouraged Han to migrate to Xinjiang, first forcibly by demobilizing army regiments in the area and sending Han youth to "learn from the peasants" (and then refusing to allow them to return home). Later, the Party used economic incentives, such as discounts on land prices. The policies worked: in 1949 the Han population in Xinjiang was 5 percent of the province's total, in 1978 it was 40 percent (Torrey, 2017).

Public choice theory asks, why does the Chinese government invests so much time, effort, and exposure to condemnation into controlling Xinjiang? A public choice analysis reveals that rational objectives, not simply an ideological disregard for human life, drives the CCP's calculus. Xinjiang has strategic and political importance.

The Uyghur homeland is a core economic and geopolitical interest for Beijing. Historically, the region has served as a link in the famous Silk Road (Chung, 2022, 10).[5] Today, it is an important component of a series of trade and investment projects, the Belt and Road Initiative, that foster Beijing's commercial presence in the world. Xinjiang also produces over a third of Chinese cotton, and the Tarim Basin is home to the country's largest fossil fuel reserves. The nation is a critical military asset allowing Beijing to project power into Central and South Asia, while also serving as a prime location to store the PLA's nuclear arsenal (Gu, 2021). Both these capabilities will only grow in importance as the CCP hedges against growing tensions with India on its Southwest flank and a potential confrontation with the US.

Controlling Xinjiang also serves an essential political purpose. The most salient objective is keeping the country unified as China deals with independence movements not just from the Uyghurs but the Tibetans, Hong Kong, Taiwan, and general skeptics of the party's authoritarian rule. Failing to hold Xinjiang or acquiescing to the demands of Uyghur nationalists will only inspire more demands from other groups, perhaps leading to a snowball effect. As a Leninist regime that revolves around a central power base rather than institutions, the CCP employs a mix of appeasement and repression to keep its population loyal. Appeasement is derived from economic growth, infrastructure investments, and public services. Repression is created by constructing a formidable national security state. Mercilessly cracking down on Xinjiang exemplifies the priorities of the CCP that are likely derived from the very nature of its governmental structure. In a one-party state, dissent and separatism must be crushed, concessions will only lead to more demands, and the example set in Xinjiang will make others think twice. In fact, the Uyghurs have served as a case study for policies and technologies to be implemented in other parts of the country to bolster the state's control and subdue resistance in problem areas (Wong, 2019).

Common Prosperity and Economic Central Planning

Beijing's increasing repression of social freedoms also coincides with a drastic shift in political-economic liberty as well. Much of the drastic re-centralization of power in the hands of the central government is in

---

[5] The silk road allowed imperial China to trade with nations as far as the Roman Empire.

reaction to the consequences of decades of decentralization. Following the proclamation of Deng Xiaoping's reform and opening period in 1978, the CCP continued down a path of power dispersal. The private sector became the dominant contributor to GDP, state-owned enterprises were reformed, and collective governance replaced the cult of personality.

For example, in the antitrust sector, Chinese regulators were laxer than their US counterparts, allowing firms to engage in what many Western observers considered to be anticompetitive conduct (Reuters, 2021). Thousands of companies violated environmental regulations, destroying the environment and causing serious public health issues (Wong, 2017). China's income inequality is one of the largest among all developed countries, and stratification exists not just among individuals but also provinces (Bloomberg News, 2021). Chinese corporations popularized an arduous work schedule known as 996, 9 AM to 9 PM 6 days a week, which has led to leaps in productivity but also serious consequences, such as workplace deaths (BBC, 2021).

This laundry list of economic griefs inspired what would become the opening salvos of Xi Jinping's Common Prosperity initiative as Chinese regulators suddenly increased the magnitude and frequency of corporate crackdowns, particularly in the technology sector, in 2021 (Che and Goldkorn, 2021). The crackdown saga began with Alibaba when it was punished with multibillion dollar fines, which was not enough to damage the company in the long-run but enough to highlight a political statement (Zhong, 2021). The ensuing regulatory onslaught spread from the technology sector into other areas, which included banning private tutoring, tightening controls on corporate debt, and artificially suppressing prices across various industries (Roberts, 2021). The "Common Prosperity" agenda's stated purpose is to address income inequality and enlarge the middle class as China's economy moves into the high middle-income bracket. This priority is sound, given that growth in China primarily occurred near the coastline, historically the center of commerce. Furthermore, industrial policies, such as subsidies, low to no interest taxes, and preferential bank loan treatment, combined with protectionist policies support unproductive companies, most of which are state-owned, and exacerbate the misallocation of resources (Scissors, 2013).

In short, "Common Prosperity" is a recognition of the adverse political-economic consequences of the CCP's transition from a Socialist planned economy to a state capitalist model. Xi understands the politically destabilizing effect of unequal economic growth and large, influential companies. Therefore, "Common Prosperity" is not just about fixing chronic issues in the Chinese economy, it reminds corporations that the CCP is in control. Xi's directive to private companies to shoulder more social responsibilities demonstrates a union of both priorities (Cai, 2021). This edict addresses important political objectives and reiterates the ultimate authority of the Party.

However, even Xi's signature domestic economic policy is not immune from politics. In April 2022, the *Wall Street Journal* reported that Beijing wished to refocus on economic growth and accordingly reduce the use of the term "Common Prosperity," after its previous pervasive touting of the term (Xie, 2022). The reasons seem like a perfect storm. Investors are losing confidence in the Chinese regulatory body's independence, and China's "Zero Covid" policy resulted in a self-induced economic downturn to address surging omicron cases (Wang, 2022).

Alongside Xi's Common Prosperity agenda are sweeping policies, such as its Military-Civil Fusion program and Made in China 2025 initiative, which integrates party ambitions with economic operations (Xinhua, 2015; State Council (China), 2015). The Military-Civil Fusion program is a national strategy to fuse private sector innovations with its military capabilities to advance the People's Liberation Army (PLA) into a "world class military" by 2049 pursuant to XI's vision of "the great rejuvenation of the Chinese nation" [中华民族伟大复兴] (State Department (US), 2022; Ministry of Foreign Affairs (China), 2022). Innovations and talent in high-tech sectors such as artificial intelligence are siphoned off to aid the military, often without the consent or knowledge of the companies involved. The benefits of bolstering the military, which is an arm of the CCP and not a branch of the government, are clear, but military-civil fusion also complicates business with Chinese firms because shared information or resources shared could be funneled to aid the military, which is a national security concern of US policymakers (Ma, 2021).

Made in China 2025 is a recognition that in order for Beijing to be the dominant economic juggernaut in the 21st century, it must transition to a high-tech, high value add economy (McBride & Chatzky, 2019). It goes without saying that this initiative goes hand in hand with Military Civil Fusion as any advancements made whether that be in establishing domestic capabilities in artificial intelligence, 3-D printing, and semiconductors will also aid the PLA. For decades, the Chinese relied on being the world source of cheap, competent labor for manufacturing. Beijing achieved this objective by opening up to foreign trade and investment while providing attractive incentives such as a lax regulatory oversight and low taxes (Bajpai, 2022). Today, not only is low-end manufacturing moving to other countries, but the CCP recognizes that the country needs to develop its own domestic corporate portfolio with cutting edge companies to overtake the US in overall global influence. Furthermore, establishing an advanced manufacturing base would ensure China can progress into higher stages of societal wealth and overcome the middle-income trap, therefore mitigating the potential unrest that accompanies economic stagnation.

The practices that accompany the industrial policies associated with Made in China 2025 have drawn international criticism. For example, the protectionist measures exercised by Beijing are far more severe than countries like Germany in that the government gives direct subsidies to domestic firms and erects substantial barriers against foreign companies doing business in China (McBride & Chatzky, 2019).

Overproduction of strategic materials such as solar panels and steel creates serious supply shocks in foreign markets as Beijing floods countries with subsidized goods, harming domestic firms (McBride & Chatzky, 2019). Finally, Chinese firms making acquisitions globally pose the risk that entire supply chains and large swaths of a country's private sector could be owned by entities that cannot separate themselves from the control of the CCP. This reality is obviously good for the Party, bad for rival states, and a mixture of domestic necessity influencing foreign policy.

A Massive Corruption Purge

Xi's China also dealt with a reckoning with rampant political corruption which not only created fault lines between reformers and conservatives within the CCP but undermined the public's faith in the government. Interestingly, Yukon Huang, a Senior Fellow at the Carnegie Endowment, explains that in many ways, corruption led to more economic growth due to the structural differences in China's system (2017). Rather than taking bribes to enact political favors or extract rents like in a typical scheme, corruption typically involves officials simply taking a cut of company profits in exchange for turning a blind eye. Essentially, corruption officials in China act more as traditional shareholders than extortionists, allowing certain companies to essentially engage in standard market behavior, rather than having to follow all the strict rules typical of a Socialist system. However, this behavior also draws the ire of the public, exacerbates inequality, and opens the door for further criminal activity. Furthermore, the growth of bureaucracy and patronage politics creates a strong interest group dynamic that is not only difficult to remove but gains inertia.

Purging corrupt officials has always been a focus of the CCP since its earliest days, however, anti-corruption prosecution, especially for high-ranking officials, increased drastically under Xi Jinping. Andrew Wedeman (2021) a professor of political science, recounts the opening of 2012 when he notes,

> In early January, newly elected General Secretary of the CCP Xi Jinping ordered a new all-out attack on corruption and vowed that he would to not only "swat flies" (low-ranking officials) but also "hunt big tigers" (senior officials). Over the next eight years, almost 300 senior state officials, party cadres, and military officers were implicated.

According to Wedeman's (2021) data, the number of "tigers" prosecuted in anti-corruption drives prior to Xi's tenure stood around four annually and then soared as high as 29, 100 percent of which are thought to have become corrupt under the Jiang Zemin or Hu Jintao eras. This campaign has often been framed as an initiative to cement Xi's power and with his nearly untouchable political capital, that is certainly plausible. The real answer is likely that the paramount leader has essentially killed numerous birds with one stone, eliminating competition, purging true bad actors, capturing the respect of the Chinese people, and trimming the fat of the party. Here we see the reoccurring public choice priorities of consolidating power, appeasing the public, and rationally addressing broad issues in society.

Unlimited Terms for Xi

Following the anti-corruption campaign, Xi did the seemingly unthinkable. He removed constitutional term limits on presidential officeholders (Bader, 2018). To many observers, this move, coupled with the backdrop of the aforementioned economic and social tightening, seems to signal a further backslide into authoritarianism. Deng Xiaoping had introduced term limits to decentralize power, thus creating more institutional legitimacy and reducing the odds of another Mao coming to power. Xi does not have the same temperament or ideas as Mao, and it is unlikely that Xi will ever be incentivized to put China through horrors like those it experienced in the mid-20th century. However, although China may still be a top-down cult of personality system, nothing simply happens because the paramount leader feels like it.

Although the National People's Congress, China's equivalent of a parliament, may function as a rubber stamp with no real authority, the politburo, which often passes on edicts to be approved by Congress, does (Reuters, 2018). In fact, deliberations at the CCP's highest decision making bodies, the politburo standing committee, the military, and state council are quite candid, and the politics very real (US-China Business Council, 2022). Xi being able to convince officials at the highest level to support him demonstrates not only tremendous political capital but also suggest that the times may necessitate such action.

For one, Xi assumed power during a critical turning point in Chinese history. His country is not only facing growing geopolitical challenges but also drastic economic and social changes at home. Furthermore, Xi's administration began a series of ambitious policy campaigns such as the Belt and Road Initiative, Dual Circulation, and Common Prosperity which likely require consistent leadership in order to complete. As a result, Xi's actions not only represent his own ambitions, but a desire of party elites to keep him at the helm because they also derive benefit from his rule.

Although breaking the two-term limit may help China maintain a level of policy stability, it may also degrade overall government effectiveness. An analysis by the Brookings Institute predicts that centralizing more power at the top of the government may likely discourage lower ranking officials to take the initiative and raise concerns (Bader, 2018). At the same time, a more centralized Chinese government may make Chinese foreign policy more predictable and easier to work with as the primary decisions that matter will increasingly lie with Xi and his closest officials, not the diverse opinions within his bureaucracy.

As a result, Chinese elites, in particular, Xi, may start to see a degradation in the quality of advice they receive from local officials and lower ranking staff leading to less informed decision making at the top, and more complacent governance on the ground. Many have raised the same concern with Russia's president, Vladimir Putin, who not only centralized more power around himself throughout the years but also increasingly isolated himself (Schull, 2022). A logical result of such political decay might be his miscalculated invasion of Ukraine and perhaps a lapse in the preparation of the Russian army leading up to the invasion (Kupchan, 2022).

From a public choice perspective, Xi's decision to break the longstanding two-term limit stands out in two distinct ways. The first is that it coincides with Xi's own power maximizing intentions and reflects on the amount of existing authority under his command. The second point is that the CCP's top leadership also found it beneficial to consent to such a bold change in the constitutional structure. Both these factors suggest a more existential driving force behind this reform, which is that both Xi and the party elite find it necessary to continue along the policy vision laid out by Xi, rather than risk the inconsistency that comes with a new president. Perhaps this speaks to possible internal stability issues, the fact that China's political and economic landscape is in an awesome state of change, and that China's foreign policy requires hyper delicate management given that Beijing and Washington are now in a great power competition. Furthermore, removing the term limit fundamentally changes the structure of Chinese politics in that Xi will need to ensure he enters the election season with strong popular support and that the CCP will not have groomed a successor anytime soon.

Xi Jinping Thought

Xi's outsized legacy and long-term intentions for the party facilitate a need to entrench his ideals into Chinese society. These ideals are articulated as "Xi Jinping Thought." The fact that his ideological contributions not only get the title "thought" and not "theory" but bear his name, places him in the same category as Mao, and above the previous three leaders (Jordan, 2017). Xi Jinping Thought is not necessarily a governing ideology more than it is an articulation of priorities and values to be adopted by the country. Much like his predecessors, Xi's doctrine reflects the general objectives and concerns of his regime, such as modernizing the military, conforming the law to the party line, and environmental sustainability (BBC, 2021).

To an outside observer, the use of the term Xi Jinping thought or Hu Jintao's "Scientific Development Concept" may come off as a sort of Orwellian form of propaganda and resembles a cult of personality (Fewsmith, 2004, 1). There is some truth to this. However, a more appropriate way to view these executive doctrines is a reflection of the intentions of the leadership and a plan to address the core problems identified by the CCP. Former president Hu Jintao's Scientific Development Concept essentially tried to reconcile the technocratic and pragmatic governance of the CCP as a coherent doctrine. Under Hu, China focused on continuing economic growth, protecting the environment, and fighting corruption by bolstering institutional structures and procedures. Many of these same logical priorities show up in Xi Jinping Thought.

Some key differences with Xi's doctrinal articulations include the depth and scale of influence. Xi Jinping Thought in many ways resembles civics education with the amount of detail and scope encapsulated in its material. The doctrine covers everything from the indoctrination of the youth into Chinese-style socialism to the importance of national security. Part of this is likely due to his own political power and influence compared to the past two presidents, who were generally viewed as lacking vision compared to Mao and Deng (Global Times, 2021). In fact, in 2021, the CCP's resolution, or rewriting, on its history minimized the role of the past two presidents, Jiang Zemin and Hu Jintao, compared to Xi and Deng (New York Times, 2022). Part of this is due to the formers' relatively smaller role in shaping Chinese politics compared to the latter. Another component is that by blaming making the last two presidents seem less significant while associating them with many of China's problems, such as income inequality and environmental degradation, Xi's power is bolstered. Furthermore, because he needs the party elite to agree to endorse the resolution, the fact that this rewriting of history passes signifies that perhaps broader leadership finds it advantageous to the CCP's ongoing rule to build a national cult of personality around Xi.

Rising Nationalism

Revising the history of the Party also feeds into the broader phenomenon of surging Chinese nationalism. Since the post-1978 downfall of Maoism as a uniting ideology fully realized during the Tiananmen Square Protest, the CCP increasingly looked to nationalism to keep the country together. In the wake of the democracy protests in 1989, the Chinese government rolled out "Patriotic Education." Patriotic Education forms the bedrock of modern nationalism in China (Zhao, 1998, 287). In essence, the CCP frames Chinese history as one of national humiliation at the hand of foreign imperialist powers beginning with the First Opium War with the British in 1849 and a quest for national rejuvenation beginning with the formal rule of the CCP over China in 1949 (Hayes, 2022). In 2022, the results of this campaign are clearly seen in China's soaring nationalism that inspires its citizens not just to defend the CCP's authoritarian system but even lash out against foreign companies that voice concerns over slave labor in provinces like Xinjiang (Ma, 2021).

Rewriting history is an important step for the long-term rule of the party as is building a state-led nationalism because it places the party in the middle of China's supposed return to greatness. In the rewritten narrative to oppose the Party is to oppose the nation. In the face of a gradually declining GDP growth and an ever-growing list of social issues, nationalism is the glue that can hold the Party in place (Bradsher, 2022). This is especially important today, not just because of socioeconomic issues, but of separatist movements in areas like Xinjiang, Tibet, Hong Kong, and Taiwan. Chinese history is incredibly complex and full of nuances that are not necessarily reflected in the CCP narrative, which includes the fact many parts of China don't actually consider themselves Chinese.

Furthermore, the socialist underpinnings of this state led nationalism to necessitate careful writing of history because most of China's allegedly 5000 years of proud history is from its feudal period (Bajoria, 2008). However, one cannot look to the grand palaces and exploits of Chinese dynasties and also attribute them to a communist party. Rather, today's nationalism is primarily focused on rallying around the CCP and its vision for what constitutes China, whether that be advancing territorial claims against other countries or repressing ethnic groups in Xinjiang (Xu, 2019). Unlike countries like the United States, which can rally around its shared values in constitutional government, or the United Kingdom, which can take pride in its respected monarchy and ancient parliament, China has no such rally point. As a result, rising levels of Chinese chauvinism and exceptionalism point towards not just China's rising power in the world, but the active efforts of the CCP to craft a national identity around supporting the Party and the state. Xi's efforts to bolster these sentiments by reforming school curriculums to reflect the CCP's priorities represent a key step in shoring up the Party's control over society and ensuring loyalty that extends beyond a social contract for economic growth and public services.

Politics and Self-Interest Apply in China

Chinese presidents like Xi are still subject to political opposition from other elites as well as popular discontent from the general population. The manner in which such challenges are handled is more so determined by the structure of the government, rather than an inherent inclination for authoritarian behavior. A Leninist system where the Party remains the most powerful political entity and National People's Congress functions more as a rubber stamp invites different behavior than a liberal democracy (Sweeney, 2018).

China does not act as a single, evil entity on the world stage. Just like every country, it is led by self-interested and rational individuals who make their decisions within the structural context they occupy. Furthermore, Chinese citizens are also rational, self-interested individuals that seek basic human desires such as economic growth, opportunity, and a secure living environment. As a result, the actions of the Chinese government are logically focused on domestic concerns first, and foreign affairs second. Furthermore, the CCP is primarily concerned with maintaining order and stability for its rule, which often requires making compromises to its own objectives and tailoring policy to appease its own people. Finally, Chinese politics are not a monolith. The individuals within the system are extremely important to the overall trajectory of the nation, whether that be the vision of one person, the compromise of factions, or the self-interested motives of entrenched constituencies. That means understanding and acknowledging the incentives that drive CCP decision-making means one cannot just predict where the Party is heading but also craft more effective policies to confront China.

5. Rooting China's Actions in Historical Reality

When assessing political processes and state transformation, Tilly (2006) writes "there is no way to create comprehensive, plausible, and verifiable explanations without taking history seriously into account." History is a powerful tool in political analysis because it connects present policies and worldviews to legacies of the past. The Chinese leadership's policies and worldviews exhibit recurring themes and sentiments shaped by memories of the past that were perceived to affect China's order, stability, and power. China's vast and rich history, from dynasty to nation-state, unveils the underpinnings of how PRC leaders choose to lead and engage with its people and other nations. Ideas, events, and policies of the past molded modern Chinese institutions and political ideology, which manifests as the decisions CCP leaders make today. Chinese intellectual debates on the lessons that should be drawn from history are ongoing, but it is abundantly clear where the leadership's priorities lie: the preservation of stability [维稳] (Feng, 2013).

We begin by first addressing three aspects most Western observers get wrong about China. History is salient because it breathes life into a "collective memory of the past" that molds a people's identity (Wang, 2008). These unique histories distinguish not only identity but also analytical frameworks in which to understand political behavior and institutions. Thus, China cannot be analyzed with frameworks derived from the Western experience, and misconceptions of China are ultimately the result of such attempts. Nonetheless, these offer essential discussion points because it shows how misunderstandings of Chinese political motivations result in erroneous conclusions and, consequently, misaligned policy objectives.

First, China cannot be understood through the lens of the liberal world order. The post-WWII world order that the US created suggested that democratic and economic development occurred in parallel. Despite China's lagging progress in fulfilling its WTO accession requirements, President George W. Bush ardently advocated for its WTO accession in 2001 because he believed that China would not only enter into a new era of economic prosperity, but more in line with America's agenda, foster democratic development, proliferate liberal ideals, and open a massive untapped consumer market to American businesses. Even prior to the turn of the century, the US-China rapprochement in 1972 launched decades of cooperation and optimism until the early 2000s when hawks sounded the alarm bells over the US's growing trade deficit with China, currency devaluations, intellectual property (IP) theft, and lack of market access. Concurrently, China's economy was growing at an unprecedented double-digit GDP growth rate, and it became an industrial powerhouse as the label of 'The World's Factory' highlights. This has incited retrospective discussions on whether the US should have played a key role in supporting China's accession into the WTO and granted it Most Favored National (MFN) trade status. However, this is the wrong question to be asking.

The question should not be whether or not the US should have promoted China's economic integration into the economic world order or why China is not a democracy today. When Chinese President Hu Jintao and US President George W. Bush made their initial opening statements to the press on April 20, 2006, an American reporter asked President Hu, "When will China become a democracy with free elections (White House, 2006)?" In the translated transcripts provided by the US Office of the Press Secretary, President Hu replied:

> I don't know. What do you mean by democracy? What I can tell you is that we've always believed that, in China, if there is no democracy, there will be no modernization, which means that ever since China's reform and opening up in the late 1970s, China, on the one hand, has vigorously promoted economic reform and, on the other hand, China has also been actively, properly, and appropriately, moved forward the political restructuring process, and we have always been expanding the democracy and freedoms for Chinese citizens.

> In the future, we will, in the light of China's own national conditions and the will of the Chinese people, continue to move ahead with political restructuring and developing socialist democracy. We will further expand the orderly participation of the Chinese citizens in political affairs so that they will be in a better position to exercise their democratic rights in terms of democratic supervision, democratic management, and the democratic decision-making (2006).

The simultaneous Chinese announcements of the meeting made no mention of the content of the interviews, let alone the question of democratic reforms raised by the reporter (China Government Network, 2013). President Hu's response made clear that China's 'democracy' is not the same as an American democratic system that values free and fair elections and the protection of the people's fundamental freedoms. Hindsight is 20/20, and it is clear that a Western governance model has not and will not apply to China's own governance model.

Thus, the question that should be asked is: What did the US misunderstand or downplay that continues to matter in China's decision-making calculus (Ritter & Johnson)? This is the fundamental purpose for this chapter. It is to identify and describe the aspects motivating the Chinese leadership's decision-making calculus.

Second, the Chinese leadership is not a monolith, and the president is not the only decision maker that matters. China's political structure is tremendously complex and misunderstood, and this results in gross misconceptions that the leader of an authoritarian regime should be the sole unit of analysis. This assumption, however, is understandable. The leader of the PRC typically possesses unrivaled power because he wields the three most powerful positions in China: President, Chairman of the Central Military Commission, and General Secretary of the Communist Party of China. In combination, these three spokes of power grant an individual tremendous discretion over the nation's course and military's usage. To contribute to the confusion, China is also a one-party state. This means that the CCP is effectively the only party allowed to occupy government positions. The Chinese Constitution enforces a one-party state model by tightly integrating the party within the very seams of political structure. Consequently, the terms 'Chinese Communist Party' and 'Chinese government' are often used interchangeably in Western media.

The power structure inherently masks the underlying complexities and perspectives of individual politicians and convinces outsiders that the only character who matters is the President. To an extent, this assumption is not entirely incorrect because China implements a top-down governance approach. Lower-level bureaucrats make rational decisions to follow the will of top leadership officials to advance in their careers. Senior-level bureaucrats in the Standing Committee of the Politburo will be purged and disgraced if their agenda threatens or interferes with that of the President's. Furthermore, the Xi Jinping's centralization of power has shifted the incentives at play, increasing the cost of deviance and the benefits of compliance.

Third, Chinese citizens are generally satisfied with the CCP, whether or not they believe it is an authoritarian or democratic government and treat it as legitimate (Harsha, 2020; Chen, 2002; Ma, 2021). The pervasive Western misconception is that the people should not accept a government or leadership that is not democratically elected. In other words, an authoritarian regime has no business governing people who do not systematically vote to be ruled by it and possess no individual rights and freedoms (Thayer, 2020). Critics of the Chinese regime have gone so far as to label it a dictatorship (Gueorguiev, 2019; Soros, 2021). Even the CCP's most revered paramount leader, Mao Zedong, attests to China being a dictatorship, more specifically a "people's democratic dictatorship" [人民民主专政。] (Mao, 1949). Mao's framing of a dictatorship draws influence from Marxist-Leninism, in which the CCP represents and leads the working class as the sole legitimate ruling party. However, the semantics of the 'dictatorship' description can only go so far in explaining the incentives underpinning Chinese politics and CCP governance.

Many scholars who study China naturally seek to answer the question of regime legitimacy because the West's ideological framework of governance does not work. In democratic states, open and fair elections proxy the periodic renewal of political legitimacy, but that is not the case in the PRC (Kwok, 2021). The PRC is a one-party state, and officials are appointed by other CCP members in power. This system of power succession is evident in the nation's highest political echelons, in which the Politburo of the CCP, a collective of China's 25 highest ranking individuals, hand pick his or her next successor. If there are no direct elections, then how does the CCP legitimize its grasp on power? The legitimacy question is also of interest to the Chinese leadership and was addressed twice. The first time was after the Tiananmen Square massacre in 1989 when Deng Xiaoping announced economic growth to be the source of the party's legitimacy. The second was in 2015 after President Xi Jinping's purge of purportedly corrupt Chinese officials in the party's ranks. In both instances, social upheaval adversely stirred public sentiments, and the party leadership perceived its reputation to be awry enough to publicly address it.

During the 2015 Chinese Communist Party and the World Dialogue [2015 中国共产党与世界对话会], Wang Qishan, head of the CCP Central Commission for Discipline Inspection (CCDI), addressed the tabooed question of legitimacy. He stated that "the party's legitimacy arises from history and is determined by popular support. The party is the people's choice." Chinese social media users and China watchers abroad responded with mixed interpretations on Wang's proclamation because the concept is shrouded with mystery and no precedent of a clear definition. A netizen cleverly responded with an ironic excerpt from the *Selected Works of Mao Zedong*: "A government that is not elected by the people, how can it claim to be representing the country?" (Ruan, 2015) If legitimacy is defined as the right to rule, then Ci Jiwei (Ci, 2019, pp. 41) offers another line of thought, which is that legitimacy is derived from the party's revolutionary legacy and reputation as founder of the modern Chinese nation, but this source of power is neither sustainable nor satisfactory to the governed in the long run. Despite ongoing discussions on the CCP's longevity, opinion surveys of Chinese public sentiments towards the regime are generally favorable (Harsha, 2020; Chen, 2002; Ma, 2021) and signal the lack of political will to overthrow a regime that is perceived externally as illegitimate. This simple statement is not to suggest that dissenting opinions do not exist because public sentiment is diverse (Whyte, 2002; Mazzocco & Kennedy, 2022), and netizens nimbly navigate the state's media censorship rules to showcase such opinions. However, just as Wang points towards history for legitimacy, we explore the historical narratives underlying the Chinese leadership's perceptions, policies, and motives.

History encompasses the events that shape key decision makers' policies and worldviews and the narratives that the party perpetuates to justify its behavior. History is a process that is recorded with a stroke onto a blank canvas. With each event and idea that takes hold in China is another stroke layered upon another to form an image. While each stroke changes the image, the unseen layers of the past are still present, and the image's interpretation is in the eye of the beholder. What this means is that the behavior of the Chinese leadership, which is informed by its perceptions of history or this canvas, is the culmination of decades if not thousands of years of conflict, prosperity, and lessons chronologically layered upon one another. Narratives perpetuated by the state exemplify the Chinese interpretation of history, and it is significant because what the leadership believes is how it legislates, governs, and engages with its people and the international community. The parts of history not addressed at all does not diminish its importance in broader historical analysis because the party's reason for exclusion reveals just as much about its insecurities as it does its perceived strengths. History ultimately unveils changes and continuity of the ideas underpinning the leadership's ideological beliefs, governance style, and economic and foreign policy.

There are at least four key areas where understanding the Chinese leadership's incentives, beliefs, and values requires a sound understanding of Chinese history and the way in which it manifests as modern policy. These aspects are threats, authority and legitimacy, notions of a nation-state, and its place in the world.

The first aspect is Chinese perceptions of threat. Throughout ancient and dynastic Chinese history, threats to Chinese territory manifested as internal social unrest and external invaders. In much more recent history, in 1991, the fall of the Soviet Union, once the leader of the Communist bloc, is also largely relevant to shaping the CCP's underlying insecurities of its regime's longevity and continues to shape China's intellectual policy discussions today (Page, 2013).

From ancient China (2070 BC – 256 BC) to the dynastic era (221 BC – 1912 AD), internal rebellions and external conflicts marked these nearly 5,000 years of history (Zhou, 2012; Zurndorfer, 1983; Kaufman, 2011). The military conquests of numerous decentralized kingdoms constantly disturbed ancient China's order and stability equilibrium until Qin Shi Huang [秦始皇], otherwise known as Huangdi [皇帝] unified China through brute military force and established the first Chinese dynasty with the title of emperor in 221 BC. While the Qin dynasty was short-lived, sinologist Michael Loewe writes that this first dynasty "exercised a paramount influence on...China's subsequent history" (Loewe, 2000, pp. 654) and marked the beginnings of a dynastic epoch, which ended with the Qing in 1911. A part of the legacy subsequent dynasties established was defining what threats were by way of engagement with such threats.

During the dynastic era, internal instability always loomed. Rulers were very susceptible to social unrest and rebellions because the sheer size and growth of their territory and population demanded resources, expansive bureaucracy, military manpower, and innovative policies that did not exist but were needed to maintain stability and control (Wang). The Lülin and Chimei (AD 17 – 23) were fractured peasant revolts that arose concurrently amidst poor governance and starvation and resulted in the Xin Dynasty's depletion of resources and, ultimately, its fall. A century later, another peasant uprising, the Yellow Turban Rebellion, broke out towards the end of the Eastern Han Dynasty in AD 184. The Tang Dynasty (AD 618 – 907), considered to be China's Golden Age (Benn, 2004), and Song Dynasty (AD 960 – 1279) both self-destructed because its expansionist desires resulted in a territory too vast to control. The Tang's centralized authority thinned, and the empire fractured into warlord states. The Song was no different, but, this time, an external threat, the Yuan Dynasty, conquered the Song's distant borderlands and replaced the Song. The uprisings of rebel units in the 1640s, which consisted of "deserting soldiers" and "starving people," were fueled by the late Ming's exorbitant taxes on peasants and resulted in continual unrest until the Qing military restored order (Wakeman, 1977, pp. 205). During the Qing Dynasty, a rapidly growing population and chronic food shortages invariably resulted in frequent protests (Wong, 1982). Thus, each uprising of peasants or ethnic minorities was accompanied with a brutal military quash ordered from the very top. Although such revolts were often violently suppressed to restore stability, this method proved unsustainable as military resources were scarce, and the depletion of these resources caused rulers to lose control and, eventually, his dynasty.

As observed by Zhou (2012), peasants were not the only source of internal instability. Military officers who broke rank with the emperor also threatened the ruler's grip on power because power and force were the main tools of control over a vast, multi-ethnic empire. Following the death of Huangdi, the Dazexiang Uprising was led by two military officers who gained popular support just as quickly as it was quelled by the imperial Qin army. The relationship between the military and power is most consequential as showcased in the fall of the Ming and rise of the Qing Dynasty. The Manchurians, who established the last Chinese dynasty, were called upon by General Wu Sangui, a Ming-loyalist, to remove the Ming Dynasty's rebel and usurper, Li Zicheng. Aided by the general, the Manchus easily penetrated Ming borders and removed Li, but he unintentionally facilitated the establishment of a new dynasty, the Qing. Thus, military control is inevitably connected to state control. In fact, in the CCP, control of the military (Chairman of the Central Military Commission) constitutes one of the three prongs of absolute power, in addition to control of the state (President) and the party (General Secretary).

Dynastic China enjoyed even less external security than it did internal stability. In this case, external security refers to security of conquered territory and the rulership. The primary threats to external security were the process, or lack thereof, of dynastic transition and the interests and ambitions of foreign civilizations. During the reign of dynasties, there were always groups vying to forcefully claim the 'mandate of heaven' [天明]. The proof of such groups is the rise and fall of dynasties because dynastic transitions occurred only when the old was overthrown with the new. Liu Bang's insurrection was the first successful attempt to overthrow and establish a new dynasty, and this trend of violent succession persisted. From the Qin-Western Han to Ming-Qing, not a single dynasty has ever transitioned without bloodshed and with consensus. The rise of new dynasties was preceded by revolts, corruption, and erosion of central power that either directly or indirectly contributed to the decline of the previous dynasty (RANE, 2013). This dynamic cycle of imperial rebirth is etched into Chinese history and rationalizes an innate motivation to exterminate any perceived external threats because, by precedent, it implies a threat to the ruler's authority and 'mandate of heaven.'

On the Asian continent and beyond, imperialist nations also posed major external threats. During the Qing's reign, bordering civilizations, like Japan and Russia, threatened the fringes of Chinese territory, which were far from Beijing's protection, while Western powers, like Great Britain, challenged both its territorial and economic sovereignty. Arguably the

Qing's most aggressive neighbor, the Japanese empire, waged war on China twice, which became known as the First and Second Sino-Japanese War. Russia and China share a history of possession over Xinjiang, a distant autonomous region of western China today. In the 1930s, Xinjiang was split between Chinese (Eastern Turkestan) and Russian (Western Turkestan) territories after the Soviets provided military assistance to separatists in 1934 (Kamalov, 2021). From across the sea, Great Britain's economic ambitions and coercive trade treaties led to the First (1839 – 1842) and Second (1856 – 1860) Opium Wars, which devastated the Chinese morale, economy, and sovereignty. So devastating were the compounding losses that, in the 1860s, the Qing reformers questioned and rejected what they perceived to be an inherently "noncompetitive, non-striving, and defensive" (Kaufman, 2011) Chinese culture. They, consequently, implemented comprehensive military, cultural, and administrative reforms. A direct solution to the foreign threat was encompassed as "self-strengthening" [自强] (Pong, 2017), which engendered the adoption of Western-inspired military and diplomatic practices.

It is this period in the 19th century that is, perhaps, the most consequential narrative perpetuated by the CCP to the masses. On July 1, 2021, President Xi Jinping (2021) gave a speech commemorating the centenary of the CCP, which marked 100 years of party control, and pushing his narrative of the "rejuvenation of the Chinese nation," a key component of his 'Chinese Dream' doctrine (Cao, 2021). The speech was framed around the idea of 'rejuvenation' and "struggle". As anticipated, Xi began with a narration of the Chinese civilization's "intense humiliation" and "great pain" experienced at the hands of foreigners. Xi credits the party with having saved the nation and "profoundly changed the course of Chinese history." This history is so salient to the CCP's grand rejuvenation narrative that students are inculcated through Deng's national "Patriotic Education Campaign" (Wang, 2008), and history museums were raised to commemorate these "dark anniversaries" (Kaufman, 2011; Wang, 2008; Callahan, 2004). Chinese intellectuals still frame international relation analysis around this period of history in addition to another outstanding historical event in recent memory: the fall of the Soviet Union.

Even after the Qing Dynasty's fall ended China's imperial epoch, the nature of threats was just old wine in new bottles. Internal warfare between political factions (Chinese Civil War) and external invasions from imperialist powers (First and Second Opium Wars, Boxer Rebellion, First and Second Sino-Japanese War) were all too nostalgic for a civilization shaped by violent dynastic transitions, authoritarian suppressions, and defending against its neighbor's territorial conquests. Chinese statesman and general Chiang Kai-Shek's description of China's threats is representative of which threat, internal or external, bore heftier weight. Amidst the Chinese Civil War (1927 – 1949) and the Second Sino-Japanese War (1937 – 1945), Chiang stated, "The Japanese are a disease of the skin, the Communists are a disease of the heart" (White, 1978). Political stability as defined by the absence of violence and structural change (Hurwitz, 1973) did not exist on the mainland, ironically, until the Chinese Communist Party (CCP) overthrew the Nationalist Party and established the People's Republic of China in 1949. The CCP repackaged familiar and recent memories of foreign invasions into a historical narrative, otherwise known as the 'Century of Humiliation.' What is less publicly advertised are the internal threats because it is often the governed that is the source of domestic instability, which Chiang would attest to as he sought to eradicate the Communists. Civilians assemble and, channeling discontent, stir protest behind ideas that challenge authority as was the case with the 1919 May Fourth Movement and the 1980s democracy movement. Thus, the CCP, whose beliefs are shaped by thousands of years of historical internal unrest, is incentivized to proactively allay unrest, or brutally silence dissenters.

The central leadership has drawn from this historical lesson that it cannot be weak. If it is, it will fall prey, either to its own people or to foreigners. China's history shows that an incompetent and weak leadership will either stir discontent amongst the populace and incite revolt or invite foreigners to invade and overtake the empire. The emperors of the past left behind a playbook to address these threats, and the main tactics are to control and suppress dissent, strengthen the state's capabilities, and conquer before being conquered. The modern Chinese leadership established in 1949 follows the same playbook albeit its own history and Marxist-Leninist ideology shaped its more pragmatic interpretation of the historical playbook. Absolute control and suppression are hallmark ideas of Marxist-Leninism and the CCP's revolutionary history, so this fits nicely into the leadership's ideological traditions and policies. The 'conquer' aspect is more complex and shapes the CCP's contemporary territorial claims.

Dynastic expansionism seems to imply that the modern Chinese leadership would be no different. The CCP's territorial claims on the Senkaku (Japanese), or Diaoyu (Chinese), Islands, Taiwan, South China Sea, or the so-called nine-dash line, Arunachal Pradesh, and Depsang Plains underpins the expansionist argument (Danner & Martin, 2019; Maldahiyar, 2021; Rolf & Agnew, 2016; Birdwell & Taherian, 2021). However, territorial claims are not the same as the dynastic appetite for conquest. Conquest was a means to exert dominance and outcompete rivals who had the same ambitions, and to conquer before being conquered was a means of survival. In contrast, China's territorial claims are a matter of nationalism and unity (Huth, 1996; Roy, 1997; Shelef 2016; Tir, 2010).

A 'complete' or unified China, whether or not that be illustrated by the CCP's historical interpretations, invariably grants credibility and legitimacy to the ruling body (Fang & Li, 2019). The survival incentives between imperial China and the CCP are not the same. In fact, according to Carnegie Endowment for International Peace Senior Associate Michael D. Swaine (2015), security behavior "varied enormously" as the dynasties transitioned and its strength waxed and waned. Nonetheless, historical internal and external threats still cast a shadow on the CCP's decision making.

Authority and Legitimacy

The second aspect is authority and legitimacy. The historical dynamics in which leaders exercise authority and people perceive legitimacy is institutionally and ideologically embedded into Chinese consciousness. Authority in the Chinese context is institutionally authoritarian and ideologically backed with legacies of the 'mandate of heaven,' Confucianism, and Marxist-Leninism.

The dominant political theory of ancient and imperial China was the 'mandate of heaven,' in which the ruler of China justly and absolutely exercised top-down mandates and commanded widespread deference to his authority. Zhao (2009) argues that this political concept was an important legitimation tool that was closely tied to performance and governance. More than just an auspicious claim to power, it was a certificate of legitimacy that can be seized if an individual possessed military prowess and political acumen and delivered on *sustainable* domestic order and stability. To sustainably uphold order and stability, even imperial China's rulers recognized the shortcomings of repression. Similarly, in modern China, the right to rule is predicated on the contributions of leaders towards the advancement of Chinese civilization, and such contributions often focus on economic growth, military capabilities, and social unity and stability. Unlike the Western notions of legitimacy, there is neither historical tradition nor a need for democratic tenets, like fair and open elections, rule of law, and limited government, to justify and exert authority.

Although its role should not be overstated (Hu, 2007), Confucianism also perpetuated a sort of paternalistic governance while most of its other tenets are recognized to be outdated. It was once a state ideology that shaped Chinese political, legal, and social norms and values in favor of the imperial governance system (Dubs, 1938; Hu, 2007). Early Confucianism, as a school of thought derived from the *Analects*, described an ideal society as hierarchical, patriarchal, and, consequently, paternalistic. In line with the Confucian concept of the 'rectification of names' [正名], every individual in society was expected to act according to his or her title (mother, daughter, husband, son, etc.). The ruler, specifically, was guided by benevolence (仁), righteousness (义), and propriety (礼) (Hu, 2007, 148). Once patronized by imperial China's emperors, Confucianism was rejected during the New Culture Movement [新文化运动] (1910s-1920s) and, again, by Mao Zedong's Cultural Revolution [文化革命] (1966-1976) (Gregor & Chang, 1979). Despite the undulations of Confucianism's acceptance throughout Chinese history, it defined the role of the leader of the Han Chinese nation and the tenets of civil governance (Sun, 2020), as well as continuing to influence modern Chinese politics.

More relevant to the modern Chinese regime's sources of authority and legitimacy is Marxist-Leninism and, more specifically, how this ideology complimented the Chinese perception of its own series of historical humiliations and failures in the 19th and 20th centuries. The CCP of the 21st century does not adhere to traditional Marxist-Leninist ideals. Rather, the leadership has embraced certain facets of the ideology that aligns with their broader political agenda and singular goal of keeping the Party in power indefinitely.

Mao Zedong, China's first paramount leader and founding member of the CCP, embraced the Marxist-Leninist ideology because of its anti-imperialist, anti-Western, and pro-working-class undertones, and his integration and endorsement of this political ideology outlived his lifetime as an effective political tool for the party. Marxist Leninism effectively delegated all authority into the hands of a small group of individuals to do the work of countless bureaucrats and a free-market economy that is typical in a democratic society. Of all the Chinese leaders, Mao's rule most closely resembled Communist ideals, but even he deviated from the original Marxist-Leninist paradigm, and it was not long after he embraced its ideas that "Mao Zedong Thought" came about, which was a revisionist Marxist-Leninist political philosophy with "Maoist" characteristics. Marxism-Leninism, as applied by subsequent Chinese leaders, was never that of the original philosophy, but a rendition that better suited China's political and economic circumstances (Wang, 2021) as well as the perceptions of a legitimacy crisis (Chu, 2013).

Despite the authoritarian historical context, legitimacy is largely understood through the state-society relationship where the people's voices and opinions matter but not in the same political sense as Western democracy. The people grant legitimacy in Western democracy through periodic public elections. On the other hand, Chinese legitimacy has historically been premised on deliverables. If not deliverables, then the next best set of tools of governance were coercion, censorship, and propaganda.

Legitimacy

Singapore and China represent two authoritarian, majority ethnic Chinese states in Asia. The former maintains a government that is quite stable and confident in its legitimacy, the latter is actively searching for reasons. Lotus Yang Ruan, notes in *The Diplomat,* "the PAP in Singapore has adjusted and appealed to the rationality embedded in the constitutional and legal system; popular support manifest in the votes won through open and competitive elections becomes the new source of legitimacy (Ruan 2015)." The Chinese government does not observe any of these important legitimizing institutions which is why the CCP has vigorous internal discussions on preserving its ruling mandate (Gilley & Holbig, 2009, 339).

The CCP has struggled to articulate a sustainable case to justify the current government and borders. Tensions between a Han Chinese ethnic state and the 55 officially recognized minority groups are especially apparent (Dede, 2023). Like other large countries such as the United

States and India, China is not a cultural monolith but numerous different groups living together under one government. During the Qing Dynasty, the Qianlong Emperor, who was both Han Chinese and Manchu, made conscious efforts to shore up his legitimacy to rule a multiethnic empire. Asia for Educators, a project of Columbia University, recounts:

> Qianlong portrayed himself as a reincarnation of one of the most important bodhisattvas of Tibetan Buddhism, Manjusri; for the Mongols he took on the role of a steppe prince who understood their steppe traditions; and to the Han Chinese he portrayed himself as a scholar and great patron of Chinese learning and art (Hearn and Zelin, 2023).

The CCP faces a similar challenge to preserve a ruling mandate from its subjects. However, unlike the Qianlong Emperor, the CCP openly alienates groups like the Uyghurs and the Tibetans, leading to a back-and-forth cycle of violence. Even among the majority Han population, the Party exerts tremendous effort to justify its right to rule, especially in the face of challenges like Covid-19, corruption, and income inequality demonstrating the primacy of this issue (Blumenthal, 2020).

Constructing Legitimacy

The CCP understands that, as a socialist revolutionary party, it has largely abandoned its ideological commitments. The government cannot draw on Marxism nor on China's dynastic institutions to garner legitimacy. This reality leads the CCP to some creative methods and conclusions. The quest for legitimacy was made explicit in 2004 when the party admitted in a document, following a high-level plenum, that: "The party's governing status is not congenital, nor is it something settled once and for all" (Resolution 2004, 1154). As a member of the Shanghai party committee research arm put it: "That statement contained within it a profound historical lesson that we learned from the Soviet collapse, namely that if we do not . . . prevent and overcome the threat of legitimacy crisis, living only by the old dictum that 'anyone can rule by force alone' then it is not inconceivable that we will follow the same path as the Soviet Union" (Zhou 2006, 250-1). Shambaugh (2008, 124) calls the 2004 declaration "probably the most important" party document since the 1978 plenum decision that launched the reform movement.

Scholars, including Oxford Professor Rana Mitter, posit that the CCP's legitimacy stems from three essential pillars, economic growth, policy deliverables, and nationalism (Mitter, 2021). Economic growth is easily the most significant and universal objective for any regime to stay in power, liberal or authoritarian. The CCP's legitimacy and right to govern derive much credence from the fact that China rose from one of the poorest countries in the world to a global commercial giant within a single generation. This is why Chinese leaders emphasize good GDP performance and withhold more information as growth statistics falter (Bradsher, 2022). Furthermore, the government talks extensively about addressing pressing societal concerns, like cleaning up China's highly polluted environment or tackling income inequality, as shown by Beijing's constant emphasis on sustainable development in presidential platforms (China.org, 2021). Wealth redistribution programs such as Common Prosperity, which attack large corporations, fulfill a dual function of appeasing the public and reminding the private sector who is in charge (Ren 2022).

The nationalist component because of its open-ended nature is of particular interest. Constructing narratives, myths, and mandates to show a government's legitimacy when objective performance falters. As China's economy slows and the CCP's policy ideas face setbacks, sparking nationalist fervor allows the government to foster loyalty. However, even nationalism can be difficult to control and inspires citizens to oppose government officials they feel are not doing enough for the nation (Holbig & Gilley, 2010).

In recent years, scholars have noted that the CCP increasingly uses culture and institutions to solidify its legitimacy (Holbig & Gilley, 2010). As early as 1986, the State Education Commission called for a revival and reinterpretation of Confucianism, one of the most ancient and significant Chinese philosophies (Holbig & Gilley, 2010). As a result, the dominant interpretation of Confucian values shifted throughout the years as different schools of thought competed for mainstream adoption. Some particularly interesting views include a justification of authoritarian government led by virtuous Confucian appointees (Holbig & Gilley, 2010). Official slogans today, such as the pursuit of "social harmony," represent a vague reference to Confucianism as a compromise to these contentious debates.

Furthermore, the CCP carefully embraces different segments of China's imperial history where most Chinese cultural symbols and achievements originate. At the 2008 Beijing Olympics, the Opening Ceremony featured China's "four great inventions," showcasing ancient achievements but made no reference to the Communist revolution (Xinhua, 2008). Alongside other symbolic measures, these actions demonstrate the CCP's attempt to frame itself as the legitimate heir to China's proud history, despite the anti-monarchy, highly progressive tendencies of the Communist party.

Furthermore, the Party actively attempts to configure ideas such as "democracy and human rights" to be interpreted in ways supportive of the government. For example, many Chinese nationals would say that China is a "democracy," but the term refers to an authoritarian system where the people can consult with their leaders, not necessarily elect them (Drinhausen 2023). Furthermore, term human rights in the Chinese context, does not refer to individual liberties but instead a collective right to economic development, making broad room for government power in pursuit of the "common good (Oud, 2023)."

Perhaps the oldest legitimacy narrative still in use is the Century of Humiliation. From the First Opium War in 1839 to the establishment of the People's Republic of China in 1949, this traumatic sequence of one national defeat at the hands of a foreign power after another forms a core historical memory that informs the Chinese about their perceived place in the world and the CCP's role in national rejuvenation (Kaufman, 2011). In short, the Century of Humiliation narrative leads one to believe: China was abused by powerful imperialists; it was China's weakness that allowed such predation; it is the CCP that will make the Middle Kingdom the most respected nation once again. This powerful story informed Beijing's view of itself in 1955 at the Bandung Conference. The Chinese framed themselves as the leaders of the third world and continue to do so to the present. The Century of Humiliation narrative also explains why taking back Taiwan, an island ceded to Japan after losing the First Sino-Japanese War, is a non-negotiable objective for the Chinese.

Beyond basic notions of economic performance and policy deliverables, the Party frames its right to rule emotionally, depicting itself as the steward that will guide China back to greatness. Chinese citizens legitimize their government through both practical tradeoffs and sentimental beliefs in institutions, national history, and pride. During Deng's Reform and Opening campaign, economic growth and public services helped carry the CCP's legitimacy into the 21st century. However, as Chinese citizens grow more affluent and more knowledgeable while growth slows and policy initiatives fail, the Party needs to establish a consistent cultural case for its authoritarian rule. Given culture's inherent flexibility and vagueness, this approach can cut both ways, which is why the CCP closely audits its historical narrative (Xiaoshan, 2021). Symbolic campaigns like Xi's "Chinese Dream" show a clear attempt to create emotional buy-in from an increasingly diverse society, both intellectually, economically, and demographically (Lee, 2014).

Although understanding the inspiration behind every single initiative to further the regime's legitimacy, one should ultimately view the CCP's strategy as prioritizing order and stability over abstract principles. Of course, every government, authoritarian or liberal, hopes to stay in control, and China's efforts are especially ambitious given the lack of structural constraints on the Party's power and the lack of longstanding, established historical support for the regime's right to rule. It is essential to consider how the CCP weighs costs and benefits as the regime actively attempts to construct a longstanding case for its right to rule all of China.

6. Nationalism and Chinese Identity

One of the most interesting and important developments in recent Chinese politics is surging nationalism. Understanding the role and origin of nationalism in Chinese politics is key to understanding how Chinese citizens view their relationship with the state. Former Secretary of State Mike Pompeo once remarked, in a famous speech at the Richard Nixon Presidential Library, that the Chinese people are separate from the CCP (2023). His words espouse an aspirational view. To Pompeo the CCP is simply an oppressive institution, completely distinct from the population that it rules.

The reality is that Chinese nationals often approve of the Party's leadership and support Beijing's quest for national greatness (Feng, 2020). Although there is some truth to Pompeo's statement, in some cases, China's citizens can be more aggressive, chauvinistic, and passionate than the CCP itself, even forcing the Party to be a moderating force at times (Burcu, 2021). Sino-Japanese relations ,for example, are emblematic of this dynamic. Hyper-nationalist fervor often complicates Beijing's attempts to pragmatically manage its relations with Tokyo and other countries as populist sentiments bump up against the more nuanced intentions of the foreign policy elite. The elevated levels of nationalism bordering on jingoism seen today are products of collective historical experience and a carefully cultivated state-led narrative (Burcu, 2021).

Nationalism, state-led and organic, is an explanation for substantive issues that arise in and around China today. Beijing is far more aggressive on the world stage than it once was, and many of its citizens approve of the CCP's leadership. China is making territorial demands in areas like the South China Sea, on the self-governed island of Taiwan, against Japan over some uninhabited islands (the Senkaku Islands), and sometimes violent exchanges with India over the Himalayas. Beijing has also endorsed the view that East Turkistan or Xinjiang has always been part of China, even though the region has been independently ruled many times throughout history. Understanding the role of national pride and belonging is essential to explaining why the CCP continues to act in the way it does.

On the one hand, the Party has cultivated a proud and loyal population that accepts the legitimacy of what may otherwise seem like an overly oppressive government. In China, love of the Party is equated to love of the nation (Burcu, 2021). However, the benefits of nationalism also have limitations and drawbacks. Nationalism may mitigate but not totally defeat the destabilizing effects of economic stagnation and societal gripes such as income inequality and environmental degradation. Although national pride may inspire a population to rally around the flag when Beijing is in its competition with America, it can easily go overboard, demanding unproductive confrontation over nuanced diplomacy. American foreign policy towards China faces the same problem.

Today, surging Chinese nationalism explains much of Beijing's recent belligerence on the world stage. Although Xi Jinping is certainly a strong man-style leader at the helm of a more powerful China, one should not discount the demands of an increasingly nationalistic and entitled population. Wolf Warrior Diplomacy is an obvious side effect of China's newfound national pride where Beijing's diplomats engage in highly confrontational behavior with foreign nations (Zhai & Wong, 2021). This tactic may coerce weak countries, but it stains China's reputation abroad but is highly attractive domestically. Although Twitter may be banned, CCP officials often take to the American social media platform to hurl insults, conduct trolling, and engage in vitriolic arguments with Western figures who criticize China (Brandt & Schafer, 2020) Diplomats and other officers approved to use of Twitter to gain political favor within the Party for engaging in such confrontational activity which is why the practice continues despite the negative backlash abroad.

At its most extreme, Chinese nationalism inspires hot-headed generals and other Chinese officials to threaten nuclear war against countries like Japan and the United States over hot-button territorial issues like Taiwan and the South China Sea. In fact, the CCP even produced a video signaling its desire to abandon its no-first-use nuclear policy with Japan specifically if Tokyo ever tried to intervene in a war with Taiwan (Business Standard, 2021). The video stated, "We will use nuclear bombs first," the video said. "We will use nuclear bombs continuously. We will do this until Japan declares unconditional surrender for the second time." The video was taken down shortly after, likely because the CCP understood that such an idea is not only counterproductive but a promise they shouldn't keep. However, this occurrence captures the surging nationalism that motivates much of China's politics and the balancing act the CCP must play in catering to public sentiment, much of which they created through their state propaganda campaigns.

The emergence of contemporary nationalism represents an obvious public choice issue as Chinese elites balance the benefits and challenges of the state narrative that they created (Zhao, 1998). On the one hand, surging Chinese nationalism based on government-approved history creates a strong cohesion that binds the country together around the leadership of the CCP. At the same time, this nationalism can often be destabilizing as Chinese patriots demand that the government do more than what is practical in forwarding the perceived interests of the nation. Contemporary Chinese notions of national identity are especially important today because they form the third leg of the stool that supports the legitimacy of the CCP (Mitter, 2021).

Much like in any society, Chinese citizens support the government and its excesses in large part because the Party delivers relatively good outcomes for society. Those outcomes form the first two legs of the stool, economic prosperity, and political performance, i.e., building infrastructure, asserting dominance on the world stage, solving local issues, and other policy deliverables. Nationalism, or an allegiance to the Party and state through a more identity-based connection, provides a sense of belonging beyond one's immediate community. The CCP, as a revolutionary, Marxist organization that adamantly disavows earlier regimes, cannot easily call upon China's proud history of achievement, and institutions like the American government can reference its constitution or the English their monarchy (Zhao, 1998).

The reasons for this include the fact that the People's Republic of China controls territories and cultures that may not think of themselves as politically connected to Beijing, such as Hong Kong, or even ethnically Han

Chinese, like the Tibetans or the Uyghurs. Furthermore, Chinese history is filled with factionalism, infighting, separatism, and other destabilizing events that undermine the notion of a concrete Chinese nation. Looking at Chinese history observers can see whatever they want to see, whether that justifies a massive empire, or a China broken into multiple different countries. Lastly, the CCP as a revolutionary party must necessarily eschew much of China's feudal past, making any attempts to leverage longstanding institutional symbols awkward. This contradiction can be seen in Xi's calls to embrace the ideas of Confucius, a towering figure in ancient Chinese thought, but a figure the CCP has long eschewed because of his feudal origins (Page, 2015). On the one hand, the government frames itself as a revolutionary Marxist party that freed China from its oppressors. On the other hand, it is necessary to leverage the history, symbols, and cultural pride inherent to the Chinese nation. This question of capturing the loyalty of the population to support the Party beyond a simple economic and political performance relationship is one that has occupied the minds of leaders since the beginning of the PRC.

During Mao's leadership, the CCP used Communism, and a narrative of struggle against imperialism, to unite the Chinese people (Brown, 2012). Mao's charisma, the success of the Communists as the victors in the Chinese civil war, and the relief of the citizenry for an end to the violence, all played a role in winning the compliance of the country. However, cynicism for the socialist project and the legitimacy of the government began to wane following the disastrous Great Leap Forward that brought about mass starvation (Brown, 2012). It also demonstrated the inability of collectivized governance to effectively allocate resources, causing many to resort to black markets and bribing officials to allow communities to engage in market-based activities. Fast forward to Deng's reform and opening policies in 1978 and by 1989 massive democracy protests are erupting in Beijing as well as other major cities.

By this time, the CCP rightly concluded that the struggle for a workers' utopia, Communism, had ceased to be a united force for the Chinese people and a source of legitimacy for the Party's right to rule. They needed a new cohesive in the form of a narrowly tailored and state-led nationalism which came in the form of the Patriotic Education Campaign, one of the most successful propaganda efforts in Chinese history (Kuang, 2021).

Nationalism has always been a driving force in Chinese politics, even before the advent of the Patriotic Education Campaign in 1994. Indeed, both major factions of the Chinese Civil War, the overtly nationalist Kuomintang (KMT), and the Communists ultimately traced their motivations to a conception of a Chinese nation state (Jia, 2023.) The father of the revolution that overthrew the Manchu monarchy, Sun Yat-Sen, famously remarked "the treasure for a state to prosper and for a nation to survive (Jia, 2023)." Sun's ideas stemmed from the collective Chinese experience of a weak and submissive monarchy that tolerated one embarrassment after another at the hands of Western invaders. He asserted the revolutionary and popular idea that the Chinese people needed to overthrow their Manchurian rulers and create a more cohesive and confident China.

The Communists, much like the KMT, leveraged the idea of a uniquely Chinese experience to advance their cause. Perhaps one of the core reasons why China's government and ideology are less exportable than its Soviet counterpart was because of its overt reliance on Chinese history as a foundation. During the Mao era, the CCP justified closing off the country from the world under the guise of defending the country from foreign imperialists, an important narrative in Chinese history (Friedman, 1994). However, as effective as the anti-imperialist rhetoric was at creating a revolution, one cannot unite an entire country in the long term simply of a shared hatred for foreign invaders, especially when the fighting stops.

Today, Han Chinese ethnic nationalism dominates the conversation (Friedman, 1994). However, during Mao's rule, he recognized that China was far too diverse and disunified and advocated for a multiethnic China. The CCP would learn during the Cultural Revolution how destabilizing these regional identities are to a cohesive Chinese nation. The disaster of the Great Leap Forward, which not only weakened the government's capacity to rule but also shattered confidence in Communism as a unifying ideology, saw the re-emergence of regional identities (Friedman, 1994). As a result, China under Mao became increasingly politically divided along regional lines because of the effects of his collectivization policies that reduced physical mobility and economic interdependence (Friedman, 1994).

Although Mao hoped to unite the nation under the banner of Communism, cynicism quickly spread as the CCP's socialist policies took their toll on the country. The country actively moved away from what Ernest Gellner, a renowned nationalist theorist, outlined as necessary for the development of national consciousness (Friedman, 1994). These factors included a commonly spoken language, universal education systems, interconnectedness, and economic integration. As a result, Mao's radical socialist policies hardened regional identities at the expense of loyalty to the central government. Furthermore, the economic failure of central planning only added to the decaying legitimacy of the CCP. The massive size of China only added to this dilemma, which is illustrated by documented tensions between Southern and Northern China.

Northern China held the nation's capital, Beijing, while southern China maintained relatively liberal values, due to its exposure to the West through port cities like Hong Kong (Friedman, 1994). The South even has its own proud language, Cantonese, which is often spoken instead of the national language imposed by Beijing, Mandarin. Furthermore, the juxtaposition of the South's liberal market values with the socialist policies imposed by rulers in the north exacerbated this regional divide to the point that Mandarin was known as "Big Brother Speech" (Friedman, 1994).

By the 1990s, after China's reform and opening policies, the northern Chinese, once the ruling, anti-imperialist saviors, were demoted to backward conservatives, compared to the sophisticated and dynamic southerners. And this is only talking about ethnic Han Chinese, who share a cultural and historical bond. China today encompasses a diverse set of ethnicities, regional identities, and formerly independent kingdoms, like Tibet and Xinjiang. Clearly, if the CCP wanted to inspire national loyalty beyond a purely transactional relationship based on economic growth and political deliverables, they had to instill a new sense of nationalism. Finally, the passing of market reforms in 1978 and the near-death experience of the Tiananmen Square Protests in 1989, dashed all remaining hopes of a population united primarily by Communist struggle.

The CCP's reaction, rolling out an entirely new Patriotic Education Campaign in 1992, successfully recaptured the imaginations of the Chinese people like never before (Wang, 2008). In 1989, the Party nearly lost control over a population that ceased to view socialism as a viable form of governance and increasingly looked to other entities be it the West or regional allegiances for inspiration. Now, in large part because of what is easily one of the most successful and ongoing propaganda initiatives,

Chinese nationals demonstrate high levels of patriotism, even when they are living in the West (Wang, 2004). Protests and advocacy from oppressed groups like the Tibetans or the Uyghurs for human rights and sovereignty are met with counterprotests from unapologetic Chinese citizens. Basic criticisms of the CCP, whether it be its authoritarian style of governance or allegations of slave labor in Xinjiang spurred a popular hashtag shared amongst the population stating #ISupportXJCotton (Yang, 2021). In 1989, millions flooded the streets calling for human rights and democracy. Today, with information more abundant than ever, Chinese citizens enthusiastically rally to support the now nationalistic objectives of the CCP.

This stark reversal and surging nationalism provide evidence for the success of China's new state-curated history that is being taught in schools across China. The reversal demonstrates the fruits of Beijing's economic and repression policies, which have increased the benefits of compliance while also increasing the cost of resistance. Rather than attempt to sell a narrative of workers' struggle and superiority to the West, the CCP opted for victimhood (Wang, 2008). Under Mao, the state framed history through the lens of Marxism and ideology, capitalism vs socialism (Wang, 2004). Not only did this narrative fall apart after China started to embrace markets but Mao's policy failures generated skepticism long before Deng's Reform and Opening. Today, far more focus is placed on a specific 100-year stretch of history from 1849-1949 known as the Century of Humiliation (Kaufman, 2011).

This period is firmly ingrained into the country's historical consciousness and forms the foundation for the CCP's legitimacy and right to rule. According to the narrative, China used to occupy a seat of power and greatness in Asia, being the largest, most prosperous empire. However, after losing the First Opium War to the more technologically advanced British Empire, China faced one humiliation after another at the hands of foreign powers (State Department, 2023).

There is much truth to this narrative. The once-great Qing dynasty began a slow decline towards collapse as Western powers and Japan carved up Chinese territory and imposed their will with little resistance. The British infamously forced China to create a number of Treaty Ports, or ports forcibly opened to foreign trade, along with ceding Hong Kong in the Treaty of Nanking (Bracken, 2018). The Chinese would later be forced to sign other treaties demanding similar access and concessions with countries like

France, Russia, and Japan. During the second Opium War, Britain and France marched into Beijing and burned down a famous structure known as The Old Summer Palace (BBC, 2015)Those ruins still stand today as a painful reminder of the Century of Humiliation.

A more technologically and politically advanced Japanese empire defeated the once-feared Chinese military, culminating in the Treaty of Shimonoseki, which granted Tokyo control over the island of Taiwan and forced Beijing to recognize Korea, a Chinese tributary, as an independent state (1895). Perhaps the most humiliating development following the treaties signed in 1895 was the creation of "spheres of influence" (University of Washington, 2023). This term refers to how diverse foreign powers from Britain to the US, to Germany, to France carved up sections of China, granting exclusive trading rights to themselves, and some even claiming the land directly. These impositions would inspire the Boxer Rebellion, which sought to expel foreign powers from China. This movement began with support from local peasants and eventually gained the endorsement of the government. However, the countries with interests in China formed an eight-nation alliance, in which the US and Japan successfully put down the rebellion. The US Marine Corps cataloged the bravery and achievements of the soldiers that successfully lifted the Boxer's siege of Beijing (Plante, 1999). In China, the event is remembered as a severe embarrassment and a brazen act of imperialism where foreign powers exercised their will on Chinese soil without remorse.

At the turn of the 20th century, things further deteriorated for the Chinese. In 1911, the Xinhai Revolution, led by the Chinese nationalist Dr. Sun Yat Sen, led to the emperor's abdication from the throne in 1912 (Cucchisi, 2002). The regime that replaces the Qing dynasty would be known as the Republic of China, led by a former Qing general, Yuan Shikai. However, with Yuan's death in 1916 and the country quickly descended into a period of feuding warlords, destabilizing the social, political, and economic life for decades (Kuo, 2019). Shortly after Beijing suffered yet another national humiliation at the Treaty of Versailles following the conclusion of World War I in 1919. Well before the outbreak of the Great War, Germany annexed the Chinese city of Qingdao in Shandong Province in 1897, widely considered the cradle of Chinese civilization (Boissoneault, 2017). In 1914, the Japanese invaded Qingdao in an attempt to expel the Germans from

Asia and to keep the territory for themselves. The Chinese wished to join the Entente (Britain, France, Russia and allies such as Japan) in an attempt to gain greater geopolitical prestige with the Europeans, but Japan blocked Beijing's official entry to preserve its position as the most important Asian power (Boissoneault, 2017).

To allow them to maneuver around Tokyo's veto, the Chinese sent over a hundred thousand non-combatant volunteers to assist the British and French in Europe, making them the largest and longest-serving non-European contingent in World War I (Boehler, 2023). After the conclusion of the war and perhaps due to the political instability of China's warlord period, Beijing received little representation at the peace talks. Adding to the insult, the Japanese kept the formerly German-occupied territories in Shandong Province after the war (Kuo, 2019). As a result of the May 4th Movement of 1919 where Chinese citizens expressed outrage to imperialism, warlordism, and traditional Chinese culture for its role in failing to compete with the West (Carnegie Council, 2019). This hyper-patriotic awakening served as one of the most important turning points in the country's history, inspiring Sun Yat-Sen to reform his Chinese nationalist party into the Kuomintang (KMT) and wage a campaign to eliminate the warlords. More importantly, the anti-imperialist, anti-traditionalist sentiments of the May 4th Movement brought together a number of intellectuals in 1921 to form the Chinese Communist Party (Carnegie Council, 2019).

From this point on, the narrative of the Century of Humiliation inched closer to its end in 1949. Following the establishment of the CCP and the KMT, the two groups soon to be sworn enemies formed the First United Front in 1922 where they worked together to purge China of warlords (Egorov, 2021). At this time, the Soviet Union played a crucial role in arming the KMT despite its more conservative leanings because they saw them as necessary to complete a Communist revolution in China (Egorov, 2021). Simultaneously, the Soviets urged the CCP to cooperate with KMT. From 1926-1928, the United Front launched Dr. Sun's Northern Expedition to eventually unite China under one rule (Cucchisi, 2002). However, Sun's death in 1925 before the campaign and placing the KMT's leadership and operations with General Chiang Kai Shek, the future first president of Taiwan. Chiang unified China but sparked a civil war in the process by purging the Communists near the end of the campaign. Chiang had been trained in the Soviet Union and had little affection for communism and refused to share power with CCP. This led the Soviets to end their support for the KMT and cease diplomatic relations.

Chiang's actions ignited the Chinese Civil War between the Nationalists and the Communists, plunging the nation into new rounds of chaos. The two factions would briefly stop fighting to form a Second United Front against the invading Japanese army in 1937 in the leadup to World War II (Egorov, 2021). Moscow subsequently reestablished its relations with the KMT because of their mutual interests in defeating Japan, all the while continuing to urge cooperation between the Nationalists and the Communists. The Japanese invasion of China now seen as the capstone of the Century of Humiliation narrative, as unspeakable atrocities were committed by the invading force. The most famous is the Rape of Nanking (USC Shoa Foundation, 2023). In December of 1937 Japanese forces, after taking the city, murdered up to 300,000 civilians and surrendered soldiers, raped tens of thousands of women, and burned numerous buildings. This uncontrolled carnage continued for two months until the establishment of a Japanese puppet government. After Tokyo surrendered to the United States in 1945, dozens of individuals were convicted at the Tokyo War Crimes Trials. Today, a memorial and mass grave site marks this horrific memory as a stark reminder to the Chinese people about the consequences of military weakness and inspiration for national greatness.

After the end of World War II, the Chinese Civil War resumed with the Russians and the Americans supporting the CCP and the KMT respectively (Egorov, 2021). Eventually, the Communists declared victory and established the People's Republic of China on October 1, 1949. The KMT evacuated to the island of Taiwan, which the Japanese relinquished to China at the end of World War II, and made plans to retake the mainland (Facts and Details, 2019). However, neither side made a successful attempt to invade the other leading to the current stalemate with Taiwan having de facto independence and the CCP claiming Taiwan as a breakaway province. To this day, Beijing considers Taiwan an integral part of the Chinese nation and a reminder of the humiliation at the hands of foreign powers that led the island to be separated in the first place (Maizland, 2015). However, it should be noted that during the 1920s-1930s the CCP and the KMT did not view the island as particularly important and supported Taiwan's independence from Japan (van der Wees, 2020). It was not until 1942-1943 when Chiang Kai Shek suggested that the island "be returned to China" and the CCP made similar statements soon after. Suggesting that much like China's broader national identity, Taiwan's significance is a product of politically motivated nationalism, not a long-standing cultural tenant.

According to the CCP's official narrative, the Century of Humiliation ends in 1949 with the establishment of the CCP (Kaufman, 2011). To their credit, from 1839 when the British kicked off the First Opium War, China suffered one humiliation after the next at the hands of foreigners, each weakening the country and preempting a downward spiral. This story of victimhood is understandably galvanizing, especially given China's historic power and current strength. The CCP derives much of its legitimacy and support from framing itself as an organization that ended this cycle of humiliation and brought forth the nation of today (Kaufman, 2011). In fact, the Party portrays itself as the only modern political organization that could have stewarded China's rejuvenation and as a result, to question the CCP is to go against the countries.

Beijing continues to invoke the Century of Humiliation narrative to justify various political goals and to rally the public around its leadership. In 2004, the former Chinese president warned that "Western hostile forces have not yet given up the wild ambition of trying to subjugate us (Kaufman, 2011)." In 2021, marking the 100th anniversary of the CCP, Xi Jinping made a similar remark stating "we will never allow any foreign force to bully, oppress, or subjugate us. Anyone who would attempt to do so will find themselves on a collision course with a great wall of steel forged by over 1.4 billion Chinese people (Xi, 2021)." This rhetoric continues even though China is no longer weak and is now increasingly viewed as the aggressor.

Despite the geopolitical reality that no country has the intention or capacity to invade China, the CCP is threatening to annex liberal-democratic Taiwan, pressing territorial impositions on Southeast Asian countries, and cooperating with international pariahs like Russia and North Korea. Furthermore, Beijing constantly claims that it maintains a uniquely peaceful and selfless foreign policy, that the West is the aggressor, and that Beijing stands up for the Global South. These claims run counter to the encroachment into other nations affairs and weaponization of financial aid to coerce developing countries like Panama to revoke their recognition of Taiwan

(BBC, 2017). China uses these narratives of victimhood and claims of solidarity with the developing to justify its great power ambitions.

Indeed, for much of Chinese history, Taiwan was considered unimportant, as it changed hands between various occupying powers. Although Taiwan is certainly part of Chinese civilization, there seems to be little deep cultural basis for integrating it into Beijing's control. Rather, much if not all of the contemporary calls for unification have come from political leaders, and the Century of Humiliation narrative, which asserts that Taiwan was taken and remains secured by imperialist foreign powers. The island provides essential strategic value, both as a launching point for military assets and for its semiconductor production, but the contemporary vitriol over the island's status is primarily a nationalistic one. Chinese leaders are conscious that appearing tough on the Taiwan question is important both for tangible national interests and in order to appease their own citizens. With this in mind, Beijing's behavior on the world stage mirrors that of a rational, power-maximizing state no different from any other country.

Although the CCP's narratives are grounded in a bit of truth, the actions are the result of the circumstances that positioned China to behave in the way it does. A weak nation cannot wage war against others, a poor nation has more in common with other poor nations, and a country with economic leverage but lacking in soft power must resort to economic coercion. Like all countries, China's behavior is confined by structural forces such as its relative power and wealth compared to its geographic and global neighbors.

These realities explain, at least in part, why Beijing is far more aggressive today than in the past. It is also why Deng Xiaoping set a precedent that China should "hide and bide." He knew that the country was far too weak in 1978 to assert itself (Rudd, 2018). But even in its earlier stages, Beijing could not resist playing great power politics by supporting the Khmer Rouge regime in Cambodia, in an attempt to counterbalance the Soviet Union and Vietnam (Wang, 2018). This move not only received global condemnation, for supporting a government actively committing genocide, but demonstrated that, whatever solidarity China had with the Global South, or even fellow Communist countries, it was superficial at best.

There is nothing about Chinese culture, beliefs, or people that fundamentally make Beijing more peaceful, socialist, or selfless than other countries. Rather, the CCP's narrative is only thinly supported by facts from historical experience and the geopolitical realities the regime faces. Although there is some support for the CCP's story, it ultimately falls apart when you consider the full fact pattern and motivations driving China's behavior on the world stage.

There is certainly a debate about whether Chinese nationalism is predominantly a top-down imposition or a bottom-up phenomenon (Wang, 2008, 783). The answer is likely at least partially both, but one can surely debate to what extent one is more influential than the other. The Century of Humiliation narrative, although factually correct does inspire many Chinese citizens to feel a certain sense of historical trauma. At the same time, it is possible to interpret history in different ways, especially in a manner that does not justify authoritarian rule and hatred of the West. Countries across the world, be it the nations of the European Union or Japan and the United States, have all come to the rational conclusion that it's better to establish mutually beneficial relationships rather than dwell on historical conflicts. However, such peaceful thinking does not make for good nationalism.

Regardless, the CCP, through its complete control over the education system, pervasive propaganda, and relentless censorship, captures the hearts of its population through this victim narrative. The people who are not convinced are incentivized to keep quiet as they enjoy the country's economic growth and refrain from actions that lead to negative consequences. The Party conveniently frames itself as the organization that revived China's greatness and the organization that will continue stewarding the nation to a brighter future. They assert that to go against the CCP is to go against one's country. Indeed, this carefully crafted victim narrative differs from the mass mobilization and revolutionary attitude initially espoused during the Maoist era (Wang, 2008, 783). Not only is the Patriotic Education campaign easier to administer than the Maoist radicalization strategy, but it also allows the state to fine-tune its message to fit its goals over time.

The victimization narrative message of Patriotic Education is quietly infused into everyday life through the school system, news media, and popular culture with technocratic precision. The CCP is actively deploying this education model to tame Hong Kong. After numerous democratic protests rocked the city, Beijing engaged in a multifront operation, infusing Patriotic Education into the school curriculums, censoring textbooks that referenced democracy protests in Hong Kong as well as the mainland, and blaming teachers for fostering seditious attitudes amongst students (Wu, 2020). In a 2020 article following Beijing's crackdown on the 2019 Hong Kong protests, *Reuters* reported that

> Hong Kong's Education Bureau said that "fostering students' sense of national identity" is a key learning goal, as it is in other countries. National education "aims to enhance students' knowledge about our country's history, culture and development," the bureau said. "As well as their awareness of the importance of national security, thereby developing in them a sense of belonging to the country (Wu, 2020)."

Much like every country, China's borders have shifted throughout history. New territories are conquered, restless provinces separated, and territorial wars alter the geopolitical landscape. The CCP's nationalist education campaign intimately acknowledges that a coherent Chinese nation-state is inherently fragile and that Beijing's contemporary nation-building project is incomplete (Wang, 2008, 783). The framing and narrative espoused by the Patriotic Education Campaign creates a foundation to legitimizing the CCP's rule over China's current borders, encompassing diverse societies with differing interpretations of identity, history, and politics.

Today, the Party's curated and self-interested narrative about Chinese history frames the organization as an inseparable part of national identity. As a result, criticizing the Party's authoritarian rule is disloyalty and sedition. Through this perspective, the Party can deflect Western accusations of human rights violations, assaults on Hong Kong's democracy, and military aggression towards Taiwan as yet another series of imperialist impositions from the same old actors. A 2009 speech given by the Chinese ambassador to Malawi illustrates this teaching,

> The Western media always hold their Cold War mindset to criticize China in various aspects from family planning policy to human rights in order to bring shame on China. We never expect them to say anything good and fair about China. You may understand very well what kind of image Africa has from the western media. How can you get hands from the west to slap your friend in the face?

The remarks attempt to frame any criticism of China's policies as an aggressive act rather than a good-faith expression of values and concerns. In liberal democratic countries like the US, subjects like the 2022 Russian invasion of Ukraine attract diverse perspectives, ranging from those that view the conflict as a fundamental assault against the global order to those that see it as a consequence of NATO expansionism, however ill-advised US forays into international conflicts may be (Carpenter, 2022).

In China state censorship and carefully crafted narratives make most questions concerning national security and external relations non-negotiable. There can be no discussion about whether the CCP should respect Taiwan's autonomy nor whether the South China Sea should be shared with other nations, consistent with international law. Questioning the Party about such matters is viewed as siding with foreign aggressors. The entire idea of the current rules-based international order is a Western construct that runs counter to the CCP's interests. If or when Beijing is in charge, things will be done differently. Cynical and self-serving as such a view may be, it is a fundamentally realist view of the world. America and its allies have the power to shape the world in their image, and the status quo reflects Western interests, albeit with mostly universally attractive ideas. Much like CCP's Century of Humiliation narrative, there is much truth that underpins this view of the contemporary.

Chinese nationalism today serves an important political purpose. It is no coincidence that Xi Jinping's rise to power paralleled a sharp uptick in nationalism and adversarial sentiment, after decades of relatively peaceful globalization. Although an organic sense of national identity and patriotism played a key role in overthrowing the Qing Dynasty and China's historic memory, today, the CCP leverages and fosters nationalism as a tool of governance. The fervor and energy of Xi's China owe much of its foundation to the implementation of the Patriotic Education Campaign, perhaps one of the most successful propaganda campaigns of the modern era. The program conveniently frames the CCP as the vanguard of China's ascendancy and that notion pervades almost every aspect of daily life. This system allows the state to tailor its message rather than attempting to unleash a massive and volatile mass mobilization common in Mao's era. Most importantly, nationalism instills a sense of loyalty to the Party that goes beyond economic growth and policy deliverables. In essence, national identity and pride are essential components of nation-building, especially for a country as large and young as the People's Republic of China.

Integration with the global economy and a spirit of cooperation with the West served an important purpose in modernizing the country and brought hundreds of millions of Chinese citizens out of poverty (Lugo, Raiser, and Yemtsov, 2021). Whereas Mao Zedong kicked off the Communist dream of an adversarial China bent on spreading the workers' revolution around the world, Deng Xiaoping recognized the value of cooperation and a low profile. His Hide and Bide doctrine set China on the path to becoming a global power deeply rooted in supply chains and commerce. The era of Xi Jinping, although a high point in Beijing's power, is also an era of living dangerously. It is a time filled with geopolitical tension, environmental degradation, economic inequality, slowing economic growth, and a more globalized and educated population. Economic growth rates and political deliverables cannot justify the CCP's authoritarian rule forever, and many of these challenges are not easily solved. An organization as astute as the Chinese politburo can easily observe that a strongman leader like Xi, combined with an increase in nationalist rhetoric, are rational tools to preserve the regime's legitimacy and power (Long, Hwang, Chingman, & Chan, 2021).

7. Economic Policy

Under Xi Jinping, China continued its shift to nationalism and aggression. Beijing's economic policy took a sharp and unexpected turn, reversing decades of liberalization. In November of 2020, the once untouchable and outspoken billionaire, Jack Ma, went missing after he criticized the Chinese state banking system (Peach, 2021). CEOs like Alibaba's Jack Ma, who have built and run outstanding companies, are starting to think that there are perhaps better ways to run the country, clearly a potential threat to the Party's authority. As a result, his fin-tech firm and the country's largest payment facilitator, Ant Group, saw a sudden cancellation of its IPO while Ma and Eric Jing, the firm's chairman, were summoned by Beijing's regulators for questioning. Shortly after, at the beginning of 2021, Xi announced the start of Common Prosperity, an ambitious wealth redistribution campaign that rocked the business world in China and beyond (Wu, 2022).

For many, the most memorable event of this campaign was an opening salvo of massive regulatory fines against successful tech companies like Alibaba (online retail), Tencent (multimedia), and Didi (ride-hailing) (Zhu, Yang & Tian, 2022). These fines also signaled the emergence of an invigorated antitrust apparatus far more active, strict, and aggressive than before as the government released the Anti-Monopoly Guidelines for the Platform Economy Sector (Evrard & Tong, 2022). For decades, China's regulators observed relatively lax enforcement practices, facilitating breakneck growth and innovation. Now companies like Didi face harsh penalties, such as being forced to delist from the New York Stock Exchange for merely ignoring the concerns of Chinese regulators on data privacy (Lu, 2022). Ant Group faced a complete government-led restructuring for Jack Ma's comments on the banking system (BBC, 2021).

Xi's regulatory salvo shocked the business sector, domestically and internationally. Not only were entire industries, like private education, effectively abolished, but overall economic growth slowed (Miura, 2022). Tech and e-commerce firms were hit particularly hard. Multibillion-dollar fines ravaged companies like Alibaba and Meituan, a food delivery service, for alleged anticompetitive and abusive conduct (Campbell, 2021). Video game companies, like Tencent, felt the pain from limitations placed on gaming hours. Corporations experienced an unprecedented level of scrutiny. The State Administration for Market Regulation (SAMR), China's anti-monopoly bureau, tightened controls on mergers and exponentially increased fines (Evrard & Tong, 2021). The CCP also unveiled a new, aggressive data protection law, prompting firms like the social media company LinkedIn to pull out of the country, despite China being one of its largest markets (China Briefing, 2021). The Microsoft-owned company cited the onerous compliance procedures created by the new law which include storing personal data to be inspected by authorities (Weise & Mozur, 2021).

Overall, investors around the world saw hundreds of billions of dollars of capital wiped out by these crackdowns (Brooker, 2022). The uncertainty generated by Xi's aggressive regulatory reform alongside recent developments such as the use of Zero-Covid policies and Beijing's tacit support for the Russian invasion of Ukraine all contributed to the country's stunted economic growth in 2022. It is uncertain when or if investors, who are responsible for much of China's growth and economic activity, will regain confidence in Beijing's market because of the political risk generated by its government.

This ordeal served as a sudden wake-up call to the world that the Communist in Chinese Communist Party still meant something and that the Party is not completely devoted to markets and the economic progress they have provided as some speculated. Instead, economic growth is a tool to be wielded to advance the goals of the CCP, whether that be supporting the modernization of the People's Liberation Army, advancing Beijing's leverage in the world, or keeping the masses economically satisfied.

Prior to 2021, the reemergence of the state's involvement in the economy was gradually signaled. In 2020, Xi proclaimed private companies should show more alignment with the objectives of the CCP (Xin, 2022). Since Xi's ascendancy to power in 2012, Beijing's central planning initiatives became increasingly ambitious, with the announcement of large industrial policy schemes and the reinvigoration of state-owned enterprises (Ruwitch, 2021).

In 2015, Xi's government announced its ambitious industrial policy scheme bent on making the nation a technological leader, a ten-year plan known as Made in China 2025 (McBride & Chatzky, 2019). In 2014, the CCP rolled out a new Military Civil Fusion strategy which now boasts its own committee chaired by Xi himself (Levesque, 2021). State mandates to translate commercial advancements into military capabilities date back to the Mao era, but the recent iteration presents far greater consequences. China now leads in many technology sectors, and its companies conduct far more global engagement. This presents a national security concern to countries that do not wish to support Beijing's military.

Even more importantly, China is actively attempting to decrease its reliance on foreign markets while increasing the world's need for its own massive domestic market. This strategy, which seeks to boost the internal dynamism of the Chinese economy while also creating self-sufficiency by making consumption more of a drive of economic growth rather than investment, is known as Dual Circulation (China Power, 2023). A massive undertaking in industrial policy, Dual Circulation requires huge interventions in the private sector and central planning to boost strategic sectors of the economy.

The sought-for result by the CCP is a China practically immune from sanctions, embargos, and external influence. At the same time, Beijing can coerce other nations that desire market access, giving China a decisive tool in geopolitics. This campaign runs counter to previous efforts towards globalism and interdependence that brought the country to its current state. These goals are also so ambitious as to be largely that it might be impossible outcomes. These disruptive and sudden government interventions will likely chill private investment for years to come, as it already has at the time of this writing. Indeed, American economists have observed that the New Deal programs meant to combat the Great Depression actually prolonged economic stagnation. One of the primary reasons was that uncertainty, the aggressive curtailment of property rights and use of state intervention reduced investor confidence (Higgs, 1997, 563).

These realities beg the question of why the CCP is engaging in such radical behavior even after years of firsthand experience with the benefits of open markets and a relatively free private sector. Although Xi Jinping played a core role in pushing China to increase state control and engagement of the marketplace, his actions came with the consent of the political establishment such as those in the politburo. Despite the perception of China being a one-man rule, there has been a spirited debate amongst Party officials in recent years on the feasibility of policies such as Common Prosperity (Bloomberg News, 2021). Using the understanding that CCP officials think independently and speak candidly amongst themselves, explaining the rationality behind the reforms driving China's abrupt and potentially self-destructive shift in economic policy making is difficult. Political survival and institutional structure provide the most plausible and satisfying explanations.

Understanding Leninism and Markets

As a single-party Leninist state, the government and its policymaking essentially serve the CCP's elite decision-makers. Although not as ideological and dogmatic as the Soviet Union, Chinese leaders still subscribe to a vision of a society stewarded by a vanguard party. The phrase heard over and over again is Socialism with Chinese Characteristics which CGTN, a state media outlet, explains,

> the concept of socialism with Chinese characteristics aims to redefine the relations between planning and socialism, and market economy and capitalism. It has preserved institutions of socialism and public ownership while importing sophisticated management experience and advanced market mechanism from developed countries (CGTN, 2023).

In essence, the CCP through the arms of the government exercises near-total discretion over economic policymaking with few checks and balances. The only counterweight to the desires of the party leadership is the reality on the ground and disagreements among each other. For example, there is no independent judiciary to review changes to the law that may easily come off as too arbitrary or overly intrusive here in the

United States (Reuters, 2017). As a result, the Party and its leaders are free to intervene in any way they see fit. Since the tenure of Deng Xiaoping, the CCP's relationship with markets and economic freedom has been the same, despite the policy differences. The uniting factor is that the Party regulates the economy in a manner that boosts the power of the country and ensures the stability of the government's rule. This point is perhaps the single greatest oversight made by some Western observers. That is that the CCP does not make decisions solely on the basis of a broad ideology like free markets or Socialism. Rather, policy directives, like they are in every society, are based on politics.

Indeed, one of the major driving forces of Chinese GDP post-1978 was not necessarily the highly innovative megacorporations we see today, but small businesses that the government simply decided to leave alone. The late Nobel Laureate Ronald Coase and Ning Wang, a professor of political economy, account on this fact by explaining that in the early stages of reform, small private businesses led the way while the government still toyed around with central planning. They explain that,

> the Chinese government was happy to leave them alone as long as they did not threaten the state sector or challenge the Party's political power. This created a room for what we called the "marginal revolutions" that brought entrepreneurship and market forces back to China during the first decade of reform (2013).

The important phrase that is especially relevant to understanding the ark of Chinese economic policy is "as long as they did not threaten the state sector or challenge the Party's political power". This is precisely why economic freedom became widely discussed in China whereas any discussion of political freedom was off the table.

One does not need to look any further than the violent suppression of the Tiananmen Square Protests or the quashing of Hong Kong's democracy. It is not uncommon to see the Chinese taking advice and inspiration from free-market thinkers in the US. From our own experience, we have met Chinese nationals taking internships at the libertarian Cato Institute, known American professors that are often solicited by Beijing to provide advice on institutional reform, and actively taught free-market ideas in Chinese

Universities. They all say the same thing; the CCP is very interested in learning more about markets because it helps them grow the economy and empower the country. Another telling development is that recently, Beijing is less receptive to such advice, given the economic shift, but they still like to request comments from Western intellectuals to claim they received an independent critique. Actions to disband the Unirule Institute, a free market think tank in Beijing and one of China's only independent think tanks in 2019 shows that desire for independent critique isn't the primary goal of such engagement. (Kuo, 2019).

The CCP's embrace of markets to the extent that it keeps the Party in power while also improving the country is apparent. China's advantage today is its massive internal market where 1.4 billion people can trade and compete against one another. During the radical Mao era, the governments suppressed markets and attempted to rule everything under collective governance. The CCP's forbearance and acceptance of private enterprise allowed the Chinese people to experiment with different business models (Coase & Wang, 2013). This sort of economic freedom started as a necessity during the later Mao era as the state lost the ability to effectively police society because of the chaos of the Great Leap Forward and the Cultural Revolution. After 1978, this sort of entrepreneurial energy became legalized and even socially encouraged as books like Adam Smith's *Theory of Moral Sentiments* were translated into Chinese and embraced by Party elites like former premier Wen Jiabao (Coase & Wang, 2013). Individualism began to spread as a natural result of market activity and as the actively shifted away from teaching radical Socialism (Steele & Lynch, 2012).

Progress Served Its Purpose

Often hitting repeated annual growth rates exceeding 10%, China was well-served by markets and integration with the global community. Indeed, the CCP's plan to leverage privatization, globalization and relative laissez-faire paid off handsomely. The country went from one of the poorest nations in the world to middle income status and overall the second largest economy in a single lifetime. In fact, the government may have been a little too invested in growth and catching up with the West.

Environmental concerns are a good example of the issue. China has some of the most polluted air in the world and its natural resources such as arable soil and fresh water are being depleted at an alarming rate (Maizland, 2021). Part of this problem stems from the country's rapid industrialization, coupled with lax enforcement of environmental protections or even basic property rights (Zhen, 2017). Local communities often have little say over their own land when the government desires to use it for industrial or commercial purposes. The incentives are weighed heavily against the citizen and the environment as aggrieved individuals have little political or legal right to push back against the state. This dilemma is worsened when the CCP's industrial policy objectives are involved. Subsidized steel production is a particularly egregious example, which has created a massive oversupply while also being the single largest polluter in the country, exceedingly even electricity generation (China Power, 2023). The state's involvement in steel production and the political interests that it creates are so great that studies have shown that Chinese overseas development aid tends to fluctuate with domestic steel production (Brazys & Vadlamannati, 2021).

Protecting the environment has since become a top priority for the Chinese government at least on paper. Virtually every president including Xi has made strong assurances of the CCP's commitment to mitigating pollution. Furthermore, the government's industrial policy has expanded to include green energy production such as solar panels and windmills (Almendral, 2022). Although these recent policies set China on the path to potentially becoming a global leader in renewable energy production, the CCP is by no means a supporter of environmentalism as a principle. Political interests are the main driver. The most obvious indicator is the fact that China continues to finance new coal-fired plants domestically and more concerningly, abroad, to advance its diplomatic leverage with developing nations (Standaert, 2021). The CCP's leadership on sustainability is representative of its broader strategy of coopting popular demand and turning it into a state initiative to maintain legitimacy. There are hundreds of protests on a daily basis, often regarding pollution and the government's inability or outright resistance to addressing the problem (Standaert, 2017). These grassroots movements threaten to destabilize the Party's rule led to the creation of the current environmental leadership narrative, while also quashing dissenters that get too far out of hand. Much like CCP's toleration of small businesses because of their low political danger, it allowed isolated protests but drew the line at things that could potentially unite the entire country in opposition. Journalist Michael Standaert explains in Yale Environment 360,

> Daniel Gardner, a professor at Smith College and author of *Environmental Pollution in China: What Everyone Needs to Know* — soon to be published by Oxford University Press — says that vested economic and political interests have long been concerned over grassroots environmental phenomena. This was evident in the crackdown on "Plastic China" and, especially, "Under the Dome," which pointed to official corruption and collusion with fossil fuel companies as root causes of the air pollution problem (2017).

Further the acceptance of corruption in China often took the side of economic development as public officials allowed companies to break environmental regulations in exchange for a cut of the profits while also boosting their standing within the Party (World Affairs, 2017). This phenomenon is supported by broad empirical research finding that corruption always hurts entrepreneurship, but in a poor business environment corruption tends to have less of a negative effect (Dutta & Sovel, 2016, 179). Today, the government is claiming to do more in protecting the environment and is succeeding in some regards. However, it is clear that the CCP's commitment to protecting the environment is more so about staying in power than it is about actually protecting the environment. With few institutional checks and balances to hold the government accountable, one should continue to expect political interest to drive most of the Party's policymaking in this and all areas.

China's regulation of capital markets represents a more notable and complicated shift in doctrine. For decades, the CCP attempted to reform the role of SOEs given their low efficiency and overall inferiority to private firms. However, rolling back the role of these publicly controlled companies proved difficult for numerous reasons ranging from the strategic role they play in industrial policy to the political weight these entities have as arms of the state. SOE not only served the government's interest in the market, often being called on to support industrial policy objectives, but have their own vested interests in suppressing private competitors (Li & Brødsgaard, 2013). Allowing private firms to grow not only requires deregulation but breaking the monopolies held by SOEs, while also relinquishing political control over the economy. This is why in recent years, SOE reform has not only stalled, but the state is also tightening its grip on the private sector as China prepares for great power competition with the United States (Lockett, 2022).

When Xi released his first major policy plan in 2013, he hailed the importance of the private sector in allocating resources, taking a page from Western political economy as well as the Chinese experience (Lockett, 2022). However, the Party has since gone in the exact opposite direction for two primary reasons: a strategic economic competition with the US and the rising threats to social stability and foreign interference posed by less tightly controlled markets. Part of the threat comes from the growing competition with the US which brings the threat of sanctions and other forms of economic leverage, such as making Chinese firms dependent on US investment (US Department of the Treasury, 2023).

A more important reason is that the CCP is afraid of its own firms, many of which are so large they not only pose a challenge to the Party's authority but often play a role in exacerbating social tensions. These tensions include soaring income inequality, work burnout, workers' rights complaints, and data privacy concerns with media platform companies (Piketty, Yang, Zucman, 2019). However, the more existential problem is what the Party noted as the "weakening, watering down, hollowing out and marginalization" of party leadership (Martina, 2017)." Decades of pragmatic market liberalization and deradicalization have taken their toll on the primacy of the CCP.

The government's 2021 regulatory crackdown, starting with the 3-month disappearance of Jack Ma and developing into an aggressive assault on the economy listed certain policy goals such as combatting income inequality and addressing anticompetitive conduct. However, it is clear that the exponential increase in antitrust fines for failing to notify the government of a merger, forcing corporations to donate to certain charities, and limiting video game usage to 3 hours a week serve a broader purpose (Cai, 2021; Zhai, 2021). Although these policies all purport to serve an important goal, their most important purpose is to reassert the Party's authority and to remind the private sector who is in charge. The authoritarian and reflexive nature of the CCP's drastic shift toward more central planning represents the concerns of a Leninist party that is not restricted by checks and balances. Xi and the broader leadership are acute students of the fall of the Soviet Union, which they attribute to the lack of unity. In early 2013, Xi assembled the country's top leadership and asked them a rhetorical question about how the Soviets fell, his answer,

> "It completely denied Soviet history, the history of the Soviet Communist Party, denied Lenin, denied Stalin," he said. "Party organizations at all levels had almost no effect, and the army was not there (Westcott, 2021)."

Governments do not tighten controls on society when things are going well, they get strict when things are going poorly. Chinese leaders understand the benefits of markets too well to toss out economic freedom for purely ideological reasons. Indeed, they have actively expanded and contracted markets in a manner that is conducive to boosting the power of the regime. Xi's remarks about the primacy of the Party reflect a growing concern amongst the CCP's more conservative members since Deng Xiaoping's economic reforms which have now become mainstream. In fact, the concerns over the destabilizing effects of the market and the loss of political control brought about by Reform and Opening surfaced prior to Xi's tenure during the previous Hu administration (Blumenthal, 2020).

A competition for power within the pro-market faction led by Hu and the previous president, Jiang Zemin created an opening for the Leninist faction to reassert itself. Although Hu initially stood for entrepreneurship and private enterprise, in the end, he was pressured into tightening regulations and expanding the public sector's role in the economy (Blumenthal, 2020). In this context, Xi's ascension to power, the amount of authority trusted to him, and his strongman rule represents a natural extension of a structural shift in Chinese elite politics rather than just the intentions of one man.

Where the Chinese Economy is Headed

Compared to the Chinese, liberal democracies, with their general ideological commitments to open markets and robust institutions, maintain a deep level of respect for the private sector. Sentiments may be changing, but regulatory bodies in the West, such as the American Federal Reserve and the Federal

Trade Commission (FTC), serve as umpires with constrained mandates. The Fed's role is to control the money supply in a manner that keeps inflation low and employment high; the FTC's job is to enforce consumer protection laws created by Congress (St Louis Federal Reserve, 2023). These constraints on the powers of executive agencies are within the constitutional separation of powers. Partisan gridlock often prevents overly-political legislation from being passed (Legal Information Institute, 2023). While both the Fed and the FTC are attempting to push the boundaries of their regulatory authority with activist antitrust and climate change conscious monetary policy, they remain largely constrained by constitutional limits.

Chinese officials operate without such constraints. They face nearly non-existent judicial oversight, a rubber-stamp National People's Congress, and little, if any, ideological respect for the institution of free markets (Saich, 2015, p. 1). Especially when there is little political threat, CCP leaders are also pragmatic enough to understand the importance of relatively objective rulemaking and enforcement. In fact, China maintains a number of highly successful Special Economic Zones, like the Shanghai Free Trade Zone and the Hainan Free Trade Port (Sun, 2022). As can be seen, the CCP is more than willing to allow such experiments and policies, when it serves their interest to do so. In the case of the Hainan Free Trade Port, for example, Beijing is in a position to benefit tremendously from its promise to increase domestic consumption and trade with Southeast Asia, a strategic region.

The legal system is where the political interest is most clearly shown. Yes, most laws and most cases are adjudicated with objectivity. This promotes confidence in important matters such as contracts and basic rule of law. Indeed, the American Bar Association and the US legal academy played a key role in advising the creation of the current judicial order. However, the Congressional-Executive Commission on China notes,

> over 68 percent of surveyed judges identified local protectionism as a major cause of unfairness in judicial decisions. Judicial authorities in China speak frequently about the problem of administrative interference and have identified the spread of local protectionism as one of the principal problems facing the courts (Congressional Executive Commission on China, 2023).

The Chinese courts, unlike American courts, have little separation from other branches of government. In accordance with the Chinese constitution, the office of the prosecutor and the legislative branch supervise the court system (Congressional Executive Commission on China, 2023). Furthermore, the CCP maintains a Political Legal Committee with an explicit goal of maintaining ideological conformity. For high-profile economic policies, such as Common Prosperity and Dual Circulation, the Chinese actually create black letter laws and documents, such as The 14th Five Year Plan (Chinese Government, 2023). However, the government tends to employ vague language and so there does not seem to be any meaningful legal constraints on how these laws are acted upon.

Leading up to the 2020s, one could see the gradual development of a stronger antimonopoly apparatus as the CCP amended its black letters laws and ultimately consolidated all economic regulatory duties under the powerful State Administration for Market Regulation in 2018 (Foster, 2018).

Although the full force of the Chinese regulatory state would not be unleashed until 2021, it could already be observed how the CCP would wield antitrust as a tool to advance its industrial policy objectives. For example, not only are some of the laws purposefully vague, such as a highly subjective prohibition on abuse of market dominance but regulators have a preference for behavioral remedies (Baruzzi, 2020). That is unlike its counterparts in the West, the Chinese antitrust apparatus tends to force misbehaving companies to perform certain mandates such as maintaining a certain price or aiding competitors to enter the market (Foster, 2018). Perhaps the most telling example that a Chinese antitrust apparatus is simply a political tool for disciplining and herding the private sector is the fact that state-owned enterprises do not have to abide by the same rules (US Chamber of Commerce, 2022). Furthermore, the US Chamber of Commerce points out that Chinese antitrust laws serve to,

> 1) reinforce a Great Wall of data protectionism, in lockstep with other laws like the National Security Law, National Intelligence Law, Cybersecurity Law, Data Security Law, and Personal Information Protection Law; (2) strengthen industrial policy to ensure China's seizes the commanding heights in emerging technologies by creating 10,000 Chinese "Little Giants" that benefit from subsidies, tax breaks,

and exemptions from regulation, and (3) push domestic champions to expand and deepen China's digital mercantilism abroad from a domestic market insulated from competition (US Chamber of Commerce, 2022).

As the economy modernized, Xi and the CCP increasingly decided that general growth had served its purpose. They decided that China's newfound strength must be directed towards strategic areas, be it establishing dominance in specific industries, strengthening the military, or creating international leverage. More importantly, the private sector, most notably tech firms, had to be taught who was in charge, leading to the Common Prosperity campaign following the Jack Ma-Ant Group scandal. The government began accusing China's large firms of exacerbating inequality, asserting data privacy posed a national security threat, and that capital was "expanding in a disorderly fashion (Bloomberg News, 2021)."

These aggressive policies do have consequences. In 2022, investors were hesitant to do anything in the current regulatory environment and megafirms like JD and Alibaba are hemorrhaging workers (Soon, 2022). Common Prosperity, once an omnipresent term in Chinese society, quietly faded from use in 2022, as the CCP takes stock of the damage to its economic growth (Brooker, 2022). China's tacit support for the 2022 Russian invasion of Ukraine, the Zero Covid policy, and the regulatory shock of 2021 has led to an unprecedented capital exodus, prompting Xi to make unsuccessful attempts to regain investor confidence (Horta e Costa, 2022). Although the 2010s saw a narrative of an ascendant China, one that continued to relentlessly grow in power, the China of the 2020s is an embattled one held back by its own contradictions. On the one hand, Xi's policies have shattered Beijing's rosy image of a well-behaved and investment-friendly nation. On the other are a set of important mandates and political promises that seem to be necessary for the CCP's long-term stability and power.

Translating Economics Into Politics

At the time of this writing, China is in the midst of an industrial plan of unprecedented proportions. Military Civil Fusion, Made in China 2025, and China Standards 2035 all represent attempts to channel economic growth into strategic industries such as advanced technology and military hardware

(Chambers, 2021). These projects not only aim to make the country more influential in the global economy but also more self-sufficient, not having to rely on countries like Japan and the US for cutting-edge technology. However, the most ambitious and consequential initiative is by far the Dual Circulation Strategy, which seeks to make China less dependent on the world and the world more dependent on China (China Power, 2023). Dual Circulation, if it is even possible to achieve, would cement Beijing's power in the world and fundamentally shift the scales of geopolitics in its favor.

This strategy is likely a product of Xi and the CCP's observations about the nature of globalization from a Chinese perspective. Although becoming interdependent with the world in terms of investment and export made China rich and more dynamic, it also exposed Beijing to events outside the government's control. Trade tensions with the US, the global shutdown from Covid-19, and the looming threat of sanctions from the collective West all demonstrated how disruptive interdependence could be. These considerations inspired the Xi regime in 2020 to begin focusing on self-sufficiency and leveraging its massive internal market of 1.4 billion people while also building greater trade relationships (Tang, 2020). As a result, external shocks, such as economic isolation over an invasion of Taiwan, would have less of an effect on China and likely be more harmful to its adversaries.

Another interpretation of Xi's Dual Circulation Strategy focuses not just on its foreign policy implications but the domestic concern with increasing consumption as a driver of growth (Carr, 2022). Although boosting internal circulation, or domestic consumption, is important for trade influence and self-sufficiency, it's also important for breaking through the dreaded middle income trap (Griffith, 2011). China is rapidly approaching the point where catch-up growth and concentrated wealth generation in its urban centers will not be enough to sustain long-term development across the country. With economic growth already slowing and up to 90 percent of Chinese citizens considered poor in 2021, China is desperately behind the curve on poverty alleviation, despite the CCP's claims it has done otherwise (Gill, 2021). This interpretation of Chinese poverty comes from a study conducted by Brookings Senior Fellow and World Bank Vice President Indermit Gill who posits that China is roughly as rich as the US was in the 1960s (Gill, 2021). They apply the US metric of poverty adopted at the time, $21.70 a day, which is ten times higher than what Beijing uses today, revealing just how far behind China is. Given that the CCP is using an inappropriate measure of poverty for a country as rich as it is, this correction puts the country decades behind schedule even though it succeeded initially in bringing people out of the most abject poverty.

The reasons for this predicament are systemic; potentially existential. Some of the most important factors include the consequences of the CCP's one-child policy, which destroyed the demographic balance, a much older population and a lower birth rate (Mullen, 2021). Mao's radical socialist policies of collectivization and self-sustaining countryside communes made migration to cities much more difficult. It is also likely that an unfree economy and society makes development harder and discourages advocacy for effective poverty alleviation (Gill, 2021). On that note, data presented at a CSIS-Stanford panel discussion suggested that China's economy is increasingly coopted by a shadow sector of informal, low-skill, high-labor work (2022). This type of employment, such as selling fruits on the street, is often a stagnating factor for developing middle-income economies, because it is not only less productive but pulls talent away from more formal jobs. It's possible that this phenomenon could be caused by a variety of factors in a growing economy, such as a need for better education, local job opportunities, and so on.

China's economic challenges are substantial and systemic. The CCP faces a conundrum. As a ruling party that must have absolute control it nevertheless is trying to run a dynamic economy. Mao's regime was able to maintain strict control over Chinese society, but it lacked the sort of productivity needed to make the country a global power. Today, the CCP's problem is the reverse, and they are attempting to thread the needle to create a powerful market economy and achieve complete social control. However, the institutional forces and social reality make this objective elusive. China cannot easily reform its state-owned enterprises, which are not only highly inefficient but disrupt the private sector as state monopolies. Furthermore, successful private corporations tend to grow large and eventually pose a threat to the CCP's authority; centrally planning an economy filled with medium-sized corporations is much easier said than done. Lastly, China's authoritarian past and present have existential consequences whether that be its declining birthrate or an exodus of investor confidence.

A heavy hand may win the CCP some flashy victories, but there is a reason why liberal democracies, like the US, are able to flourish economically and adapt to challenges. China's political system cannot tolerate multiple centers of influence. Furthermore, corrective change is far more difficult when a centralized authority rules most decision-making given the lack of constructive feedback mechanisms and incentives to point out issues in society. As the CCP confronts contemporary challenges, be it income inequality, disruptive corporations, or geopolitical tension, it cannot help but prioritize internal stability first. The reversion back to a more centrally planned economy is a clear reaction to the growing disorder in Chinese society. A disorder that keeps Xi and other CCP elites up at night.

8. Social Policy

China commits egregious human rights violations.[6] Human rights abuses in China feed a never-ending media cycle, as the CCP discovers new ways to shock the consciousness of humanity and push the limits on how Orwellian an industrialized country can be. Beijing's behavior is especially egregious to Western observers because, unlike North Korea, the PRC is not a crackpot regime. It is not even like the Soviet Union. The Soviet Union was quite powerful but still could not produce remotely comparable living conditions for its citizens to those free societies like the US did (Morton, 2007). China boasts gleaming skyscrapers, innovative companies, and dynamic society and at the same time Chinese citizens are nevertheless subject to constant censorship, surveillance, and repression. However, the Chinese government, or any government, does not tighten its grip on society merely for the sake of abusing its population. Rather, the trajectory of the CCP's policies towards civil and political rights seems to mirror its growing concerns with controlling its population.

As Chinese society continues to grow richer and more dynamic, so too does the government's involvement in social life. Although it would be easy to simply paint the CCP as inherently spiteful of minorities, free expression, and religion, there is a clear rational progression to Beijing's policy making. It does not make sense to expend precious resources and political capital on repression for repression's sake. Furthermore, cracking down on society

---

[6] See the internment of Uyghur Muslims in Xinjiang, or the pervasive censorship of speech nationwide, or what is easily the most sophisticated online content moderation regime, dubbed "the Great Firewall" (Chan et al 2011).

not only makes the country less productive but also wears out the patience of the citizenry. A closer look reveals that the CCP's treatment of human rights follows a rational political calculus that is enabled by its authoritarian structure and inspired by its core goals.

Censorship in China is industrial in scale. YouTube, Twitter, Facebook, and Google are all banned (Human Rights Watch, 2022). Citizens are thereby compelled to use highly-regulated Chinese equivalents. Authorities suppress online content deemed not in line with "core socialist values" (Xinhua, 2013). The forced disappearance of Alibaba CEO and the scrubbing of actress Zhao Wei's presence from the internet are just two examples of many crackdowns on "misbehaving" celebrities (Gan & George, 2021). The MIT Technology Review noted that,

> On June 17, the internet regulator Cyberspace Administration of China (CAC) published a draft update on the responsibilities of platforms and content creators in managing online comments. One line stands out: all online comments would have to be pre-reviewed before being published (Yang, 2022).

The move rides on a growing tide of increased internet censorship as the digital sector flourishes and more people can broadcast their opinions. In 2018, major Chinese media companies, like Tencent, ramped up hiring for content moderators in response to criticism from the CCP for lack of policing. As one would expect, in 2021, the discussion platform, Clubhouse, was rapidly shut down after authorities discovered conversations involving Uyghurs.

Since 2010 Beijing has devoted more resources to domestic security than its military, and that number is only increasing (Tan, 2018). Those resources are most concentrated in unstable areas such as Xinjiang and Tibet, far exceeding the national average in spending per person. Coming in third and fourth place are Beijing and Shanghai. Furthermore, ethnic discrimination is overt as non-Han Chinese individuals are subject to far more scrutiny (Tan, 2018). For example, in Xinjiang, ethnic minorities receive barcodes with their personal information, often placed on their house doors. Indeed, the CCP appears more afraid of its people than external adversaries.

Human Rights Watch reports that Chinese law makes room for only five religions, and the government strictly controls how the faith is practiced within the country (2023). Practitioners of faith are often targeted by authorities, which the CCP sees as a threat to its control because religion offers an authority beyond the government. State control over religion has only increased since in 2016, "President Xi called for "Sinicization" of religions—which aims to ensure that the Chinese Communist Party is the arbiter of people's spiritual life—state control over religion has strengthened (Human Rights Watch, 2023)."

Sexual minority rights are increasingly threatened, even though the government decriminalized same-sex activity in 1997. In July 2021, the Associated Press reported that the Chinese social media giant, WeChat, deleted dozens of lesbian and gay accounts (Ting, 2021). In September of the same year, the government banned the appearance of effeminate men on TV (Associated Press, 2021). Chinese state media outlets blamed the rise of feminine men on Japanese culture, which they claim was influenced by the US to pacify Tokyo following World War II (Yang, 2021). Furthermore, the rise of nontraditional male behaviors is a product of the retreat of politics from style, allowing for more self-expression. Regardless of if this is true, curtailing personal style makes sense as the CCP seeks to reassert itself in more aspects of daily life while also preparing the country for geopolitical competition.

Beijing's handling of the Covid-19 pandemic illustrates the CCP's attitude toward human rights when pursuing its policy objectives. From the outbreak of Covid-19 in 2020 and extending into 2022, China's Zero Covid Policy shut down entire cities at a moment's notice while providing a backdrop to restrict already non-existent political rights (Morrison , Kennedy , & Huang. 2022). Human Rights Watch provides examples by writing,

> In August, a Beijing court sentenced activists Chen Mei and Cai Wei to 15 months in prison after convicting them of "picking quarrels and provoking trouble." They were detained in April 2020, for archiving censored online articles and social media posts about the pandemic. In the same month, imprisoned citizen journalist Zhang Zhan became seriously ill following a hunger strike. In December 2020, Zhang was sentenced to four years in prison after traveling to Wuhan to

document the pandemic in February. Citizen journalist Fang Bin, who was detained in April 2020 in Wuhan, remained missing (2023).

China proclaimed that its harsh Covid policies mitigated the pandemic and allowed it to be the first country to begin a post-covid recovery befor (Kuo L. , China becomes first major economy to recover from Covid-19 pandemic, 2020)e the end of 2020, which may have been true initially (Kuo, 2020). However, by April of 2022, the world looked in horror as Shanghai, a city of over 26 million people, choked under the grip of an aggressive lockdown that created supply shortages (Sharwood, 2022). Drones patrolled the city, broadcasting commands to "control your soul's desire for freedom" as citizens protested from their balconies.

Cities across China implemented the Zero Covid Strategy, and Xi Jinping only doubled down on the government's commitment to the policy as criticisms about its effect on the economy and actual effectiveness grew (Davidson, 2022). Indeed for Xi, Zero Covid is not just about suppressing the virus but about his personal authority and the perceived infallibility of his administration leading into the next Party Congress in November 2022 (Hadano, 2022). A meeting where Xi will receive the chance to be appointed for an unprecedented third term. Furthermore, China's authoritarian response to the pandemic represented a key difference from the West, which the CCP hoped to portray as hindered by its emphasis on individual rights.

The Politics of Rights

The US frames rights through the lens of negative rights, focusing on freedoms from government action (Currie, 1986, p. 864). These liberties include free speech, due process, and equality under the law. Negative rights protect individuals from an imposition on their autonomy, whereas positive rights grant individuals an entitlement, such as healthcare. The Chinese government does not recognize political rights as the discretion of the CCP, a political party, is central to the regime. Rather, the Chinese speak profoundly of what they define as economic rights or the right to development. Beijing ratified the International Covenant on Economic, Social, and Cultural Rights (ICESCR), whereas the US did not (United Nations, 1966). The US ratified the International Covenant on Civil and Political Rights, whereas China did not (United Nations, 1966). This dichotomy demonstrates ideological differences between the two governments and highlights the political nature of both governments in approaching the idea of rights.

From their very inception, the two human rights covenants represented political compromises. Both documents originated during the Cold War and demonstrated the global divide between regimes that saw a more limited role for government and a more active one. Although many countries signed both covenants, it is clear that economic, social, and cultural rights justify government intervention, and civil and political rights serve as restrictions on power. Countries like the Soviet Union and China were more than happy to provide government access to education and healthcare, while they could not afford to provide rights such as free speech. The United States is the opposite; while civil rights and other negative liberties fit well within Washington's political framework, providing so-called economic and cultural rights does not fit so neatly. To paraphrase the Reagan Administration, economic and cultural rights are merely aspirations (Amnesty International, 2008). The Chinese follow a similar line, proclaiming that civil rights are luxuries to be enjoyed once a country is sufficiently developed (Ministry of Foreign Affairs (China), 2022).

Choosing to honor certain rights over others has political underpinnings and is often tied to institutional structure, whether that be a liberal democracy or a Communist dictatorship. The CCP seems to understand the value of human rights, given their use of rights-based terminology. Indeed, Ren Danhong from the China Society for Human Rights Studies advocates for his government by writing,

> The Communist Party of China (CPC) and the Chinese government always respect and ensure human rights. For a long time, China, by connecting the universality principle of human rights with China's reality (China Human Rights, 2023).

The key phrase is "China's reality," which serves as an easy excuse to curb the extent of rights, either partially or entirely in pursuit of the Party's political goals. These goals may be laudable, such as maintaining stability to create the conditions necessary for societal growth, or they could be entirely self-serving, such as aggressively crushing protests to preserve power (Amnesty International, 2022). The key component in understanding how the CCP will act is a political calculation of how respecting or dismantling rights serves long term goals.

Certain policies, such as curating what Chinese citizens can see on the internet, serve obvious ends of maintaining Party control and ensuring favorable information consumption (Wang, 2020). Other restrictions, such as what protests are allowed, factor in more complicated considerations. There are hundreds of protests daily in China on issues ranging from environmental degradation to local corruption (Fisher, 2012). The government can't crack down all the time as that would not only offend the population, but such civic demonstrations can serve the Party's interest.

Often, protestors raise their concerns out of patriotism rather than a disdain for the state, which allows the government to address the problem and boost its legitimacy. However, even when these movements start as means to improve the country, the CCP is still suspicious that well-intentioned movements may spin out of control into social unrest. For example, authorities harassed and broke up a demonstration against an incinerator plant in Wuhan, even though the protestors held a banner with the words of China's Premier Li Keqiang reading "War on Pollution (Bloomberg News, 2020)." However, one must consider that the CCP sees threats in civil unrest, especially those with the potential of expanding to uncontrollable levels, even if the activity is seemingly in support of the government.

A Tale of Two Cities: China's Hong Kong Crackdown and Macau's Peace

The CCP's pragmatism and rational calculus with human rights are readily apparent when comparing its treatment of Hong Kong and Macau. Both cities are former European colonies that returned to China at the end of the 20th century and are designated Special Autonomous Zones because of their Western political and economic systems. However, Hong Kong's autonomy is violated far more than Macau's.

The CCP's relationship with the city of Hong Kong is especially complicated given the contrast between Communist Beijing and the city's unique democratic system. Following the conclusion of the first Opium War, the British controlled the city as a colony from 1840-1997 (Ministry of Foreign Affairs (China), 2023). As a result, Hong Kong returned to Chinese control with robust Western attributes such as democracy, civil liberties, and one of the highest degrees of economic freedom in the world (Feulner, 2021). Furthermore, Hong Kong's handover from the British came with agreements to respect the city's autonomy contained in the Sino-British Declaration (Cheung, 2021). The document was signed in 1984, over a decade before the actual handover, and took two years to negotiate.

Taming and ultimately integrating Hong Kong into China poses a complicated task for the CCP, especially because of the vast differences between the government. Although Beijing promised 50 years of autonomy, the political reality is that many Hong Kongers likely do not want to lose their freedoms as China shows little sign of liberalizing. Furthermore, Beijing likely views the city's autonomy as a liability for social stability, especially given its highly globalized culture and position as an international trade hub. In particular, both Western and Chinese thinkers see the potential for democracy movements in the city to spread northward towards the mainland (Illmer, 2021). However, Beijing has been more proactive in gradually curtailing the city state's liberal impulses. The greatest escalation in China's involvement in Hong Kong's internal affairs occurred after a series of massive protests against an extradition agreement with the mainland rocked the city in 2019 (Maizland, 2022).

Following Beijing's crackdown, many Western experts proclaim that the CCP violated the One Country, Two Systems Agreement (Overhold, 2019, p.13). Although the central government may have intervened in Hong Kong in the past, such interference did not rise to the level observed post-2019. The escalation represents a clear political cost-benefit analysis and a rational move to advance the CCP's interests. Hong Kong's open society presents a clear security issue. The CCP cannot afford to let ideas such as liberal democracy spread from the island to the mainland.

Furthermore, Beijing does not maintain the same legal powers to regulate social behavior as it can on the mainland. At the same time, the Chinese government understands that Hong Kong's productivity and social stability require a level of autonomy. Many Hong Kongers still treasure the freedoms leftover from British rule. Furthermore, the city's dynamism and productivity stems from its political-economic system. For example, in 2021, Hong Kong's GDP per capita stood close to $50,000, whereas mainland China stood at the lower end of $12,000 (Country Economy, 2023).

Together the dismantling of Hong Kong's democracy and the gradual assertion of Beijing's authority in the Special Autonomous Zone demonstrate a clear enmity for civil rights. In this case, the CCP is not only restricting political expression but actively rolling back freedoms, even after making promises to allow Hong Kong to maintain much of its democracy (Overholt, 2019, p. 1). Beijing passed the infamous National Security Law following the 2019 anti-extradition protests, which represented the final straw for the CCP after numerous other protests (Datt, 2021). The law contains vague restrictions on "separatism, subversion, terrorism, and colluding with foreign forces," punishable up to life in prison (Hong Kong Government, 2020). What constitutes a violation is intentionally vague as to provide the government the discretion to target virtually any political enemy, such as closing down and arresting members of Apple Daily, a Hong Kong newspaper (Enos, 2021).

Although the National Security Law may sound like a policy to mitigate violent threats, it functions as a means of direct control over the political freedoms of Hong Kong residents. Passing the law degrades the One Country Two Systems framework as Beijing now exerts direct control over the social and political life of Hong Kongers. Following the 2019 protests, the CCP's efforts to blur the lines between Hong Kong and the mainland only accelerated. In July of 2021, the South China Morning Post reported that Carie Lam, the city's Chief Executive, pledged to ""boldly push ahead" with patriotic education, which she called an important policy the city has failed to implement even after its return to Chinese rule, to rectify the moral values of the younger generation (Cheng, 2021)." Political indoctrination combined with the punitive powers of the National Security Law enabled Beijing to slowly flatten Hong Kong's liberal spirit.

However, while the world watches in horror as the CCP systematically dismantles Hong Kong's free society, there is little news about such conflict in Macau, another Special Autonomous Zone. Macau is geographically and culturally similar to Hong Kong, except the Portuguese ruled the city-state until its return to China in 1999 (BBC Travel, 2019). Although the One Country Two Systems Model failed in Hong Kong, the residents of Macau and Beijing coexist peacefully, mostly because of the city state's unique history with the mainland. One of the first major differences is the inward-facing role of the city's economy compared to Hong Kong. Macau is a gambling hub with a population in the hundreds of thousands, not 7.4 million. ABC notes,

> While both Macau and Hong Kong are governed under the "one country, two systems" formula, national security and Indo-Pacific expert at RAND corporation, Derek Grossman, said Macau was fundamentally different to Hong Kong because the nature of economic development was "much more geared toward the gaming industry and less about interconnectivity with the Western economy (Zhou, 2019)."

ABC also cites political scientist Bill Chou Kwok-ping who notes that nearly half of Macau's population was born in mainland China compared to only around 20 percent of Hong Kong residents (Zhou, 2019). As a regime that is currently dealing with ethnic tension in many of its frontier provinces, such as Tibet and Xinjiang, Beijing understands the difference demographics makes in social stability.

Another key point is that many of the political institutions the CCP desires are already present in Macau because of its Portuguese heritage. Not only were the Portuguese more willing to (Cohen, 2019) hand over their colony than the British (Lisbon attempted to return the colony during the Cultural Revolution, but Beijing rejected the offer because it had to deal with ongoing turmoil on the mainland), but they also did not share the same legal systems as the British (Cohen, 2019). Jerome Cohen, a law professor at New York University, explains that

> Portugal brought to Macau a continental European civil law system and a criminal process that rested on different philosophical, religious, and political developments and traditions that were reflected in the legal institutions established. Often, those continental traditions proved too malleable in Lisbon to resist the demands of politicians who sought to impose authoritarian government (2019).

Lisbon did not instill the fierce commitment to a common law tradition and rule of law that London brought to Hong Kong. The British forced the CCP to make several promises as a condition for handing over Hong Kong, among them: respecting the existence of an independent judiciary, freedom of speech, and multiple political parties.

On the other hand, Chinese authorities were given key positions in Macau's legal system, a system less resilient to authoritarian rule than what the British left. Furthermore, to the CCP's credit, Beijing provided much-needed social stability during the 1999 handover. With the approval of many of the city's residents, the CCP cleaned up gang violence over casinos which at the time caused instability and a recession (Zhou, 2019). As a result, Macau is far less suspicious of Beijing and is considered one of the only areas where the one country, two systems model works. The CCP understands this difference acutely, which explains not just why Hong Kong receives far more punishment from Beijing but also why there are diverse opinions on taming the city.

Many of Hong Kong's liberal democratic institutions are fundamentally incompatible with China's authoritarian system, especially as the Party tightens its grip on society. In 2021, the 13th National People's Congress authorized the Standing Committee to reform Hong Kong's electoral system (Ministry of Foreign Affairs (China, 2023). The result was a vetting mechanism that now approves all candidates running for the Legislative Commission, the city's law-making body. Furthermore, rather than having 50% of the body democratically elected, that number is now 22%, and virtually all of them are sympathetic to Beijing.

It is clear to the CCP that the one country, two systems model as understood in 1997 is unsustainable given the level of resistance and liberal resiliency exhibited by Hong Kong. The question to look for is how Beijing will act after 2047 when it is no longer legally obligated to uphold the current system. Some believe that a full integration of the city is impossible and may jeopardize social and economic stability. Others assert that full integration is necessary for ensuring Hong Kong is fully tamed, and perhaps China should rescind its 2047 promise and act in its interests sooner. The *BBC* writes,

> There is no need to change after 50 years," Shen Chunyao said at a legal conference in the weeks leading up to the 25th anniversary of the handover.
>
> However, he suggested that "timely improvements" needed to be made, saying that otherwise "its potential cannot be achieved in the long run".

But others have taken a stronger stance (BBC, 2022).

> "As an inalienable part of China, we cannot afford to be a country that undermines the security of China," said Regina Ip, one of Hong Kong's most well-known pro-Beijing lawmakers.

For the Chinese government, respecting the political and civil rights of its two autonomous zones represents a rational calculation rather than a purely ideological desire to undermine universal liberal values. On the one hand are the benefits of respecting such rights, whether it be maintaining productivity and avoiding backlash. On the other, most notably in the case of Hong Kong, are serious national security and integrity concerns that stem from free expression. A city like Macau, where the CCP is already deeply integrated and popular, does not require much suppression.

A city like Hong Kong requires not just the systematic dismantling of its political system but indoctrination, which is why the Party is actively attempting to introduce its Patriotic Education program into the city (Liu, 2022). Indeed, Beijing is actively learning from the governance of Hong Kong and will potentially apply those lessons to Taiwan. In August of 2022, the South China Morning Post reported that the CCP released a white paper on the reunification of Taiwan and the mainland, noting,

> It also keeps the "one country, two systems" model on the table, but a number of conciliatory measures contained in an earlier paper published in 2000, including the offer of "a high degree of autonomy for Taiwan", are missing from the latest version.
>
> Statements that "the central government will not deploy military and administrative personnel to Taiwan" and "any matter is up for negotiation under the one-China principle" also do not appear in the latest version (Lau, 2022).

Such a development seems to demonstrate a rational reaction to the governance of Hong Kong to which Taiwan may be even more difficult. Taiwan not only possesses robust liberal institutions, a strong position in global commerce, and prevalent Western influences but is also separated by 100 miles of ocean from the mainland. If the special autonomy given to Hong Kong produced social unrest and challenged CCP authority, similar freedoms would cause greater problems if Taipei were to be reintegrated. If a Chinese flag flies over Taiwan, one should expect the CCP to attempt to play an intensive balancing game in finding the right mix of freedom and control for governing the island.

Beijing's lack of respect for human rights as a universal principle is clear. Rather, the Chinese government takes a pragmatic approach whereas they allow such freedoms as necessary for productivity and social stability. Beyond the careful calculation of individual rights on the one hand and appeasing citizens on the other, the CCP tends to treat society like a garden. A garden which they carefully prune with extreme attention, whether that be curating everything their citizens see on the internet to limiting the number of hours children can play video games (Buckley, 2021). All these factors indicate a growing sense of insecurity regarding the Party's control over society and challenges that may complicate Beijing's ambitions.

However, one can see the true extremes of how far Beijing is willing to go in molding a population into compliance in its frontier provinces, namely Tibet and Xinjiang. In these two provinces, the CCP not only has to contend with restless citizens who disagree with its authoritarian policies but also oppose the government on ethnic, religious, and cultural grounds. Without a binding agreement resembling a Special Autonomous Zone or a Sino-British Declaration and a history of violent resistance, Tibet and Xinjiang know how far the Chinese will go to establish order. Furthermore, unlike Hong Kong or Macau, these regions do not possess dynamic and productive economies that force the CCP to take pause in exercising power. Indeed, the imagination and general disregard for human dignity that Beijing exhibits in repressing and taming its westernmost provinces is nothing short of extraordinary.

Breaking Tibet and Xinjiang

Tibet and Xinjiang, two former independent kingdoms home to unique ethnic groups like the Tibetans and Turkic Muslims known as Uyghurs, present unique challenges for the CCP. Although the government prioritizes social stability across the country, the ethnic and cultural distinctness of Tibet and Xinjiang present major difficulties in pacifying and integrating the local populations. Ethnic and racial tensions are an ever-present problem across the world, however, in China, these tensions often lead to violence (Hillman & Tuttle, 2023, 280). Ben Hillman, a professor at Australian National University, notes that "China's leadership sees a rise in "ethnic consciousness" as a challenge to the authority and legitimacy of its political institutions (2023, 8)."

Polarization along ethnic lines has motivated a number of Tibetans and Uyghurs to commit acts of civil unrest or outright terrorism. These include self-immolation demonstrations in Tibet and protests that lead to clashes between ethnic Tibetans and police forces (Flynn, 2018). Ethnic Uyghurs are an even greater problem for the CCP as individuals have resorted to acts of terrorism, such as hit and run strikes in the Taklamakan Desert or driving trucks into civilians as far east as Beijing (Leibold, 2016, 224). In February of 2014, 8 assailants identified by Chinese authorities as Uyghur extremists killed around 29 people and injured over 140 with machetes at the Kunming railway station (BBC, 2014).

The ethnic differences between the Han Chinese and the minority Tibetans and Uyghurs are only worsened by China's status as an invading force and the history of oppression by the CCP. For Tibet, hatred of the CCP began when the People's Liberation Army marched into the capital Lhasa in 1951 after the kingdom had enjoyed de facto independence since the fall of the Qing Dynasty (Jian, 2006, 56). Being a province on the frontier of the Chinese empire and its own independent kingdom at times, Tibet's history with China is complicated. Tibetan culture is uniquely Himalayan, a melting pot of Indian, Nepalese, as well as Chinese influences, and a unique nomadic lifestyle. Tibet's political leader is also a Buddhist religious figure, the Dalai Lama, who the Tibetans believe is perpetually reincarnated. Despite these differences, the Chinese national rejuvenation project called for the reintegration of Tibet, and the Tibetan army, especially without international recognition, was too weak to resist (Jian, 2006, 54).
Chinese forces invaded Tibet in 1951 and swiftly brought Lhasa to the negotiating table for a peaceful integration into the PRC. Chen Jian, a global fellow at the Wilson Center, explains that,

> Chinese officials also emphasized that in the long run Tibet would have to be transformed into a "people's democratic" society—a

> phrase that in the Maoist discourse meant destroying Tibet's traditional political, economic, and social structures and replacing them with socialist ones. But to ensure that a peaceful settlement in Tibet could be achieved, Mao was willing to accept a series of key compromises, including temporarily allowing the feudal economy and polity to exist in Tibet, in exchange for the Dalai Lama's acknowledgment of Chinese sovereignty (2006, 60).

Following the conclusion of the invasion, the Tibetans, under duress, signed the 17 Point Agreement, which among many things, justified Chinese control over the kingdom and mandated gradual Socialist reforms (Lama, 2021). The gradual nature of the reform policies represented a clear understanding by Mao and the CCP that Tibet's drastically different culture and political economy made peaceful, rapid integration impossible. Indeed, Mao and the Party elites understood that making concessions to the Tibetans was necessary to pursue some semblance of voluntary change. Chen Jian notes,

> For Mao and his fellow CCP leaders, the postponement of the "democratic reforms" in Tibet was no more than a tactical action. In the same "September Fourth Instruction," the CCP leadership also made it clear that making concessions to the Tibetan upper-class elites was by no means a "passive policy design." On the contrary, the CCP leaders emphasized, "we must do our job in active ways (2006, 65)."

During the initial occupation, the CCP made efforts to preserve segments of Tibetan life while supporting efforts to improve their quality of life. Perhaps the most telling example of Beijing's tactical generosity was when the Dali Lama went into exile in India, and the CCP tried to convince him to return. Zhou Enlai, the PRC's foreign minister at the time, even offered to delay political-economic reforms in Tibet even as the rest of China entered the Second Five-Year Plan (Jian, 2006, 68).

However, the Chinese occupation was ultimately unsustainable as both Chinese and Tibetans understood that Lhasa's cherished way of life had to give way to the grand vision of the CCP. Furthermore, Tibet's rural infrastructure struggled to support the population and Chinese army garrisons, exacerbating tensions (Jian, 2006, 62). By 1958, guerillas sprang up in provinces like Qinghai and Sichuan, which encompass significant Tibetan cultural sites and a region of Tibet known as Amdo (Jian, 2006, 78). The CCP neglected to exempt these regions from political reforms, which only exacerbated ethnic tensions by the time the Great Leap Forward's radical policies swept throughout China. By 1959, as guerilla forces fled to Lhasa, followed by the Chinese army, all of Tibet was in full-scale rebellion, which the CCP saw as an opportunity more than a threat, given that they now had an excuse to take full control over the kingdom's political system. According to Chen Jian, Mao reacted to the rebellion by stating, "if the reactionary forces in Tibet dare to start a full-scale rebellion, this without any doubt will mean that working people [in Tibet] will benefit from an earlier liberation (2006, 73)."

Much like how the Tibetan army didn't stand a chance in 1951, the rebellion was crushed, and the Dalai Lama permanently fled to India, where he now serves as the leader of the Tibetan Government in Exile (2023). During the uprising, Chinese forces bombed Tibetan cultural sites, such as monasteries, to exact vengeance, a practice that foreshadowed the horrors to come (Lama, 2021). After 1959, with Beijing in control, the tensions between a theocracy like Tibet and an atheist Communist dictatorship like China grew exponentially. During the Cultural Revolution, when radical Communist ideology ran rampant throughout the PRC as Mao targeted his political enemies, Tibet presented a unique target. According to the Central Tibetan Administration,

> When it ended with Mao's death in September 1976, more than 6,000 monasteries and religious institutions in Tibet laid in ruins. Millions of ancient and priceless manuscripts were burnt. Statues made of gold, silver, or bronze were removed from the temples and shipped to China. The physical torture and psychological traumas endured by Tibetans during public "struggle sessions" and imprisonment were beyond human comprehension. At least 92,000 Tibetans who were subjected to "struggle sessions" died or committed suicide and around 173,000 Tibetans died in prison, or in "Reform Through Labor Camps (2022)."

Even before the Cultural Revolution kicked off in 1966, the Panchen Lama, the second highest figure after the Dalai Lama, sent a petition to Beijing in 1962 stating that over 97% of Tibet's monasteries and nunneries were destroyed, displacing 93% of monks and nuns (Central Tibetan Administration, 1998).

Following several protests in the beginning of the 21st Century, Chen Quanguo, then Party Secretary for Tibet, built an unprecedented police state. Some of the policies implemented in the region include Grid Style Social Management, which works similarly to a panopticon (Dolma, 2020; Habich-Sobiegalla & Plümmer 1, 2022). This surveillance system employs a decentralized security apparatus where non-police individuals such as taxi drivers and sanitation workers are tasked with reporting suspicious activity to a grid manager. This mechanism conserves specialized state resources, such as trained security forces, so that they only need to be deployed towards identified threats. Such a system was recently applied to police Covid-19 lockdowns and compliance. Often, Beijing sees regions like Tibet and Xinjiang as testing grounds for innovative security practices. The differences in repression, Tibet being less restricted than Xinjiang, can likely be explained by the differences in perceived threat, as well as the comparative economic viability of Tibet.

However, the CCP's solution to address ethnic violence and tension is not only to subjugate these regions with a massive security state but to force Tibet and Xinjiang to become more Chinese. This process is known as Sinicization. Part of the strategy includes investing in infrastructure and education while also incentivizing Han Chinese citizens to populate the regions. Another component of Sinicization is coopting religious institutions to become instruments of the CCP. For example, Apa Lhamo writes on the extent of these programs in The Diplomat by explaining the, "campaigns include tightening control over monastic affairs, monitoring activities of the monks and nuns, increasing mandatory indoctrination training sessions in monasteries and nunneries across Tibet (2021). Furthermore, "trainings especially emphasize the CCP's "Measures on the Management of the Reincarnation of Living Buddhas in Tibetan Buddhism," developed in July 2007 and aimed at controlling the appointment of the 14th Dalai Lama's reincarnation (Lhamo, 2021)."

Such policies are meant to pacify the regions by reducing the cultural and ethnic differences with the rest of the country. Indeed, Xi Jinping remarked in 2020 on the need to increase Sinicization efforts when he stated a "new modern socialist Tibet that is united, prosperous, culturally advanced, harmonious and beautiful" would be achieved primarily via secondary school reforms that "plant the seeds of loving China deep in the heart of every youth (Dorje, 2020)." Although such a policy does have logical underpinnings for creating stability, it remains to be seen whether these efforts will successfully subdue Tibet and Xinjiang or invite more backlash.

The CCP Is Trying to Change The Meaning of Human Rights

China's rhetoric about human rights is strategic. Although Beijing is subject to endless audits and criticisms on its social policies, the Chinese are actively attempting to shift the meaning of the term human rights to fit their own political goals. The CCP frequently boasts about its accomplishments in the world of human rights and often encourages developing countries to follow. This contradiction is based on an emphasis on "development rights," not individual rights or what can be described as universal values like bodily autonomy. Decoding China, a European website run by the China Media Project, Heidelberg University, and the Swedish Center for China Studies, quote Liu Huaqiu, a late Chinese politician, by noting,

> For the vast number of developing countries to respect and protect human rights is first and foremost to ensure full realization of the rights to subsistence and development. The argument that human rights are the precondition for development is unfounded. When poverty and lack of adequate food and clothing are commonplace and people's basic needs are not guaranteed, priority should be given to economic development. Otherwise, human rights are completely out of thc question (Oud, 2023).

The logic and political reasoning are clear. The Chinese authoritarian model cannot tolerate the prevailing universal values regarding personal autonomy, but it does prioritize state-based assistance. One can easily argue that liberal democracies like America, Taiwan, Japan, Denmark, Germany, and so on prioritize human rights and have living standards far exceeding the Chinese. However, that is not the point. The point is that "development rights" create an excuse for a powerful authoritarian state that provides social stability, allowing some semblance of economic growth. This point is then juxtaposed with the notion that one cannot enjoy their rights if they are desperately poor and deprived. Indeed, a Chinese whitepaper asserts

> The right of education is an important prerequisite for the overall, free development of human beings. In old China, the majority of the working people did not have such a right. With only less than 20 percent of school-age children going to school, more than 80 percent of the total population were illiterate (Ministry for Foreign Affairs, 2022).

This theme of providing opportunities rings throughout China's human rights discourse. Furthermore, this conception of rights finds much grounding in Chinese history, where the power vacuum created by the fall of the Qing dynasty led to decades of chaos and violence. This convenient backdrop allows the CCP, as the victor of the Chinese Civil War and the unifying government of China, to claim that it successfully created the conditions necessary for the development and, therefore, the possibility for other rights to be enjoyed.

The CCP consistently stresses the necessity of order and authority in making human rights possible, not just because it supports their authoritarian system but because it can criticize the perceived problems of liberal democracies. AP News quotes a Chinese human rights professor who remarked,

> And that is the two political parties would sometimes do everything they can to advance their own interests. ... They would incite division and violence among the people. So, can U.S. society continue to prosper under its current democratic system? I would put a question mark on it (Moritsugu, 2021).

The professor's remarks concern America's poorly managed Covid policy in 2020. At the time, Washington's democratic system seemed to be fumbling, while Beijing's decisive actions seemed to be working. The Chinese frequently stress that civil and political rights are luxuries that can be enjoyed when a society is sufficiently stable. This idea often justifies government intervention to address various issues from income inequality to environmental degradation.

Although the CCP attempts to sell this more nebulous vision of human rights as merely an alternative to the Western orthodoxy, China's model is merely a return to a more Machiavellian view of government. That is that the state should focus on forwarding the objectives of the nation and those in charge, be it economic growth, prestige, and social stability, with little concern for universal principles or morality. Such a vision is a natural reflex for any ambitious political leader unchecked by elections, constitutions, an armed population, or any robust structure of limited government.

The incentives of political actors within the system itself, often point towards greater repression, not less. Those who use innovative and effective means for pacifying resistance often receive promotions, such as Wang Junzheng, formerly head of security in Xinjiang and now Party Chief in Tibet (Mai, 2021). Wang's promotion not only represents a signal from the CCP's top brass that they are defying Western sanctions but also an endorsement of his harsh policies used to control ethnic minorities. Much like how local officials can receive promotions by facilitating economic growth, they can also and, in many cases, must forward social stability.

China's human rights rhetoric, emphasizing the necessity for economic development and social stability, is based on two general motivations beyond the thin veil of emphasizing the necessity for order and prosperity before one can enjoy other rights. One of the primary motivations is to promote and justify the CCP's social policies to gradually shift the meaning of the term human rights. Beijing hopes to frame the discussion about human rights as a subjective matter where the West has its conceptions, the Chinese their own as well, steeped in their historical experience (Oud, 2023). That historical experience is one of recovery from decades of civil war and chaos, which they claim underlies the need for a heavy-handed government to create social stability. The other motivation is to internationalize this malleable definition of human rights to create an international order less concerned with domestic human rights abuses.

The current Western consensus on individual rights as an inalienable and inherent component of a person's humanity is a foreign and inconvenient concept for the CCP. Although the Party should not be described as sadistic or inherently attracted to violating human rights, Beijing views such rights as commodities to be enjoyed by well-behaving citizens that can be retracted and extended at will. Such a perspective stems directly from the government's authoritarian structure and doctrine, just like the American commitment to inalienable individual rights stems from its form of government. And even then, politicians in the US have diverse views about rights and often defend ideas such as free speech when it is politically in their interests and attempt to curtail speech when it is not. The structural component that prevents American leaders from censoring their citizens is the checks and balances inherent to a republican system of government.

Washington's invocation of human rights as criticism of China plays a role in the broader geopolitical competition with Beijing. Although the US generally promotes such values globally, much of the spotlight shines on China, not just because the CCP authorizes egregious social policies, but because these criticisms are a convenient weapon for the US. Although Washington's leveraging of human rights in the US-China rivalry may be a common CCP talking point, it is nonetheless rational and expected (Jia, 2022). The same goes for the Chinese attempts to shift the definition of human rights by playing semantic games that paint authoritarian practices as congruent with a more flexible definition of human rights. The way the Americans and the Chinese discuss the notion of human rights is not necessarily a cultural divide but instead one of political objectives and interests.

9. Foreign Policy

Beijing wishes to change the world in its favor. This contributes, in no small part, to why China is so especially relevant today. The important question is "in what way and to what extent." Those who overestimate the CCP's ambition claim that China seeks world domination in the territorial sense. They liken China's aims to those Nazi Germany or Imperial Japan had in mind. But even in the worst-case scenario, it is extremely unlikely that the People's Liberation Army (PLA) will be marching down Pennsylvania Avenue anytime soon, if ever.

World conquest is largely impossible in the age of nuclear weapons, and it is not politically or practically apt. Those who underestimate China's ambitions assert the CCP talking point that China is an inherently peaceful country and only seeks mutual respect and cooperation (Ministry of Foreign Affairs, 2023). This view is clearly ahistorical and neglects the reality of geopolitics. The CCP will never be secure in a world where China does not throw around its weight, be it securing strategic value in far-off places or coercing countries to cease criticizing its human rights abuses. Rather than taking Beijing word for word or attempting to construct an overly complicated theory, one should use public choice and look at the rational interests of Chinese leaders.

The best way to frame Beijing's ambitions is to start with what has been explicitly stated, which is the great rejuvenation of the country (National People's Congress, 2021). Graham Allison, a decorated China scholar at Harvard University, explains rejuvenation entails establishing dominance in Asia, annexing territory it views as its own, and gaining the respect of world leaders (Allison, 2017). Kevin Rudd, perhaps one of the most respected China experts in the world, explains that another component entails being able to fundamentally shift the global order to serve its own interests (ANU TV, 2022). John Mearsheimer, one of the most respected living international relations scholars predicts,

> China will seek to grow its economy and become so powerful that it can dictate the boundaries of acceptable behavior to neighboring countries, and make it clear they will pay a substantial price if they do not follow the rules. After all, this is what the United States has done in the Western Hemisphere.

In examining the Belt and Road Initiative Greg Caskey points towards the work of Portuguese statesman Bruno Maçães who writes on China's Belt and Road Initiative as an extension of "Tianxia ("All-under-Heaven") and its connection to the historical Tributary System (Caskey, 2020)." This vision seeks to place China in the center of commerce and elevate Beijing's status to a country where all others look to with awe, perhaps paying tribute and closely aligning themselves.

In summary, China seeks influence in the manner currently enjoyed by the US due to its standing in the world. Countries should seek to emulate, or at least respect, China's political system and its accomplishments. Governments, NGOs, and civil society will yield to the CCP's demands. If told to refrain from criticizing China or to Beijing's priorities first, they will comply. Enemies of China, whether rival nations or terrorist groups, will fear the power of the Chinese military and its allies, just as they today fear Washington and NATO. This is a far more open-ended and familiar goal than either world conquest, on the one hand, or peaceful coexistence, on the other.

There is nothing particularly novel about these grand ambitions. They simply represent the logical interests of a great power and those that rule it. American foreign policy evolved based on a calculation of national and private interests, be it a desire to secure trade routes, combat terrorism, defeat peer competitors, secure domestic popularity, among many other explanations. As China's power grows and contracts relative to the rest of the world, we should expect their interests and willingness to pursue them with coercive force to change as well.

Today, the CCP is moving into the next stage of its ascent to this position of influence. We see a far more assertive navy in the South China Sea, with incursions into Taiwanese waters (Council on Foreign Relations, 2022). We can safely assume this expansionist activity is driven both by collective grand strategy as well as individual interest groups within the Chinese system (such as maritime security) attempting to gain prestige and resources. Xi's Belt and Road Initiative spans the world, while private and state-owned entities make large investments in Africa and Latin America (Roy, 2022). In the 2022 Russian invasion of Ukraine, Beijing dragged its feet on implementing any meaningful sanctions on Moscow.

Meanwhile, the CCP continues to establish relationships with savory and unsavory actors, whether that be a fruitful trade partnership with Europe or cooperation with rogues like Iran, North Korea, and the Taliban (Myers, 2021). China is also in the process of building a blue-water navy to project force across the world, which is by no means necessary if all Beijing wanted was to defend its sphere of influence (Maclaren, 2021). All these developments represent a rational response to the challenges and opportunities the CCP perceives for the nation rather than a doctrinal commitment to a uniquely "Chinese foreign policy."

Every state has a place in the geopolitical order. As empires rise and fall, enemies, allies, hegemons, and clients rearrange themselves according to their interests and capabilities. Throughout history, China's role in the world has waxed and waned. At times China has been the most powerful nation, and at times China has been a subject nation. From 1949 onward, the leaders of the People's Republic of China dreamed of a great rejuvenation. They envisioned a world where Beijing would, once again, be respected and feared (Doshi, 2021, 1). But during Mao's reign, the country was too distracted by its own internal struggles to conduct any sort of meaningful geopolitical activity. It was Deng Xiaoping's economic reforms that set the country on track to develop the military and diplomatic power Beijing wields today. Deng's strategy of hide and bide, never taking the lead, slowly building up the country's power, integrating itself into the global order, and never showing too much aggression, was a brilliant strategy that served its role (Tsang & Cheung, 2021). China's leaders before Xi would often downplay Beijing's rise to power and thereby avoid scrutiny. They understood that an uninterrupted rise, economically, militarily, and diplomatically would be the best strategy to avoid premature conflict with a more powerful West.

Under Xi, the era of hiding one's power and never taking the lead is over. Beijing is openly challenging the United States in great power competition, coercing countries across the world to respect its interests, building a more advanced military, and supporting authoritarian regimes. For decades, the CCP cast itself as a peaceful state, devoid of the ambitions and aggression that characterized countries like America. This is no longer the case (Ministry of Foreign Affairs (China, 2022). The creation of a larger nuclear arsenal, blue water navy, and growing interest in affairs outside of Asia, like Latin America, suggest Beijing has interest in extending its ambition beyond Asia. (Roy, 2022).

Making Sense of Beijing's Tactics

The CCP's strategy of economic integration, amoral international relationships, gradual military buildup, and posturing as an international development advocate seem a carefully-executed masterplan. This strategy has required decades of patience, but has allowed Beijing to ascend to power quietly, not provoking an international backlash. Ultimately, Beijing maintains a deep realist perception of global affairs. The CCP understands the nature of power. It diligently perceives the geopolitical balance and prioritizes its national interests over vague notions of right and wrong.

The CCP will not charge into battle alongside its allies just for the sake of forwarding some common cause. This can be seen in China's apprehension toward involvement in Ukraine or in helping the North Koreans fend off the Americans. China fought the US on the peninsula during the Korean War in the early 1950s (Yufan and Zhihai, 1990, 94). Mao's decision to intervene on behalf of North Korea was highly self-interested. The CCP initially had little intention to get involved. It only did so after weighing the odds and concluding that Beijing could be in danger if Pyongyang fell (Yufan and Zhihai, 1990, 95).

The Chinese will not exert their resources for the sole sake of a good cause, such as attempting to pacify Afghanistan, unless they actually believe such actions yield results. Indeed, Beijing has closely observed the burden Washington carries of being a global hegemon and a policeman of liberal democracy (Menzel, 2021). The CCP understands that the current rules-based order is still beneficial to China and that attempting to build an alternative system comes at a massive cost in military and economic resources.

Part of China's patience and steadiness in this matter can be attributed to its authoritarian system. The CCP does not need to concern itself with elections every four years. But a closer understanding of Beijing's strategic place in the world sheds even more light on why the CCP conducts foreign policy the way it does and provides insight on where it might be going. Rather than a secret master plan that must be uncovered and decoded, China's geopolitical statecraft follows a rational and logical calculus that is not set in stone. Understanding America's rise to power can provide key lessons for understanding Beijing's behavior.

The United States dominates the world militarily. It dominates the world economically. And it dominates the world diplomatically. Washington's military dominance stems primarily from North American geography. America has the unique benefits of having friendly neighbors in Canada and Mexico, as well as two coastlines (Leffler, 2021). As America's power grew, it sought to exclude European powers from the Western Hemisphere to solidify a sphere of influence, the Monroe doctrine. This was the foundation that made an American-led world order possible. China understands the necessity of a sphere of influence both through observation and rational circumstance. Mearsheimer explains,

> A much more powerful China can also be expected to try to push the United States out of the Asia Pacific region, much as the United States pushed the European great powers out of the Western Hemisphere in the nineteenth century. We should expect China to devise its own version of the Monroe Doctrine, as imperial Japan did in the 1930s (2016).

After establishing a secure sphere of influence, Beijing would be able to insulate itself from external pressure, dominate states in the region, and establish a launchpad to push outwards into the world. An essential element of this strategy is controlling the independently governed island of Taiwan. Taiwan is an essential link in the island chain which stretches from Japan downwards (Yang, 2021). Historically, Japan used Taiwan during World War II. It was an essential point of operations to move forces south towards

Australia and east towards the broader Pacific. A Western-aligned Taiwan confines the Chinese navy and negates an essential base of operations.

Initially, the Chinese military focused on area denial doctrines, which focused on keeping the US out of its territory if a war broke out (Doshi, 2019). Facets of this strategy include Beijing's considerably large missile arsenal which although relatively short-ranged compared to American technology, is perfect for leveling the playing field against Washington's multi-billion-dollar aircraft carriers. Furthermore, satellites in orbit work to create a defensive bubble, helping to triangulate missile targets and tracking enemy ship movements (Yeo, 2020).

Like America in the 1800s, China is establishing a defensive backyard; no other great powers may enter. The military began its a transition under the Hu regime, purchasing aircraft carriers and continuing general modernization (Doshi, 2019). Hu articulated the need for the navy to protect sealines and fulfill new missions away from China. Xi echoed by stating that China must become a "maritime great power," fulfilling missions in the "far seas," and securing Chinese overseas interests (Doshi, 2021). In July of 2021, China upped the ante, testing an unprecedented hypersonic glide craft. It circled the Earth in low orbit, evaded detection systems, and launched a weapon. Effectively, it performed orbital bombardment.

Although it is uncertain what exactly this new weapon could be, its mere existence demonstrates a capability lacked by the US and grants China the ability to strike anywhere in the world (Bugos, 2022). All these facts point to a clear and explicitly articulated intention for China to become a global military presence. If Beijing is able to establish an Asian sphere of influence, combined with a capable navy, then the CCP will be able to project influence across the world and use military force to advance its interests, much like any rational actor would.

If China achieves hegemon status, the CCP will have its own forces engaged throughout the world. Due to America's global military presence, Beijing constantly accuses America of imperialism, but this military presence is merely the reality of great power politics (Fink, 2022). If Xi's recent expansionary actions are not ample proof, one can simply look at China's growing interest in foreign countries. It is unlikely that American leaders at any time period sat down and explicitly signaled their intentions to have the military presence Washington has today. Two world wars brought US forces to Europe and Northeast Asia, a Cold War created interest in Latin America and Southeast Asia, fossil fuels necessitated a presence in the Gulf States, and so on.

If, or when, China achieves the military strength to enforce its own interests abroad, it will not be because the politburo devised a grand scheme to take over the world. Instead, it will be because China feels the need to protect trade routes, protect investments in Africa and Latin America, develop regional alliances, and protect rising energy imports from the Middle East (Aluf, 2021). As the United States and Britain have learned previously, the burden and benefits of being a global hegemon are being a security giant. China will not be exempt from the geopolitics of global dominance. They will be compelled to take opportunistic and strategic actions to advance their interests as they are doing now.

However, Beijing understands that Asia is not North America, and China cannot easily establish military dominance as there are fierce rivals and competitors in the region. China has more neighbors, 16, than any other country in the world (World Atlas, 2023). These include great powers like Russia, India, and Japan as well as numerous middle powers like South Korea and Vietnam. Furthermore, states like Australia, although not directly in China's backyard, have a direct alliance with the United States and are committed to advancing liberalism in the region. Taiwan, as mentioned before, is clearly aligned with the West and acts as a barrier to Chinese expansion past the first island chain. Southeast Asia, although composed of relatively weak states, some aligned with Beijing, has the ability to act collectively to enforce its interest through ASEAN, an equivalent to the European Union (2023). As a result, Chinese foreign policy often needs to be creative, complex, and subtle in order to address challenges on the world stage while also cultivating domestic support.

Beijing's actions during the 2022 Russian invasion of Ukraine exemplify the CCP's rational and opportunistic calculations regarding foreign policy. On the one hand is China's security partnership with Moscow, an essential marriage given the two countries' opposition to the West. On the other is the threat of sanctions and China's standing in the international global system which the Chinese benefit greatly from. As a result of these two competing interests, Beijing attempted to create a compromise between not overtly condemning Russia's invasion but also not supplying aid to avoid the wrath of the West (U.S.-China Economic and Security Review Commission, 2022). China also postured itself to be a peacemaker in the conflict, making calls for "both sides" to come to a peaceful solution.

However, the CCP still ingeniously found ways to aid Moscow. The US State Department uncovered Chinese efforts to amplify Russian disinformation campaigns and censor pro-Ukraine messages at home (2022). Furthermore, while other countries moved away from the Kremlin's fossil fuel exports, Beijing significantly increased its oil purchases by 80 percent in the year (Zibang, 2022). Finally, Xi announced a new "Global Security Initiative" which centered around China's core interest of respecting the policy decisions of governments and non-interference in other's internal affairs (Freeman & Stephenson, 2022). Although Xi did not specifically mention the Western sanctions on Russia, he reiterated China's opposition to unilateral sanctions and long-arm jurisdiction. Such an announcement reflects the importance of Putin's position in the international order declining, China's military role in the world expanding, and an election for Xi for an unprecedented third term on the horizon.

In short, China is boxed in by formidable actors that must be appeased, confronted, or coerced. As a result, the CCP must be more creative in advancing its interests overseas, which requires more than just military force. This dilemma explains China's second major strategy, economic integration, and sharp power (Walker, 2018, 9). Unlike hard power, which concerns military force, and soft power, which leverages diplomacy and voluntary respect for a country's attributes, sharp power

> takes advantage of the asymmetry between free and unfree systems, allowing authoritarian regimes both to limit free expression and to distort political environments in democracies while simultaneously shielding their own domestic public spaces from democratic appeals coming from abroad (Walker, 2018, 9).

In essence, leveraging investment, trade, media, and other non-military means to coerce other countries into following the CCP's interests. During the 2019 Hong Kong protests, China forced HSBC, a British Bank with significant dealing in China, to freeze the accounts of democracy protesters (Brunnstrom & Martina, 2022).

Hollywood's abstinence from casting any movie with China as the antagonist is another clear example of Chinese sharp power; the CCP leverages the West's urge to sell movie tickets against itself (Nicolaou, Barker, & Shepherd, 2021). The sudden remake of Red Dawn 2, the sequel to the popular Cold War movie, initially cast the Chinese as the invaders of America, but ultimately had to edit the film to cast the antagonists as the North Koreans (Dargis, 2012). Not only was this a clear capitulation to Beijing and degradation of free speech principles, but also just a silly plotline as Beijing was clearly the appropriate villain. The James Bond franchise made changes to please Beijing's censors by making the villains nationally ambiguous, although some scenes are still removed prior to release on the mainland (Gunning, 2021).

Chinese investments in developing countries serve a clear national interest. Global infrastructure projects like the BRI gain Beijing favor with developing countries, often neglected by the more market-driven investment of the United States (Shullman, 2019). Pumping infrastructure spending into countries like Nepal or Zimbabwe may not gain Beijing leverage against the US, but it does gain client states. Client states that will support the CCP's authoritarian objectives such as the Nepalese government cooperating with Beijing to police Tibetan refugees and diaspora communities (Poudel, 2022). These countries also serve as purchasers for products like steel, which are currently overproduced as a result of faulty industrial policy (Shullman, 2019). BRI countries also receive technology to advance authoritarianism, serving a dual purpose of making states more like China and neutralizing external ideological threats to Beijing, such as democracy activists. *Nikkei Asia* explains,

> "The Carnegie Endowment for International Peace released the report amid concerns that authoritarian regimes would use the technology to boost their power and data could be sent back to China."
>
> "Technology linked to Chinese companies -- particularly Huawei, Hikvision, Dahua and ZTE -- supply AI surveillance technology in 63 countries, 36 of which have signed onto China's Belt and Road Initiative," it said (2019).

States like Panama and the Dominican Republic ceased recognizing Taiwan as a country after the CCP started offering generous development funds (BBC, 2017). Such behavior also explains much of the CCP's posturing as a champion of the Global South, investing, and working with otherwise low-level geopolitical players and pariah states. States like Iran, North Korea, and recently Russia after Washington cut Moscow out of the dollar-denominated financial system all use the Chinese Yuan to transact in one form or another (Allen-Ebrahimian, 2022). The circulation of Beijing's currency as a form of international tender not only spreads Chinese influence but also insulates China from US sanctions, a key objective in economic warfare.

The Belt and Road Initiative, which spans the world gaining Beijing many client states in South East Asia, Africa, and Latin America, is a clear example of this global influence strategy. Furthermore, the Belt and Road is one of a number of projects that Beijing hopes to fundamentally change global norms surrounding economic and industrial behavior. For example infrastructure projects, such as 5G broadband technology built by Chinese companies like ZTE, means many areas will abide by China's broadband standards, not the West. Chinese companies that follow Chinese data privacy norms and laws becoming dominant in foreign markets means that the CCP's data privacy doctrine becomes more influential (Liu & Yang, 2022).

Ultimately, China's economic statecraft, be it the BRI or general penchant for cooperating with all countries regardless of their wealth or human rights records, serves a clear purpose beyond their stated doctrine of "win-win cooperation" (Lin, 2009). A key goal is to make the world more tolerant of authoritarianism by leveraging economic and diplomatic relationships to incentivize or coerce countries into respecting Beijing's interests. The CCP understands that they are in a complicated situation geopolitically, given the geography of Asia and the dominance of the West. In order for China to become "the biggest player in the history of the world" while still being an authoritarian country, there is little room for miscalculation or rash policy making (Allison, 2017).

China's Taiwan Calculus

One of the greatest examples of the rational calculating nature of Chinese foreign policy is the Taiwan question. In this deceptively simple question of when and if to invade, there are diverse factors ranging from geopolitical reality, cost-benefit analysis, and domestic politics. It is not merely about the dream of a more powerful China. In the eyes of the CCP, there is one more step in concluding the Chinese Civil War and that is taking the self-governing island. The island has a complicated history, but the most important component is that the losing faction of the civil war, the KMT, fled to Taiwan and established its own government that still exists today. For this reason, Beijing believes that the island is an inseparable component of the Chinese nation and is necessary for the great rejuvenation of the country (Xinhua, 2021). More importantly, there are essential domestic and foreign policy calculations that drive the CCP's decision-making on whether or when to take the island by force.

From an entirely geostrategic perspective, Taiwan is a key outpost for any Asian power. A Chinese flag over Taipei give's control to the CCP access to deep water ports that can unleash Beijing's navy while also providing a key point of operations to kick the Americans out of Asia (Pietrucha, 2022). In a memo written by the late World War II general Douglas MacArthur, Taiwan is essentially an unsinkable aircraft carrier and submarine base given its prime location. Controlling Taiwan gives an aggressor the ability to launch operations against the Chinese mainland or toward other countries in the region (1950). Furthermore, the Japanese understand that Taiwan is essential to their own security because the CCP can use the island to subjugate Tokyo by cutting off its trade and undersea cables (Axe, 2021). This strategic reality is so apparent that Japan, a pacifist nation since its defeat in WWII, has recently made increasingly strong signals that it is willing to defend Taiwan's democracy.

The outcome of a war over Taiwan also serves a monumental symbolic purpose for the geopolitical state of the world. Of course, controlling the island gives Beijing real strategic power in terms of being able to secure its own Asian sphere of influence and exclude the Americans. However, the sheer image of a defeat or victory has massive ramifications for each side. If Beijing takes the island without a successful American counteroffensive, the CCP effectively signals to the world that Washington has failed at one of its core security objectives. Onlookers will no doubt see the reigning global hegemon decisively defeated by a challenger; the narrative of American decline will feature in every headline. Kevin Rudd predicts that losing Taiwan could essentially be Washington's Waterloo moment, an analogy to the famous European battle that marked the end of Napoleon's rule (ANU TV, 2022).

With that said, China is in no hurry to take the island. Although China is getting increasingly aggressive, especially as the Taiwanese become increasingly hostile to the idea of unification (Maizland, 2022), a Chinese defeat would be a sheer embarrassment for the CCP and perhaps a hard ego check that shatters the image of an ascendant China. It is also likely the domestic consequences for the CCP may destabilize the regime. Although Chinese fighter jets frequently intrude on Taiwanese airspace, these are likely grey zone tactics to probe Taipei's nerves and to intimidate the island into submission (Jalil, 2022). Mock invasions of Taiwan certainly serve as a more direct message, but it is already known that China is willing to invade the island (Austin, 2015). Training serves more of a contingency role if the worst-case scenario occurs and assurance of intentions much like US military exercises with partners in Asia demonstrates the same (CBS, 2022).

Beyond geopolitics, Xi and the Party are working with a considerable domestic mandate to take the island as part of their national rejuvenation narrative. For decades, the CCP has made so many assurances and proclamations about retaking the island that a failure to do so would result in a massive loss of domestic legitimacy (Culver & Hass, 2021). However, the incentives to kick the can down the road, as the CCP has done for decades, are substantial. Deng, the great pragmatist of the CCP, switched China's stance from imminent invasion to peaceful reunification in 1978 (Liao, 2021, 25). Much of this strategy involved the use of diplomacy and economic integration to incentivize the Taiwanese to join the mainland. Proposals often included significant compromises on Beijing's part, such as a one country two systems model where Taiwan keeps much of its political institutions (China.org, 2021). At the same time, Beijing actively works to exclude Taipei from important international institutions and pressures countries not to recognize the island as a country, even though the US does not formally acknowledge Taiwan's government. Eventually, the two sides met during the 1992 Consensus where representatives agreed to respect a vague understanding of a "One China Principle" albeit each side has its own interpretation of what that means (China Daily, 2022).

The status quo continued as ties between the two states warmed until the 2016 election of Tsai Ing Wen, a member of the more nationalist

Democratic Progressive Party. Tsai never fully accepted the 1992 Consensus and her more pro-sovereignty stance led Beijing to cut official ties with her administration (Maizland, 2022). After Beijing's crackdown on Hong Kong's democracy in 2019, a city that was promised "one country, two systems", maintaining de facto independence became bipartisan in Taipei (Maizland, 2022). Although the CCP actively attempted to influence Taiwan's election to sway the public toward voting for a Pro-China candidate in 2020, Tsai's administration won with the greatest popular landslide in the island's history (Kurlantzick, 2019). The growing mistrust for Beijing alongside the deepening relationship between Taiwan and the West has led Xi to lean into the more coercive measures seen today. Although the CCP still hopes to achieve a peaceful reunification in the future, today's aggression is an acknowledgment of the failure of attempted diplomacy alongside China's newfound strength. Although this new provocative stance is the reason for pessimism and increases the chance for escalation, it is still unlikely that the Chinese favor an unprovoked invasion anytime soon.

Taiwan is an incredibly difficult island to invade. It has few landing zones, treacherous oceans, harsh mountains, a decently equipped military, and potential allies like the US (Ullman, 2022). The invasion force to take the island would need to be larger than the one used in D-Day to invade Normandy. With over a hundred miles of ocean separating China and Taiwan, logistics are a nightmare. Beijing lacks the military capability to even contemplate such an offensive and even if the PLA does achieve such abilities, the losses may be unsustainable. Furthermore, the surprisingly effective resistance the Ukrainians demonstrated against a more powerful Russian army during the 2022 invasion demonstrates the capabilities of emerging asymmetric warfare doctrines (Kessler, 2022). Despite the overwhelming numbers and resources of the Chinese military, taking a competently defended fortress island like Taiwan remains a daunting task.

Finally, economic sanctions from the West could hit Beijing hard. China's economy relies on foreign commerce heavily. Taiwanese companies have a large commercial footprint in China. Technology manufacturing giant Foxconn employs over a million Chinese workers (The Economist, 2022). If a war broke out, Taipei alone could render millions of China's citizens jobless overnight. Beijing understands this reality. This is why Xi launched the dual circulation campaign, to better insulate China's economy from shocks while deterring adversaries from economic warfare. Although it remains to be seen whether the CCP ever achieves this goal, it is clear that the costs of breaking the peace in the Taiwan Strait are considerably high and Beijing understands that, for now.

At the same time, popular opinion in China doesn't necessarily demand the island be taken by a certain date. According to John Culver, a veteran of the Central Intelligence Agency, the CCP seeks to avoid a military conflict over Taiwan to the greatest extent possible as long as Taipei does not posture for formal independence (Culver & Hass, 2019). Beijing has waited since 1949 to retake the island and multiple leaders have proposed various compromises to Taipei to entice a voluntary unification. Although Xi seems more willing to use force given the changing power dynamic, increasing nationalism, and fraying cross-strait relations, war likely promises more problems than benefits. It is also possible that Xi aggressively posturing t gain domestic favor and also to put Taiwan and its potential friends on the defensive. As a result, the Chinese seem content waiting much longer than the five years some in the American defense establishment suggest (Oswald, 2021). One complication may be that Xi, in an attempt to put his ego before the Party, tries to take the island during his tenure. Although plausible, the CCP still has a diverse and powerful leadership structure that can dissuade rash decisions, especially on such a consequential move.

However, with tensions increasing and Chinese capabilities growing, the chance of premature escalation also worsens. Perhaps the most important factor in the triangle relationship between China, Taiwan, and the US is the risk of an overly zealous Taiwanese or American leadership provoking Beijing. Culver fears that Washington may do something, either to show up the Chinese or demonstrate unnecessary solidarity with Taipei, that forces the CCP's hand (Culver & Hass, 2019). This point goes back to public sentiment in China that is generally ambivalent about when Taiwan is reintegrated but cannot stand to see the island independent. Such a problem arose during the George W. Bush administration when former Taiwanese president Chen Sui Bian began making highly provocative statements to Beijing, likely emboldened by US assistance (Knowlton, 2003). Bush had to remind Taipei to respect the status quo of ambiguous de facto independence as this frustrating reality was preferable to war. Although the current Tsai administration has done a fair job at balancing Taiwan's odd status with assertiveness over her nation's values, it remains to be seen if such discipline maintains in the future.

Chinese Soft and Sharp Power

Beijing's foreign policy follows a self-interested, rational pattern that seeks to exploit opportunities in the most effective way possible. China uses military force when it can, shoring up its territorial claims in Asia and denying the US and its allies free reign in the Asia pacific. At the same time, Beijing understands that its geographical misfortune means that it cannot easily establish military dominance in its own region, much less the world (Yang, 2022). In order to project influence and exert force over far-off countries in Africa, Europe, and North America, Beijing must leverage its deep integration with the global economy. Chinese soft power is quite weak, although countries trade with China, the CCP understands that the West dominates in the realm of cultural influence (Nye Jr, 2012). However, the CCP must silence criticism and extract political deliverables in other countries, leading to its frequent use of sharp power by limiting free expression and spreading deceptive information overseas (Carminati, 2020).

Few societies look up to Beijing's political system or culture the same way they admire America's freedoms, Europe's tourism, or Japan's media (Carminati, 2020). Although China's political-economic development model provides an inspiring growth story for the Global South, many observers can't ignore the systemic distortions of the CCP's authoritarian policies. Some of those concerns include an existential birth rate decline, environmental degradation, and fears of hitting a middle-income trap. The CCP understands that its greatest soft power tool is economic clout as Beijing stands willing to outspend liberal democracies like the United States in international development financing through projects like the Belt and Road Initiative (Carminati, 2020).

According to AidData at the College of William and Mary, Chinese aid to foreign governments expanded from $2.6 billion in 2000 to 37.3 billion in 2014 whereas the US spent $13.4 billion and 29.4 billion respectively (2023). This radical increase in spending serves a clear strategic purpose and also expresses the current administration's concerns for both countries. During the Mao era, Beijing's international aid followed the regime's deep ideological struggle, going toward fellow Communist states like North Korea and Vietnam (Regilme & Hodzi, 2021, 114). Today development aid serves a variety of purposes and targets diverse countries. Perhaps one of the most notable facets of Chinese lending is its prevalence in the Global South, particularly in Africa and Southeast Asia. Beijing has effectively established a first-mover advantage over the US by targeting these states. These are regions of the world that have long complained about Washington's lack of attention and now the Americans are playing catchup (Chang & Koh, 2021).

At the same time, Chinese aid serves the CCP's desire to make the world safe from authoritarianism. Unlike American aid, which often targets civil society groups, promotes democracy, requires market reforms, and human rights scrutiny, China's aid goes directly to the state with almost no strings attached (Regilme & Hodzi, 2021, 114). One of the strings of course would be not recognizing Taiwan (Parks, 2022). This formula not only serves Beijing's desire to create a world where nations cooperate without any concern for the other's internal problems, but it also emphasizes the state's role in development. Furthermore, many developing countries often have governments that only offer limited civil liberties and market institutions making China a more attractive partner (Fraser Institute, 2022). Lastly, the institutional structure of the Chinese government, which does not need to be concerned with democratic sentiments or structures of limited government, can wield foreign aid in a more discretionary manner than Washington. Former President Trump's antagonism towards foreign aid, Congress's desire to maintain the program, and the subsequent loss of global credibility that followed, are key examples of this institutional difference (Regilme & Hodzi, 2021, 114).

However, Chinese aid is not entirely political. Some have frequently cited the idea of "debt-trap diplomacy" and the use of high-interest rates as evidence that the CCP's foreign investing is entirely an instrument to serve geopolitical goals. In particular, the idea of Beijing giving aggressive loans to poor nations to entrap them in debt or seize strategic assets as collateral comes from a sensationalized instance in Sri Lanka (Jones & Hameiri, 2020). Here, the Chinese seized Hambantota Port as a result of the Sri Lankan government's inability to pay off its loan. However, more examples of this practice are limited, and it is clear that this incident stemmed from the Sri Lankan government's own incompetence combined, which was merely exacerbated by the terms of the loan. Most countries are able to manage their public finance relationship without such problems and it is clear that Beijing wouldn't get very far if they actually practiced debt-trap diplomacy.

In fact, Bradley Parks, director of AidData, presented research at a Hoover Institution-Stanford University collaboration detailing that much of China's high-interest-rate loans served the traditional purpose of profit (2022). Although the economic investment and aid fulfilled a geopolitical goal of spreading Chinese influence, many of the players in this operation were out seeking good returns on investment, not to secure foreign policy objectives, much less partake in debt trapping. In fact, the projects financed by high-interest rate loans and loans that are effectively grants vary based on basic economic principles (Parks, 2022). Loans that are given by the Ministry of Commerce often come with low-interest rates and some are basically grants; they go to finance gift projects like presidential palaces. These funds serve a clear diplomatic purpose. Loans given by the Chinese development bank or state-owned commercial banks employ high-interest rates and finance profitable projects like oil pipelines. The nature of Chinese loans follows a rational benefit maximizing pattern based on the structure of the entity providing the funds.

Although both the United States and the Chinese may try to paint their foreign aid as charitable endeavors, their policies all serve clear strategic goals and are influenced by their respective domestic circumstances. The CCP's aid program is framed through the rhetoric of Win-Win Cooperation and being a champion of the Global South (Ministry of Foreign Affairs (China, 2022). The reality is that China's lack of reform requirements, preference for aiding states not private entities, and a focus on beating the US to developing regions serve a key interest in the CCP's foreign policy.

China's economic engagement with a country, although initially lacking any formal requirements, nonetheless develop strings later on during the relationship. This is when soft power becomes sharp power. Either unspoken or explicit, Chinese aid and market access come with the expectation of conforming to the CCP's political wishes. For example, a Hoover Institution research panel described that African nations may benefit from Chinese media training but,

> many of these reporters are required to tell stories that tout the Chinese model of government and are censored by Beijing

> headquarters from providing coverage of issues such as corruption and human rights in their home country. The underlying message that Beijing would like to convey is that Africans can achieve a high level of prosperity even if their political leaders govern (like the Communist Party of China) in a manner that is lacking in accountability and transparency (2022).

The United States benefits tremendously from educational collaboration with Beijing, from the hundreds of thousands of Chinese students attending American colleges to exciting research opportunities. At the same time, it is a well-documented problem that Chinese international students, faculty, and programming all have the potential to function as an arm of the CCP's sharp power apparatus. Problematic behavior includes the active degradation of free speech and academic freedom on campus through organized pressure campaigns, disinformation spreading, surveillance of sensitive topics or individuals, and high-level advocacy to push a CCP agenda (Lloyd-Damnjanovic, 2018, 14). Such a strategy is especially ingenious as it leverages American openness, internationalism, and desire for high-quality, tuition-paying Chinese students against its own people. Furthermore, it is worth reiterating that silencing NBA protests and constraining Hollywood from creating movies where China is the antagonist are classic examples of sharp power.

China's geopolitical statecraft follows a rational, opportunistic, and pragmatic pattern. Rather than drawing analogies to an entirely evil or benign China, one should look to traditional conceptions of great power politics and rational self-interest in domestic politics. The CCP, which is ultimately in charge of all components of the state, has an interest in protecting its domestic hold on power and advancing Chinese influence in the world (The US China Business Council, 2023). As a result, one can frame the otherwise never-ending news cycle about Beijing's foreign policy exploits in an understandable and even predictable light. More importantly, such framing allows one to see through hyperbolic interpretations and make more precise and accurate judgments on the nature of the CCP's decision-making in geopolitical statecraft.

10. How the US Can Engage China

The US-China rivalry will define the 21st century. However, the goal of either side is not primarily world domination but a battle for influence. Neither Washington nor Beijing wishes to live in a world where one of them has to play second fiddle. A world where China is the most influential country is a world hostile to the values America holds dear and a world where US interests take a back seat. A world where the US is the most influential country is detrimental to the long-term interests of the Chinese and the power of the CCP. Judging by what Beijing does with the amount of power it has now: pressuring countries to keep quiet about human rights, exerting sharp power on open societies, and spreading sympathy for authoritarian ideas, Washington has a large stake in pushing back. The question for the 21st century is how do the two countries coexist and compete without blowing up the entire world? The answer and or magic buzzword is managed strategic competition (Rudd, 2022)

Framing the Competition

Two countries existing in a tense and competitive fashion is nothing new in history. The issue, especially in the age of nuclear weapons, is ensuring that the whole ordeal does not spiral into a hot war. Furthermore, given the unprecedented levels of globalization and the benefits interdependence has brought, it would also be preferable if the US-China rivalry doesn't tear apart the fabric of the world order even if guns aren't involved. There must be, and there is a way to ensure that the two countries can safely compete where they need to, cooperate where they can, and let passions flow where they must.

In areas such as economic and political influence, there should be general rules of fairness that ensure that victory is achieved through merit. If one system of economic organization is better than the other, that experiment should occur without trying to stifle the other with unjustified sanctions. Washington can isolate strategic technologies such as semiconductors and telecommunications as important enough to place special restrictions on, but let the market for steel, soybeans, and iPhones go where it may. Both countries can compete to see who can develop the best military, the best laws, the best companies, who can get to Mars first, and so on.

Competition makes those competing better as they seek to improve and gain advantages. When competing for friends and partners across the world, each country should put its best foot forward and allow the states themselves to choose who they wish to align with. On mutually beneficial things like vaccine development, climate change, taming North Korea, preventing the next pandemic, fighting terrorism, and so on, Beijing and Washington can cooperate. On important redlines like Taiwan, human rights, and the South China Sea, we must have level-headed but firm conversations, fully willing to defend our interests with force if need be. However, it is worth noting that it is difficult to stay completely disciplined on this matter, especially with the competing interests and incentives that drive both the US and China's leadership. Furthermore, many of these objectives, such as drawing a productive hard line on semiconductors exports or cooperating on North Korea are much easier said than done. Kevin Rudd, one of the foremost proponents of managed strategic competition, notes that such a framework will not prevent either side from trying to disadvantage the other through cunning statecraft. However, such a framework will drastically decrease the chance of war and increase the ease of coexistence, which in the context of great power rivalries, is far preferable to the tragedy of the Thucydides trap. He writes,

> the United States and the Soviet Union, following the near-death experience of the Cuban Missile Crisis, eventually agreed on a political and strategic framework to manage their own fraught relationship without triggering mutual annihilation. Surely, it's possible to do the same between America and China in the arguably less trying

geopolitical circumstances of today. It is from this hope that the idea of managed strategic competition comes (Rudd, 2022).

Nobody knows where we are in the story of the US-China rivalry. There has yet to be a Cuban Missile Crisis-style event that reminds both sides how high the stakes are and to turn down the temperature. At the same time, Washington, and Beijing both deeply understand the lessons of the Cold War and the bilateral relationship is leagues ahead of the US-Soviet one.

The Biden administration seems committed to maintaining open dialogue and communication with its counterpart in Beijing. The results varied, ranging from a screaming match in Alaska to a civil virtual talk between Biden and Xi to lower tensions. (BBC, 2021; Madhani and Long, 2021) In terms of cooperation on mutual interests, climate change seems to be back on the table with the signing of the US-China Joint Glasgow Declaration on Enhancing Climate Action in the 2020s (US State Department, 2021) Although it remains to be seen whether the Declaration is mere words, such cooperation is a good sign after relations on the energy issue grew sour with the escalation of bilateral tensions (Victor, 2021).

A large component of the breakdown in climate cooperation stemmed from the need for both sides to look tough on the other, whether that be pushing back against US demands or weaponizing environmental audits against Beijing. The Covid-19 pandemic is a more salient issue where both sides could have cooperated, but politics had its way. Initially thought to be a unifying event for the world, the coronavirus outbreak in Wuhan, China only exacerbated finger-pointing and blame, albeit, not without good cause. Much of the hostility about Beijing's mismanagement of the pandemic stemmed not just from the understandable criticism of the CCP's behavior but from the partisan politics that followed. Politicians in both the West and China took the opportunity to use the outbreak as a cudgel to beat the other side and appease their base.

Hawks in the US have stressed the ever greater need to get tough on China, and CCP officials level criticism at Washington for the perceived failure of its democracy to handle the crisis. A particularly emblematic example of domestic politics superseding national interests was when conservative Australian leaders unilaterally called for a probe into the pandemic origins (Burgess, 2021). Although an investigation is justified, a medium power like Australia jumping the gun instead of first gathering a coalition of democracies to pressure a behemoth like China is a clear case of rash decisions to appear strong for a domestic audience. In response, Beijing levied bans on Australian coal, a major export, which dealt a hurtful blow to Canberra (Skidmore, 2022). However, China's leaders were no better; rolling blackouts ensued as the country faced an energy shortage in part due to the CCP's move to punish the Australians.

Much like devising a framework for a government here in the United States, we must understand how individuals respond to structural guardrails and incentives. We know that the Chinese and the Americans have competing interests and have the means to violently fight over them. Both sides should identify areas where not offending the other side ought to be the utmost priority. For the Chinese, that means no military invasion of Taiwan and refraining from creating a military presence in Central and South America. For the US, that means not recognizing the independence of Taiwan and refraining from overly militarizing Beijing's front yard.

For the US and other observers who seek to understand the US-China relationship, understand that the world at large does not have as large of a stake in a great power rivalry with China as the US and its allies do. This reality suggests that American leaders should attempt to work with allies and partners in ways that are mutually agreeable to confront China when necessary. Simply charging in headfirst and expecting everyone else to follow is a recipe for failed policy. Not only will the US likely receive little help, but rash decisions that jeopardize the interests of other countries and the US is likely to lose friends in the process. Every country is different and self-interested in terms of what it seeks to obtain from the US-China rivalry.

Australia and Japan, where China is an immediate threat, might be more willing to get involved in the confrontation, particularly over the island of Taiwan. India has border disputes with Beijing and is an emerging superpower in its own right with ambitions of having influence of its own (Bhatnagar & Sandhu, 2018). New Delhi and can continue to be a key partner for the US in working to contain Chinese activity. It is unlikely Indian forces will risk their resources to defend Taiwan, as it simply is outside their own interests. South Korea maintains an alliance with Washington and its president Yoon Suk-yeol seems to be in favor of strengthening ties with America while carefully balancing relations with Beijing (Snyder, 2022).

The important caveat here is that Seoul, as a middle power country, is no match for China militarily or economically. That means South Korea may be privy to reassess its alignment if the power dynamic swings too far in Beijing's direction. Southeast Asian countries play a delicate balancing game between the necessity of Chinese trade, on the one hand, and their status as nominal US allies on the other. Russia, Iran, and North Korea seem to be completely adversarial to Washington and logically side with Beijing on just about everything, but their relations are by no means simple or uniformly common in their interests.

This brief list of nations and their interests shows the diversity of the international community and how nuanced US foreign policy must be if it is to compete with China for influence. Such a strategy will require active engagement diplomatically, economically, and militarily. It will require a level of respect and understanding of the interests of different societies. Very few, if any countries would like to have their arms twisted by the US to take confrontational actions against China. Indeed, the European nations were reluctant if not outright opposed to getting militarily involved in the Russia-Ukraine conflict for a variety of good reasons. Likewise, no nation or leader would desire to take a stance against Beijing unless they see it to be in their own interest.

The Biden administration seems to understand this reality relatively well, although there is room for improvement. Statements from current Secretary of State Anthony Blinken seem to suggest that the administration is aiming to compete with Beijing, not fight (Johnson, 2022). The Secretary made statements in a May 2022 speech stating that Washington will not try to force countries to side with the US but instead view Washington as a more attractive option. He stated,

> We know that many countries, including the United States, have vital economic or people-to-people ties with China that they want to preserve. This is not about forcing countries to choose.

Much like the US, other countries should be able to pick what areas they want to work with Beijing on, what areas they want to resist, and so on. States that feel backed into a corner will likely side with the opposite power to create a balancing effect, which is exactly what China is learning in Asia with its territorial expansionism. Furthermore, competing with China is different from a cold war. Peacefully, but competitively coexisting entails that the goal is not to erase the other side from existence. Both sides, to the greatest extent possible, should view the US-China rivalry through this lens.

Perhaps the closest analogy of what ideal policy would look like is the competition between the US and the EU, although the stakes, consequences, and differences are less pronounced, and the regimes across Europe have substantially different political systems. Despite these differences there are some useful parallels that help to illustrate that ideal policy.

The US knows how to coexist peacefully and compete productively. Although China is more hostile and precarious, America already knows what it looks like to strive for greater economic, military, and cultural influence. Washington also already knows the stakes of losing ground to a competitor; they are much higher when it comes to Beijing. If China's economy and innovation significantly surpass the US, more countries will look to the CCP for inspiration. Even if countries understand that the Chinese economy is fundamentally flawed, Beijing's sheer consumptive, regulatory, and innovative capacity will still influence the world. If the Chinese military exceeds the capabilities and contributions of the Americans, then more countries will look to Beijing for strategic alignment.

If Xi Jinping calls the shots on the world stage, brokering trade deals, leading conferences, and engaging with other nations, then it will be China that leads the global order. For reasons both practical and emotional, it is in America's interest to compete. And of course, the US does not, and should not attempt to shoulder the burden of shaping the world. This effort can, and should be collective, involving many like-minded partners such as Europe, Japan, Australia, and other countries that share similar interests. Furthermore, banking on the collapse of Communist China will likely not bear results anytime soon, nor is such an event going to be pleasant for global stability. To the greatest extent possible, the Washington should work with Beijing wherever it can.

Why a Cold War is Not the Answer

It is tempting to look at the rivalry between Washington and Beijing as a cold war akin to what America had with the former Soviet Union. However, one should be incredibly cautious with this terminology and mindset. At the moment, there is no cold war, but both sides can certainly escalate the relationship so that it becomes one. Brookings Senior Fellow Ryan Haas elaborates on this point by noting significant differences between the US-Soviet and the US-China relationship (Hass & Weiss, 2021). The most apparent being that Washington and Moscow had very few economic ties during the Cold War, and both sides were actively creating competing alliances that carved up the world, leading to proxy wars. Hung Tran from the Atlantic Council, furthers this point by noting that Beijing and Washington are not engaged in an existential ideological struggle to make the world more capitalist or socialist (Tran, 2021). Indeed, both sides expect the other to exist for the foreseeable future and do not intend to erase the other from existence.

The US and China are not by necessity fierce enemies rather they are rivals or competitors. Beijing is deeply integrated into the international order, which contrasts greatly with the former Soviet Union, the Russian Federation, and North Korea, which all seek to disrupt the current geopolitical status quo. Chinese behavior is far more cautious and conscious of established norms and rules compared to states like North Korea, which cause headaches for both adversaries and allies alike. In the case of Pyongyang, that entails developing nuclear weapons and testing ballistic missiles by launching them over Japan, behavior that even Beijing takes issue with (Lendon & Bae, 2022).

Although Beijing seeks to shift the international order in its favor, it does so in ways that are far more subtle, often leveraging international law to its advantage while making use of multilateral institutions. Such behavior is similar to a hegemonic power like the United States rather than a rogue state. Aristyo Rizka Darmawan writes in The Fletcher Forum of World Affairs that Beijing's attempt to establish new or influence existing international institutions is similar to Washington's behavior during the 20th century (2022). That is that America used its newfound power post World War II to shift the global order through Bretton Woods, the United Nations, the World Bank, and the International Monetary Fund. China's involvement in multilateral institutions such as UN peacekeeping operations and establishing the Belt and Road all represent moves to establish Beijing as the global leader (Gowan, 2020). This is different from the Soviet Union, which sought to fundamentally destroy the global order and establish a Communist utopia.

China's intention is not to destroy the US government or spread Socialism with Chinese characteristics, rather they seek to situate themselves in a position of respect and centrality much, while seeking to minimize the associated costs. Such a goal would shift the norms and balance of power in the world in a way that makes it safer for China's authoritarian system, but it also requires a fundamentally different strategy than a Cold War. Rather, China's current strategy is to become the most influential and respected country, which entails less aggressive strategies such as creating a dominant economy, an innovative tech sector, and playing a leadership role in world affairs (Sun, 2015). Much like how the US plays an integral role in security partnerships, international trade, and shaping global norms, Beijing seeks to do the same (Sun, 2015).

Although the chance of war increases as China becomes more powerful, particularly over disputed areas like Taiwan, the South China Sea, and the Senkaku Islands, Cold War-style containment policies will do little except increase the chances of war. It is not in the CCP's interest to start a war. Yes, a more powerful China means a more active and aggressive Chinese military. However, Beijing's behavior will seek to advance its interests within the global order, much as the US has done. Although this future is worth resisting, pushing back requires a different strategy than waging a cold war. Not only is there no justification for attacking a country merely for becoming more influential, but the practical consequences of starting a war with a country like China are beyond salvaging.

There's a common saying by those who often warn against using the cold war terminology that the US and China are not in a cold war, but you'll get one if you keep using that word. Much good comes from the current peace between Washington and Beijing, profitable trade relationship, and deep connections with each other and the rest of the world. Escalating toward a cold war would not only put everyone's lives in danger but will also throw away a fruitful relationship and replace it with a potentially deadly one. There can be no overestimating the disruption that can come from a breakdown in US-China relations, be it in global supply chains, cultural exchange, or diplomatic alignments.

How to Compete

If we had a perfect step-by-step plan for the US to prevail against China in a great power competition, we would likely be too busy sipping whiskey and smoking cigars with State Department officials to write this book. However, as one can guess from the theme of this book, an important step we advocate for is a sober, detailed, and honest understanding of the challenges at hand. China is not ten feet tall, the US is not in inevitable decline, the CCP is not trying to conquer the world, nor does the world simply bend to Washington's wishes. Two countries engaged in a cold war do not maintain the level of connection that Beijing and Washington have. Beijing has serious problems at home, and much of its attention is aimed at addressing its internal interests rather than catering to a set plan for world domination. It is also those internal problems that will play a substantial role in determining the course of Beijing's decision-making, contrary to a common narrative that Chinese policies follow the grand strategy of the CCP or Xi Jinping.

The big takeaway from this book should be that China's leaders respond to incentives and have rational priorities. Policymakers should exercise honest judgment about how they think Chinese leaders will react to US actions and what the CCP could realistically hope to achieve with its capabilities. That means that the two extremes of complete world domination and benevolent altruism to the international community are unrealistic. Decision makers should instead attempt to understand what interests China maintains and how they are willing to go about fulfilling them. In areas like Taiwan, one should expect Beijing to be incredibly sensitive and willing to threaten and potentially take military action. However, much like in any country, the elites in charge of decision-making are far more pragmatic and thoughtful about the use of force than the general population. This likely explains why the CCP often publicly reacts to symbolic gestures, such as Speaker Pelosi's visit to Taiwan or former Taiwanese president Lee Teng Hui attending a school reunion at Cornell University, but takes only limited military actions (Ross, 2000, 87).

Although Chinese military and political leaders likely understand the actual insignificance of such events, these actions signal to the Chinese general population that their government is not being respected. As a result, the CCP may either be forced to pushback or even escalate depending on how things may be perceived domestically. In the case of Pelosi's visit to

Taiwan in the summer of 2022, some would say that launching missiles over the island is an overreaction (Rogin, 2022). This accusation may be justified knowing what we know about the overall purpose of the visit, a stop at a longtime Asian partner in the Speaker's tour of Asia. However, the Chinese may have seen it as one more treacherous act committed by the US in a string of many, gradually eroding the One China Policy and increasing support for Taiwanese Independence.

Beijing felt compelled to make an aggressive statement to demonstrate while also taking the convenient opportunity to rehearse a blockade of the island (Mastro, 2022). Military force will continue to grow as a preferred solution to the Taiwan question if the CCP feels that the likelihood of retaking the island by other means is fading. Furthermore, that timeline may be accelerated if the Party feels it is losing domestic legitimacy, either from its own failures at home or from challenges abroad. As a result, Washington should be conscious of how Beijing and the leaders of the CCP will react to its actions. If the US wishes to escalate tensions or assert dominance, it should also do so with the strength and long-term strategy to back it up. Deciding to push the envelope on a sensitive matter like Taiwan requires an honest understanding that violence is likely, the will and capability to engage in conflict, and a coherent strategy that justifies the consequences (bloodshed, economic upheaval, diplomatic chaos) in America's interests. On issues like Taiwan, where both sides seem at least potentially willing to posture about resorting to violence to protect their interests, Washington needs to be conscious of its capabilities relative to China before making any threats.

In most areas of competition, like trade and investment, one should understand the CCP has diverse and sometimes contradictory interests. On the one hand, Beijing and the CCP leadership needs to cultivate lucrative relationships and grow its standing amongst other countries. On the other, are political objectives that often alienate or alarm the countries it seeks to do business with. For example, China values its economic relationship with Europe, but the two societies have drastically different views about human rights, which is increasingly becoming a problem for the Europeans (Oud, 2022). Therefore, one should expect the Chinese to exercise more caution and restraint when they have to think about maintaining lucrative relationships with other countries. This was perhaps most apparent during the

2022 Russian Invasion of Ukraine in which Beijing was careful to distance itself from its Russian ally to not just avoid US sanctions but also to conduct damage control in Europe to protect its standing (Kusa, 2022).

Beijing's Belt and Road project seeks to make the world more interconnected and boost growth in all the countries it runs through. At the same time, it also serves a quasi-colonial purpose, as Chinese workers staff investments made in host countries, Beijing leverages its assistance to extract geopolitical favors and heavily subsidized Chinese goods flood foreign markets (Kleven, 2019). Furthermore, China's ambivalence to domestic politics in those nations and implicit enablement of those regimes through loans and technology sales play a role in supporting authoritarianism across the developing world (Massari, 2022). As a result, many local residents, such as those in Africa, are skeptical of Chinese engagement (Hanauer & Morris, 2014). If Washington is concerned about negative influence from Beijing, then it should understand where global engagement efforts can contain negative Chinese influence while benefiting US interests. In Africa, for example, many aspects of the Belt and Road are positive and promote development, which is good for everyone. The US may be able to gain from collaboration. On the other hand, strengthening economic, strategic, and diplomatic engagement with various African countries may help forward American interests on the continent while providing a backstop against Chinese efforts to nudge countries in a direction that Washington finds objectionable.

The US should think carefully about how it hopes to compete for influence in these situations as emulating the Chinese would likely not yield good results. Does Washington want to create its own version of the Belt and Road, or can it accomplish more through traditional modes of engagement? Does the US want to implement its own industrial policies in response to counter the Chinese in strategic areas like semiconductors or will a more market-based approach yield better results as it has for generations.

Furthermore, Washington must be realistic about how other countries feel about their place in the US-China rivalry. Although many countries value their alignment with the US, liberal democracy, and the rules-based international order, it is also in their interests to get along with China. It is difficult for countries to get around to taking sides against China just as it was during the Cold War. Beijing represents a major player in the economic and diplomatic order. As a result, Washington must be able to understand

and leverage these openings to create opportunities for cooperation when it fulfills a mutual interest.

For example, India, the rising superpower and essential US partner in the Indo-Pacific region, has border disputes with Beijing and a problematic reliance on Russian military equipment. If Washington seeks to work with the Indians to contain Chinese expansionism, it can exploit the situation by selling New Delhi more weapons, which, as of May 2022, Congress seems to be preparing to do (Sen & Martin, 2022). This move would not only bring New Delhi closer to the US, but also ensure that India is able to push back against Chinese border incursions, a shared interest for Indian and American policymakers (Tennant, 2022). At the same time, India-China trade relations are quite strong, and Washington should recognize that the Indians will continue to value such productive activity as long as they feel comfortable with Chinese actions (The Economic Times, 2022). At the same time, the US should vigorously compete for economic influence by deepening trade ties with India, not just because it's mutually beneficial but to create resiliency in the face of coercive Chinese behavior.

As Howard French, a professor of Journalism at Columbia University and Foreign Affairs columnist, puts it: China is trying to become the world's indispensable nation (2022). Just like how the US became deeply ingrained in the global order, in aspects of geopolitics from trade to security, to diplomacy, Beijing is positioning itself to do the same. That is ultimately China's endgame. As a result, Washington's strategy should focus on reinvigorating everything that made the US indispensable. Unleashing its economic innovation, inspiring awe with its political culture, and cunning statecraft. Today, the narrative of an ascendant China is salient for two basic reasons: Beijing is doing a relatively decent job at growing its power, and the US has stumbled in recent years, diminishing its international standing (Devlin, 2018).

Some contributing factors include failed wars in the Middle East, a slowing economy, political disorder, and, more recently, an unnecessarily alienating diplomatic doctrine. It is unlikely that anyone that pays attention to politics believes the US is at a high point in its reputation abroad or even domestically. However, democracies follow cycles, whereas autocracies are far less reactive and can't make course corrections as easily. The US has been here before. During the latter half of the 20th century, the US faced one setback after another, be it stagflation, disastrous war in Vietnam, a powerful Soviet Union, a failed Iranian hostage rescue attempt, social division, the Watergate Scandal, and much more (Devlin, 2018).

President Ronald Regan ran on a platform of national renewal. Although we do not wish to get into the pros and cons of the Reagan presidency, the narrative shift in America's story cannot be ignored (Ronald Reagan Presidential Foundational, 2023). National pride increased, the economy roared back, the Berlin Wall fell, the Soviet Union collapsed, and, at the end of it all, Washington stood the sole superpower. Liberal democracy and free markets defeated Communism, and the world entered decades of relative peace and prosperity. Francis Fukuyama observed this trajectory and famously penned The End of History, proclaiming that humanity had moved beyond ideological struggle as liberal democracy and capitalism were the inevitable political order (1989).

Of course, there are countless caveats and arguments about everything we just said, and Fukuyama was clearly wrong, but the general point remains. Things can change quickly in a democracy, and the US has picked itself up before and accomplished tremendous things after decades of perceived decline. The Chinese do not possess the same corrective mechanisms. Deng's reform and opening policies that turned the People's Republic around only occurred after Mao's death; even then, the damage was largely irreparable, the One Child Policy is a powerful example (Mullen, 2021). Today, as Xi Jinping positions himself for an unprecedented third term while the Chinese political system solidifies around him, one can only imagine how difficult a meaningful change will be. China's economy is slowing, investors are losing confidence, the Party is tightening its grip on society, and countries worldwide are growing weary of Beijing's behavior.

Conclusions

These facts lead us to two general points that should guide how we think about China. The first is that China's intentions follow a rational path linked both to its national interest and the interests of its leaders in the CCP. Beijing does not seek to dominate the world, nor does it seek to be a global charity bank. The CCP seeks to exploit its standing in the world to pursue its own interests within the structural barriers presented.

Chinese policy moves in positive or negative directions, depending on how the US and other countries choose to engage, and how its domestic concerns play out. It is possible, and preferable, for the US to have a very productive relationship with Beijing. The US should compete directly, cooperate where possible, and confront when necessary.

The second point is that China's government and the Chinese people follow basic notions of rationality. They are not exclusively governed by grand abstract notions of Socialism or Confucianism, or any other ideology or identity. Chinese people are just as prone to compliance, unrest, and revolution as any other person would be. Government officials are just as power-hungry, intelligent, and cunning as their counterparts in other countries. Rather than subscribing to convenient narratives about Chinese society, we should recognize that basic notions of political and economic principles apply, and that the lessons of public choice apply to China and its leaders just as they do everywhere.

Bibliography

Agency, C. I. (1959). *Comparison of the first Five Year Plans of Communist China and the USSR.* Washington, DC: Central .

AidData. (2023). *China's Development Finance.* Retrieved from AidData: https://www.aiddata.org/china-development-finance

Allen, C. (2021, December 07). Ambassador. (C. T. Bea, Interviewer)

Allen-Ebrahimian, B. (2022, March 8). *Russia turns to the renminbi.* Retrieved from Axios: https://www.axios.com/2022/03/08/russia-turns-renminbi-yuan

Allison, G. (2017, June 9). *The Thucydides Trap.* Retrieved from Foreign Policy: https://foreignpolicy.com/2017/06/09/the-thucydides-trap/

Allison, G. (2017, May 31). *What Xi Jinping wants.* Retrieved from The Atlantic: https://www.theatlantic.com/international/archive/2017/05/what-china-wants/528561/

Almendral, A. (2022, February 3). *China built more wind power than the rest of the world combined in the run-up to the Olympics.* Retrieved from Quartz: https://qz.com/2119406/china-outpaces-the-rest-of-the-world-in-wind-and-solar-energy

Aluf, D. (2021, December 30). *China's reliance on Middle East oil, gas to rise sharply.* Retrieved from Asia Times: https://asiatimes.com/2021/12/china-to-rely-more-on-middle-east-for-oil-and-gas/

Ana Lugo, M., Raiser, M., & Yemtsov, R. (2021, February 24). *What's next for poverty reduction policies in China?* Retrieved from Brookings: https://www.brookings.edu/blog/future-development/2021/09/24/whats-next-for-poverty-reduction-policies-in-china/

Anderson, S. (2020, September 3). *China's population to drop by half, immigration helps U.S. labor force.* Retrieved from Forbes: https://www.forbes.com/sites/stuartanderson/2020/09/03/chinas-population-to-drop-by-half-immigration-helps-us-labor-force/?sh=146b58e13d65

Armees, M. D. (2019). *France AND Security in the Indo-Pacific.* Retrieved from France in the US: https://franceintheus.org/IMG/pdf/France_and_Security_in_the_Indo-Pacific_-_2019.pdf

ASEAN. (2023). *About ASEAN.* Retrieved from ASEAN: https://asean.org/about-asean

Asia-For-Educators. (2023). *The confucian classics & the civil service examinations.* Retrieved from Asia For Educators: http://afe.easia.columbia.edu/cosmos/irc/classics.htm

Austin, G. (2015, August 11). *China's military trains for Taiwan invasion with mock-ups*. Retrieved from The Diplomat: https://thediplomat.com/2015/08/chinas-military-trains-for-taiwan-invasion-with-mock-ups/

Axe, D. (2021, July 15). *In A warning to China, Japan's new strategy paper mentions Taiwan for the first Ttme*. Retrieved from Forbes: https://www.forbes.com/sites/davidaxe/2021/07/15/in-a-warning-to-china-japans-new-strategy-paper-mentions-taiwan-for-the-first-time/?sh=320e65a834a9

Bader, J. (2018, February 27). *7 things you need to know about lifting term limits for Xi Jinping*. Retrieved from Brookings: https://www.brookings.edu/blog/order-from-chaos/2018/02/27/7-things-you-need-to-know-about-lifting-term-limits-for-xi-jinping/

Bajoria, J. (2008, April 2). *Nationalism in China*. Retrieved from Council on Foreign Relations: https://www.cfr.org/backgrounder/nationalism-china

Bajpai, P. (2022, June 18). *Why China Is "The World's Factory"*. Retrieved from Investopedia: https://www.investopedia.com/articles/investing/102214/why-china-worlds-factory.asp#:~:text=7%EF%BB%BF%20Additionally%2C%20consumer%20products,to%20produce%20low%2Dcost%20goods.

Barkin, N. (2022, June 1). *Watching China in Europe - June 2022*. Retrieved from German Marshall Fund: https://www.gmfus.org/news/watching-china-europe-june-2022

Barron-Lopez, L. (2020, October 14). *Democrats' coming civil war over police unions*. Retrieved from Politico: https://www.politico.com/news/magazine/2020/10/14/police-reform-police-unions-qualified-immunity-democratic-party-420122

Baruzzi, S. (2020, December 16). *China releases anti-monopoly guidelines for its platform economy*. Retrieved from China Briefing: https://www.china-briefing.com/news/china-releases-anti-monopoly-guidelines-for-its-platform-economy/

BBC. (2012, October 23). *Profile: Jiang Zemin*. Retrieved from BBC: https://www.bbc.com/news/world-asia-china-20038774

BBC. (2015, October 12). *Profile: China's fallen security chief Zhou Yongkang*. Retrieved from BBC: https://www.bbc.com/news/world-asia-china-26349305

BBC. (2015, February 2). *The palace of shame that makes China angry*. Retrieved from BBC: https://www.bbc.com/news/magazine-30810596

BBC. (2017, October 23). *Charting China's 'great purge' under Xi*. Retrieved from BBC: https://www.bbc.com/news/world-asia-china-41670162

BBC. (2017, July 13). *Liu Xiaobo: Chinese dissident and Nobel Peace Prize winner*. Retrieved from BBC: https://www.bbc.com/news/world-asia-40403811

BBC. (2017, June 13). *Panama cuts ties with Taiwan in favour of China*. Retrieved from BBC: https://www.bbc.com/news/world-latin-america-40256499

BBC. (2017, June 13). *Panama cuts ties with Taiwan in favour of China*. Retrieved from BBC: https://www.bbc.com/news/world-latin-america-40256499

BBC. (2018, March 11). *China's Xi allowed to remain 'president for life' as term limits removed.* Retrieved from BBC: https://www.bbc.com/news/world-asia-china-43361276

BBC. (2019, May 7). *The night the US bombed a Chinese embassy.* Retrieved from BBC: https://www.bbc.com/news/world-europe-48134881

BBC. (2021, September 16). *Aukus: UK, US and Australia launch pact to counter China.* Retrieved from BBC: https://www.bbc.com/news/world-58564837

BBC. (2021, April 13). *China forces Jack Ma's Ant Group to restructure.* Retrieved from BBC: https://www.bbc.com/news/business-56728038

BBC. (2021, August 25). *China schools: 'Xi Jinping Thought' introduced into curriculum.* Retrieved from BBC News: https://www.bbc.com/news/world-asia-58301575

BBC. (2021, September 2). *China steps in to regulate brutal '996' work culture.* Retrieved from BBC: https://www.bbc.com/news/world-asia-china-58381538

BBC. (2021, September 2). *China's media cracks down on 'effeminate' styles.* Retrieved from BBC: https://www.bbc.com/news/business-58394906

BBC. (2021, February 10). *Clubhouse: The controversial chats that angered China's censors.* Retrieved from BBC: https://www.bbc.com/news/world-asia-china-55984854

BBC. (2021, March 10). *US and China trade angry words at high-level Alaska talks.* Retrieved from BBC: https://www.bbc.com/news/world-us-canada-56452471

BBC. (2022, January 18). *China's Xi Jinping defends 'common prosperity' crackdowns.* Retrieved from BBC: https://www.bbc.com/news/business-60034050

BBC. (2022, July 1). *Hong Kong's handover: How the UK returned it to China.* Retrieved from BBC: https://www.bbc.com/news/world-asia-china-40426827

BBC Travel. (2019). *A trading and military past.* Retrieved from BBC Travel: https://www.bbc.com/storyworks/travel/specials/get-to-know-macao/history/

Bhatnagar, A., & Sandhu , J. (2018, June 6). *India's thinking global. It should act regional first.* Retrieved from Global Policy: https://www.globalpolicyjournal.com/blog/06/06/2018/indias-thinking-global-it-should-act-regional-first

Bloomberg News. (2021, September 5). *China's 'Mr. Income Distribution' explains Common Prosperity.* Retrieved from Bloomberg News: https://www.bloomberg.com/news/articles/2021-09-05/china-s-mr-income-distribution-explains-common-prosperity?leadSource=uverify%20wall

Bloomberg News. (2021, September 9). *What Xi means by 'disorderly capital' Is $1.5 trillion question.* Retrieved from Bloomberg News: https://www.bloomberg.com/news/articles/2021-09-09/what-xi-means-by-disorderly-capital-is-1-5-trillion-question?leadSource=uverify%20wall

Bloomberg News. (2022, June 14). *China city accused of using Covid health codes to stop protests.* Retrieved from Bloomberg News: https://www.bloomberg.com/news/articles/2022-06-14/china-s-iphone-city-may-be-using-covid-controls-on-protesters?leadSource=uverify%20 wall

Bloomberg News. (2022, June 22). *China's property slump ios a bigger threat than its lockdowns.* Retrieved from Bloomberg News: https://www.bloomberg.com/news/articles/2022-06-22/china-housing-market-slowdown-drags-economy#:~:text=The%20slump%20began%20last%20year,prices%20 and%20reduce%20financial%20risks.

Bloomenthal, A. (2022, January 31). *6 factors driving investment in China.* Retrieved from Investopedia: https://www.investopedia.com/articles/economics/09/factors-drive-investment-in-china.asp

Blumenthal, D. (2020, June 04). *China's Steps Backward Began Under Hu Jintao.* Retrieved from Foreign Policy: https://foreignpolicy.com/2020/06/04/china-xi-jingping-hu-jintao-aggression-ideology/

Boehler, P. (2023). *The forgotten army of the first world war.* Retrieved from South China Morning Post: https://multimedia.scmp.com/ww1-china/

Boissoneault, L. (2017, August 17). *The surprisingly important role China played in WWI.* Retrieved from Smithsonian Magazine: https://www.smithsonianmag.com/history/surprisingly-important-role-china-played-world-war-i-180964532/

Bong, C. (2019, December 04). *Cambodia's disastrous dependence on China: A history lesson.* Retrieved from The Diplomat: https://thediplomat.com/2019/12/cambodias-disastrous-dependence-on-china-a-history-lesson/

Borst, N. (2021, April 15). *Has China given up on state- owned enterprise reform?* Retrieved from The Interpreter: https://www.lowyinstitute.org/the-interpreter/has-china-given-state-owned-enterprise-reform

Bracken, G. (2018). Treaty ports in China: Their genesis, development, and influence. *Journal of Urban History*, 168-176.

Bradsher, K. (2022, October 17). *China delays indefinitely the release of G.D.P. and other economic statistics.* Retrieved from The New York Times: https://www.nytimes.com/2022/10/17/business/china-gdp-delay.html

Bradsher, K. (2022, January 16). *China's economy is slowing, a worrying sign for the world.* Retrieved from The New York Times: https://www.nytimes.com/2022/01/16/business/economy/china-economy.html

Brandt, J., & Schafer, B. (2020, October 28). *How China's 'wolf warrior' diplomats use and abuse Twitter.* Retrieved from Brookings: https://www.brookings.edu/techstream/how-chinas-wolf-warrior-diplomats-use-and-abuse-twitter/

Brazys, S., & Vadalamannait, K.C. (2021). Aid Curse with Chinese characteristics? Chinese development flows and economic reforms. *Public Choice*

Brooker, M. (2021, March 11). *Whatever happened to Common Prosperity?* Retrieved from Bloomberg: https://www.bloomberg.com/opinion/articles/2022-03-11/absence-of-common-prosperity-hints-at-a-lost-moment-for-china#xj4y7vzkg?leadSource=uverify%20 wall

Brown, C. (2012). *China's Great Leap Forward.* Retrieved from Association for Asian Studies: https://www.asianstudies.org/publications/eaa/archives/chinas-great-leap-forward/

Brunnstrom, D., & Martina , M. (2022, 14 March). *U.S. lawmakers demand HSBC explain actions against Hong Kong activists, Americans.* Retrieved from Reuters: https://www.reuters.com/world/us-lawmakers-demand-hsbc-explain-actions-against-hong-kong-activists-americans-2022-03-03/

Buchholz, K. (2021, June 29). *Private sector is China's main economic driver.* Retrieved from Statista: https://www.statista.com/chart/25194/private-sector-contribution-to-economy-in-china/

Buckley, A. R. (2019, November 16). *The Xinjiang Papers.* Retrieved from The New York Times: https://www.nytimes.com/interactive/2019/11/16/world/asia/china-xinjiang-documents.html

Buckley, C. (2018, February 26). *Xi Jinping thought explained: A new Ideology for a new era.* Retrieved from New York Times: https://www.nytimes.com/2018/02/26/world/asia/xi-jinping-thought-explained-a-new-ideology-for-a-new-era.html

Buckley, C. (2021, August 30). *China tightens limits for young online gamers and bans school night play.* Retrieved from The New York Times: https://www.nytimes.com/2021/08/30/business/media/china-online-games.html

Buckley, C. (2021, November 7). *To steer China's future, Xi Is rewriting its past.* Retrieved from New York Times: https://www.nytimes.com/2021/11/07/world/asia/china-xi-jinping.html

Buckley, J. (2022, April). *2022/4 "Vietnam's Labour Reforms: Drivers and Implications".* Retrieved from Yusof Ishak Institute: https://www.iseas.edu.sg/articles-commentaries/iseas-perspective/2022-4-vietnams-labour-reforms-drivers-and-implications-by-joe-buckley/

Budhathoki , A., & Dahal, B. (2021, July 28). *Nepal's cautious approach to the tibetan question.* Retrieved from The Diplomat: https://thediplomat.com/2021/07/nepals-cautious-approach-to-the-tibetan-question/

Bugos, S. (2022, January). *Chinese hypersonic glider said to fire projectile.* Retrieved from Arms Control: https://www.armscontrol.org/act/2022-01/news/chinese-hypersonic-glider-said-fire-projectile

Burcu, O. (2022). The Chinese government's management of anti-Japan nationalism during Hu-Wen era. *International Relations of the Asia Pacific* , 237-266.

Burgess, M. (2021, July 16). *Australia's Morrison repeats call for probe into virus origins.* Retrieved from Bloomberg News: https://www.bloomberg.com/news/articles/2021-07-16/australia-s-morrison-repeats-call-for-probe-into-virus-origins?leadSource=uverify%20 wall

Burgess, M. (2021, July 16). *Australia's Morrison repeats call for probe Into virus origins.* Retrieved from Bloomberg: https://www.bloomberg.com/news/articles/2021-07-16/australia-s-morrison-repeats-call-for-probe-into-virus-origins

Cai, J. (2021, November 10). *China's path to common prosperity puts pressure on private enterprise.* Retrieved from South China Morning Post: s/article/3155367/chinas-path-common-prosperity-puts-pressure-private-enterprise

Cai, X. Z. (2016, March 11). *Charting China's rising individualism in names, songs, and attitudes.* Retrieved from Harvard Business Review: https://hbr.org/2016/03/charting-chinas-rising-individualism-in-names-songs-and-attitudes

Campbell, C. (2021, September 10). *Why 'Common Prosperity' has China's billionaires running for cover.* Retrieved from Time: https://time.com/6095560/china-common-prosperity/

Carminati, D. (2020, July 3). *The state of China's soft power in 2020.* Retrieved from https://www.e-ir.info/2020/07/03/the-state-of-chinas-soft-power-in-2020/: E-International Relations

Carnegie Council. (2023). *Why is the May 4th Movement a turning point in modern Chinese history?* Retrieved from Carnegie Council: https://www.carnegiecouncil.org/explore-engage/classroom-resources/1919-the-year-of-the-crack-up/china-protests

Carr, E. (2022, April 10). *China's dual circulation and its global implications.* Retrieved from China US Focus: https://www.chinausfocus.com/finance-economy/chinas-dual-circulation-and-its-global-implications

Caskey, G. (2020). Book Review: Belt and Road A Chinese World Order. *Independent Review.* Retrieved from The Independent Review.

CBS Mornings. (2022, May 24). U.S. marines train for a possible future Chinese invasion of Taiwan. *CBS Mornings.* CBS.

Center for Preventive Action. (2022, May 4). *Territorial disputes in the South China Sea.* Retrieved from Council on Foreign Relations: https://www.cfr.org/global-conflict-tracker/conflict/territorial-disputes-south-china-sea

Central Intelligence Agency (US). (1959). *Comparison of the first five year plans of communist China and the USSR.* Central Intelligency Agency. Retrieved from CIA.

Central Tibetan Administration. (2022). *Revisiting the "Cultural Revolution" in Tibet.* Retrieved from Central Tibetan Administration: https://web.archive.org/web/20201101012258/https://tibet.net/revisiting-the-cultural-revolution-in-tibet/

CGTN. (2023). *What does 'path of socialism with Chinese characteristics' mean?* Retrieved from CGTN: https://www.cgtn.com/how-china-works/feature/What-does-path-of-socialism-with-Chinese-characteristics-mean.html

Chambers, A. (2021). Study on People's Republic of China (PRC) policies and Influence in the development of international standards for emerging technologies. *Federal Register*, 60801-60802.

Chan, C., Dao, A., Hou, J., Jin, T., & Tuong, C. (2011). *Free speech vs maintaining social cohesion*. Retrieved from Stanford CS181: Computers, Ethics, And Public Policy Final Project: https://cs.stanford.edu/people/eroberts/cs181/projects/2010-11/FreeExpressionVsSocialCohesion/china_policy.html

Chang, J., & Koh, C. (2021, September 15). *US engagement in Southeast Asia: How much will be enough?* Retrieved from The Interpreter: https://www.lowyinstitute.org/the-interpreter/us-engagement-southeast-asia-how-much-will-be-enough

Chang, P. T. (2021, September 9). *US must learn to share global stage with China and adapt to the reality of a diverse, multipolar world*. Retrieved from South China Morning Post: https://www.scmp.com/comment/opinion/article/3147966/us-must-learn-share-global-stage-china-and-adapt-reality-diverse

Che, C., & Goldkorn, J. (2021, August 2). *China's 'Big Tech crackdown': A guide*. Retrieved from The Chine Project: https://thechinaproject.com/2021/08/02/chinas-big-tech-crackdown-a-guide/

Cheng, L. (2021, July 10). *Hong Kong leader vows to push 'patriotic education' in city's schools to stop children being misled*. Retrieved from South China Morning Post: https://www.scmp.com/news/hong-kong/education/article/3140616/hong-kong-leader-vows-push-patriotic-education-citys

Chen-Weiss, J. (2014, November 25). *Chinese nationalism: the CCP's 'eouble-ddged sword'*. Retrieved from The Diplomat: https://thediplomat.com/2014/11/chinese-nationalism-the-ccps-double-edged-sword/

Cheung, G. (2019, July 4). *What is the Sino-British Joint Declaration and what does it have to do with Hong Kong's extradition crisis?* Retrieved from South China Morning Post: https://www.scmp.com/news/hong-kong/politics/article/3017318/explainer-what-sino-british-joint-declaration-and-what-does?module=inline&pgtype=article

China Briefing. (2021, August 24). *The PRC Personal Information Protection Law (Final): A full translation*. Retrieved from China Briefing: https://www.china-briefing.com/news/the-prc-personal-information-protection-law-final-a-full-translation/

China Daily. (2011, January 30). *Jan 30,1995: President Jiang Zemin puts forward eight propositions on development of relations between two sides of Taiwan Straits*. Retrieved from China Daily: https://www.chinadaily.com.cn/china/19thcpcnationalcongress/2011-01/30/content_29715090.htm

China Daily. (2022, August 5). *How was the 1992 Consensus reached?* Retrieved from Peoples Daily: http://en.people.cn/n3/2022/0805/c90000-10131577.html

China Power. (2023). *Will the dual circulation strategy enable china to compete in a post-pandemic world?* Retrieved from China Power: https://chinapower.csis.org/china-covid-dual-circulation-economic-strategy/

China Power. (2023). *Is air quality in China a social problem?* Retrieved from China Power: https://chinapower.csis.org/air-quality/

China.org. (1984, June 22). *One country, two systems.* Retrieved from China.org: http://www.china.org.cn/english/features/dengxiaoping/103372.htm

China.org. (2021, May 9). *Scientific outlook on development.* Retrieved from China.org: http://www.china.org.cn/m/english/china_key_words/2021-09/21/content_77765465.html

Chinese Government. (2021, March 13). *The Fourteenth Five-Year Plan for the national dconomic and social development of the People's Republic of China and outline of long-term goals for 2035.* Retrieved from Gov.cn: http://www.gov.cn/xinwen/2021-03/13/content_5592681.htm

Chinese Government Network. (2006, April 21). *Hu Jintao holds talks with Bush, reaching consensus on issues of common concern between China and the US.* Retrieved from Gov.cn: http://www.gov.cn/ldhd/2006-04/21/content_259420.htm

Chiu, D. (2017). The East Is Green: China's Global Leadership in Renewable Energy. *New Perspectives in Foreign Policy Issue 13, Summer 2017*, 3-12.

Christie, J. (2008, April 8). *Pro-Tibet activists scale Golden Gate Bridge.* Retrieved from Reuters: https://www.reuters.com/article/us-olympics-torch-goldengate/pro-tibet-activists-scale-golden-gate-bridge-idUSN0723796620080408

Chun, H. (2019, April 7). *China's hard edge: The leader of Beijing's muslim crackdown gains influence.* Retrieved from The Wall Street Journal: https://www.wsj.com/articles/chinas-hard-edge-the-leader-of-beijings-muslim-crackdown-gains-influence-11554655886

Chung, C.-p. (2002). China's "War on Terror": September 11 and uighur separatism. *Foreign Affairs*, 8-12.

CNBC. (2019, July 10). *Antiwar candidate Bernie Sanders faces backlash over the $1.2 trillion war machine he brought to Vermont.* Retrieved from CNBC: https://www.cnbc.com/2019/07/10/bernie-sanders-faces-backlash-over-war-machine-he-brought-to-vermont.html

Coase, R. H., & Wang , N. (2013). *How China became capitalist.* Retrieved from Cato Institute: https://www.cato.org/policy-report/january/february-2013/how-china-became-capitalist

Cohen, J. (2019, December 21). *Macau and Hong Kong are too different for Beijing to treat them like peas in a pod.* Retrieved from South China Morning Post: https://www.scmp.com/comment/opinion/article/3042815/macau-and-hong-kong-are-too-different-beijing-treat-them-peas-pod

Congress, L. o. (2023). *U.S. trade with China: selected resources.* Retrieved from Library of Congress: https://guides.loc.gov/us-trade-with-china

Congressional-Executive Commission on China. (2023). *Judical independence in the PRC.* Retrieved from Congressional-Executive Commission on China: https://www.cecc.gov/judicial-independence-in-the-prc#:~:text=China's%20judiciary%20continues%20to%20be,the%20independence%20of%20individual%20judges.

Cook, S. (2017). *Falun Gong: Religious Freedom in China.* Freedom House. Retrieved from Freedom House: https://freedomhouse.org/report/2017/battle-china-spirit-falun-gong-religious-freedom

Costa, S. H., & Horta e Costa, S. (2022, March 29). *Xi battles distrust by global Investors burned in China before.* Retrieved from Bloomberg: https://www.bloomberg.com/news/articles/2022-03-29/xi-battles-distrust-by-global-investors-burned-in-china-before#xj4y7vzkg?leadSource=uverify%20wall

Council on Foreign Relations. (2023). *What happened when China joined the WTO?* Retrieved from World 101: https://world101.cfr.org/global-era-issues/trade/what-happened-when-china-joined-wto

Country Economy. (2023). *Country comparison Hong Kong vs China.* Retrieved from Country Economy: https://countryeconomy.com/countries/compare/hong-kong/china

Cruz, B. H. (2020). Between theory and practice: the utility of international relations theory to the military practitioner. *Wild Blue Yonder.*

Csikszentmihalyi, M. (2020, March 31). *Confucius.* Retrieved from Stanford Encyclopedia of Philosophy: https://plato.stanford.edu/entries/confucius/

Cucchisi, J. L. (2002). The causes and effects of the Chinese Civil War, 1927-1949. *Seton Hall University Dissertations and Theses* .

Culver, J., & Hass, R. (2021, March 30). *Understanding Beijing's motives regarding Taiwan, and America's role.* Retrieved from Brookings: https://www.brookings.edu/on-the-record/understanding-beijings-motives-regarding-taiwan-and-americas-role/

Cunningham, M. (2022, March 07). *Looking Ahead to China's 20th Party Congress.* Retrieved from Heritage Foundation: https://www.heritage.org/asia/report/looking-ahead-chinas-20th-party-congress

Currie, D. P. (1986). Positive and negative constitutional rights. *University of Chicago Law Review.*

Custer, S., Russell, B., DiLorenzo, M., Cheng, M., Ghose, S., Sims, J., . . . Desai , H. (2018). *Ties That Bind: Quantifying China's public diplomacy and its "good neighbor" effect.* Williamsburg: AidData at William & Mary.

Dargis, M. (2012, November 21). *He's lost the game. Can he beat the Koreans?* Retrieved from The New York Times: https://www.nytimes.com/2012/11/21/movies/red-dawn-remake-trades-soviets-for-north-koreans.html

Darmawan, A. R. (2022, April 19). *Leveraging international law: Is China positioning itself for hegemony?* Retrieved from The Fletcher Forum for World Affairs: http://www.fletcherforum.org/home/2022/4/19/leveraging-international-law-is-china-positioning-itself-for-hegemony

Datt, A. (2021, September 8). The impact of the national security law on media and internet freedom in Hong Kong. Washington, DC, USA.

Davidson, H. (2022, May 6). *Xi Jinping attacks 'doubters' as he doubles down on China's zero-Covid policy.* Retrieved from The Guardian: https://www.theguardian.com/world/2022/may/06/xi-jinping-attacks-doubters-as-he-doubles-down-on-chinas-zero-covid-policy

Dede, K. (2023). *Ethnic minorities in China.* Retrieved from Asia Society: https://asiasociety.org/ethnic-minorities-china

Department of International Trade (United Kingdom). (2021, January 30). *UK applies to join huge Pacific free trade area CPTPP.* Retrieved from Gov.uk: https://www.gov.uk/government/news/uk-applies-to-join-huge-pacific-free-trade-area-cptpp

Department, U. S. (2023). *Monroe Doctrine, 1823.* Retrieved from Office of the Historian: https://history.state.gov/milestones/1801-1829/monroe

Devlin, K. (2018, December 17). *International relations experts and U.S. public agree: America is less respected globally.* Retrieved from Pew Research Center: https://www.pewresearch.org/fact-tank/2018/12/17/international-relations-experts-and-u-s-public-agree-america-is-less-respected-globally/

Dikötter, F. (2016, June 22). Understanding China's Cultural Revolution. (R. Johnson, Interviewer)

Dollar, D. (2018, September 14). *U.S.-China trade war has its seeds in the financial crisis.* Retrieved from Brookings: https://www.brookings.edu/blog/order-from-chaos/2018/09/14/u-s-china-trade-war-has-its-seeds-in-the-financial-crisis/

Dolma, K. (2020, August 31). *Tibet Was China's first laboratory of repression.* Retrieved from Foreign Policy: https://foreignpolicy.com/2020/08/31/tibet-china-repression-xinjiang-sinicization/

Dorje, Y. (2020, September 3). *Rights groups slam Xi's latest calls to 'Sinicize' Tibetan Buddhism.* Retrieved from Voice of America: https://www.voanews.com/a/east-asia-pacific_rights-groups-slam-xis-latest-calls-sinicize-tibetan-buddhism/6195382.html

Doshi, R. (2019, January 22). *Hu's to blame for China's foreign assertiveness?* Retrieved from Brookings: https://www.brookings.edu/articles/hus-to-blame-for-chinas-foreign-assertiveness/

Doshi, R. (2021). *The long game: China's grand strategy to displace American order.* Oxford: Oxford University Press.

Drinhausen, K. (2023). *Democracy / 民主*. Retrieved from Decoding China: https://decodingchina.eu/democracy/

Duffy, C. (2020, April 27). *Bill Gates explains how the United States can safely ease coronavirus restrictions*. Retrieved from CNN: https://www.cnn.com/2020/04/26/business/bill-gates-coronavirus-reopening-gps/index.html

Dutta, N., & Sobel, R. (2016). Does corruption ever help entrepreneurship? *Small Business Economics*, 179-199.

Economist, T. (2021, June 23). *https://www.economist.com/the-economist-explains/2021/06/23/how-did-confucianism-win-back-the-chinese-communist-party*. Retrieved from The Economist: https://www.economist.com/the-economist-explains/2021/06/23/how-did-confucianism-win-back-the-chinese-communist-party

Egorov, B. (2021, Janauary 14). *How the USSR helped the Communists seize power in China*. Retrieved from Russia Beyond: https://www.rbth.com/history/333268-how-ussr-helped-communists-china

Enos, O. (2020, June 1). *The closure Of Apple Daily: Another nail in the coffin for freedom in Hong Kong*. Retrieved from Forbes: https://www.forbes.com/sites/oliviaenos/2021/07/01/the-closure-of-apple-daily-another-nail-in-the-coffin-for-freedom-in-hong-kong/?sh=55d80f9b61ba

European Commission. (2022, May 6). *European Commission Trade Department.* Retrieved from European Commission: https://trade.ec.europa.eu/doclib/docs/2006/september/tradoc_122530.pdf

Evrard, S., & Tong, B. (2022, February 11). *Antitrust in China – 2021 year in review*. Retrieved from Gibson Dunn: https://www.gibsondunn.com/antitrust-in-china-2021-year-in-review/

Facts and Details. (2019). *Taiwan after World War II: Kuomintang take control and the 2-28 Incident.* Retrieved from Facts and Details: https://factsanddetails.com/southeast-asia/Taiwan/sub5_1a/entry-3799.html

Falun Info. (2023). *The 6-10 Office.* Retrieved from Falun Info: https://faluninfo.net/the-6-10-office/

Feng, E. (2020, September 23). *As U.S. views Of China grow more negative, Chinese support for their government rises*. Retrieved from NPR: https://www.npr.org/2020/09/23/913650298/as-u-s-views-of-china-grow-more-negative-chinese-support-for-their-government-ri

Feulner, E. J. (2021, April 5). *Hong Kong Is no longer what It was.* Retrieved from Heritage Foundation: https://www.heritage.org/asia/commentary/hong-kong-no-longer-what-it-was

Fewsmith, J. (2004). Promoting the scientific development concept. *China Leadership Monitor.*

Fink, A. (2022, April 29). *Russia and China team up to accuse America of 'Imperialism'.* Retrieved from The Dispatch: https://thedispatch.com/article/russia-and-china-team-up-to-accuse/

Fisher, M. (2012, January 05). *How China stays stable despite 500 protests every day.* Retrieved from The Atlantic: https://www.theatlantic.com/international/archive/2012/01/how-china-stays-stable-despite-500-protests-every-day/250940/

Florek, S. (2020, March 09). *Middle Kingdom.* Retrieved from Australian Museum: https://australian.museum/learn/cultures/international-collection/chinese/middle-kingdom/

Flynn, J. (2018, March 17). *Self-immolation for Tibet: Why the Dalai Lama's silence is costing lives.* Retrieved from Brown Poltical Review: https://brownpoliticalreview.org/2018/03/self-immolation-tibet-dalai-lamas-silence-costing-lives/

Foster, A. L. (2018, November 12). *China's antitrust regulator ramps up scrutiny, enforcement of behavioral remedies.* Retrieved from Skadden: https://www.skadden.com/insights/publications/2018/11/chinas-antitrust-regulator-ramps-up-scrutiny#:~:text=The%20most%20common%20types%20of,any%20illegal%20tying%20or%20bundling

Fraser Institute. (2022). *Economic Freedom Ranking 2019.* Retrieved from Fraser Institute: https://www.fraserinstitute.org/economic-freedom/map?geozone=world&page=map&year=2019

Freeman, C., & Stephenson, A. (2022, October 5). *Xi kicks off campaign for a Chinese vision of global security.* Retrieved from United States Institute of Peace: https://www.usip.org/publications/2022/10/xi-kicks-campaign-chinese-vision-global-security

French, H. (2022, May 9). *While America slept, China became indispensable.* Retrieved from Foreign Policy: https://foreignpolicy.com/2022/05/09/us-china-competition-africa-central-asia-infrastructure-development/

Friedman, E. (1994). Reconstructing China's national identity: A southern alternative to Mao- Era anti-imperialist nationalism. *The Journal of Asian Studies*, 67-91.

Fukuyama, F. (1989). The end of history? *The Nationali Interest,* 3-18.

Galen Carpenter, T. (2022, February 24). *Ignored warnings: How NATO expansion led to the current Ukraine tragedy.* Retrieved from Cato Institute: https://www.cato.org/commentary/ignored-warnings-how-nato-expansion-led-current-ukraine-tragedy

Gan, N., & George , S. (2021, August 30). *Why is the Communist Party clamping down on China's biggest stars and fan clubs?* Retrieved from CNN: https://www.cnn.com/2021/08/30/china/china-entertainment-crackdown-mic-intl-hnk/index.html

Ghosh, P. (2020, September 18). *The Exodus of Chinese manufacturing: Shutting Down 'The World's Factory'*. Retrieved from Forbes: https://www.forbes.com/sites/princeghosh/2020/09/18/the-exodus-of-chinese-manufacturing-shutting-down-the-worlds-factory/?sh=24c3e0d3c2f2

Gill, I. (2021, January 25). *Deep-sixing poverty in China*. Retrieved from Brookings: https://www.brookings.edu/blog/future-development/2021/01/25/deep-sixing-poverty-in-china/

Gilley, B., & Holbig, H. (2009). The debate on Party legitimacy in China: a mixed quantitative/qualitative analysis. *Journal of Contemporary China* , 339-358.

Glaser, B. S. (2020, November 2020). *Online Event: China's Power: Up for Debate 2020 - Debate 1*. Retrieved from Center for Strategic and International Studies: https://www.csis.org/events/online-event-chinas-power-debate-2020-debate-1

Goldkorn, J. (2019, December 23). *Why did so many foreigners believe that Xi would be a reformer?* Retrieved from The China Project: https://thechinaproject.com/2019/12/23/why-did-so-many-foreigners-believe-that-xi-would-be-a-reformer/

Gowan, R. (2020, September 14). *China's pragmatic approach to UN peacekeeping*. Retrieved from Brookings: https://www.brookings.edu/articles/chinas-pragmatic-approach-to-un-peacekeeping/

Griffith, B. (2011). Middle-tncome trap. In R. N. al., *Frontiers in development policy.* World Bank elibrary.

Griffiths, R. (2019). *Engagement With China: was it a mistake?* Retrieved from The Foreign Service Journal: https://afsa.org/engagement-china-was-it-mistake

Gu, V. (2021, July 27). *Scientists discover a massive field of nuclear silos in China, signaling a significant nuclear expansion in the country*. Retrieved from Insider: https://www.insider.com/china-constructing-massive-nuclear-base-silos-xinjiang-2021-7

Gunning, C. (2021, February 14). *James Bond: Everything that was censored from Skyfall In China*. Retrieved from Screen Rant: https://screenrant.com/james-bond-skyfall-china-deleted-scenes-explained/

Habich-Sobiegalla, S., & Plümmer, F. (2022). *Topologies of power in China's grid-style social management during the COVID-19 pandemic.* SSRN.

Hadano, T. (2022, April 12). *China to hold party congress in November: report*. Retrieved from Nikei Asia: https://asia.nikkei.com/Politics/China-to-hold-party-congress-in-November-report

Hall, H. a. (2022, November 27). *Clashes in Shanghai as COVID protests flare across China*. Retrieved from Reuters: https://www.reuters.com/world/china/shanghai-hit-by-covid-protests-anger-spreads-across-china-2022-11-27/

Hanauer, L., & Morris, L. (2013, December 13). *China in Africa implications of a deepening relationship.* Retrieved from Rand Corporation: https://www.rand.org/pubs/research_briefs/RB9760.html

Hasanli, J. (2019, May 4). *The Soviet archives and xinjiang, 1944-1949.* Retrieved from Wilson Center: https://www.wilsoncenter.org/blog-post/soviet-archives-and-xinjiang-1944-1949

Hass, R. (2021, September 9). *Assessing China's "common prosperity" campaign.* Retrieved from Brookings: https://www.brookings.edu/blog/order-from-chaos/2021/09/09/assessing-chinas-common-prosperity-campaign/

Hass, R., & Chen-Weiss, J. (2021, July 12). *The Cold War is a poor analogy for today's US-China tensions.* Retrieved from Brookings: https://www.brookings.edu/on-the-record/the-cold-war-is-a-poor-analogy-for-todays-us-china-tensions/

He, H. (2022, January 6). *Why are China's Gen Z women rejecting marriage, kids more than their male counterparts?* Retrieved from South China Morning Post: https://www.scmp.com/economy/china-economy/article/3162221/why-are-chinas-gen-z-women-rejecting-marriage-kids-more-their

Hearn, M., & Zelin, M. (2022). *The Kangxi and Qianlong Emperors.* Retrieved from Recording the Grandeur of the Qing: http://projects.mcah.columbia.edu/nanxuntu/html/emperors/

Higgs, R. (1997). Regime Uncertainty: Why the Great Depression Lasted So Long and Why Prosperity Resumed after the War. *The Independent Review,* 561-590.

Hillman, B. (2016). Introduction: Understanding the current wave of conflict and protest in Tibet and Xinjiang. In B. Hillman , & G. Tuttle, *Ethnic Conflict and Protest in Tibet and Xinjiang: Unrest in China's West* (pp. 1-17). New Yorl: Columbia University Press.

Holbig, H., & Gilley, B. (2010). Reclaiming legitimacy in China. *Politics & Policy,* 395-422.

Hong Kong Government. (2020). The Law of the People's Republic of China on Safeguarding National Security in the Hong Kong Special Administrative Region. Hong Kong , China .

Hoover Institution, Stanford University. (2022, March 22). *China's sharp power In Africa: A handbook for building national resilience.* Retrieved from Hoover Institution: https://www.hoover.org/events/chinas-sharp-power-africa-handbook-building-national-resilience

Howell, J., & Duckett, J. (2018). Reassessing the Hu–Wen Era: A golden age or lost decade for social policy in China? *The China Quarterly* , 1-14.

Huang, C. (2012, September 9). *Long after retirement, Jiang Zemin continues to exert his influence.* Retrieved from South China Morning Post: https://www.scmp.com/news/china/article/1032511/long-after-retirement-jiang-zemin-continues-exert-his-influence

Huang, Y. (2017, December 1). Yukon Huang: Debunking Myths About China's Economy. (N. B. Pickering, Interviewer)

Huifeng, H. (2021, July 28). *China's state-owned enterprise reform: Shenzhen tries to lure loyal party cadres into oversight roles.* Retrieved from South China Morning Post: https://www.scmp.com/economy/china-economy/article/3142870/chinas-state-owned-enterprise-reform-shenzhen-tries-lure

Human Rights Watch. (2021, May 6). *Dismantling a Free Society.* Retrieved from Human Rights Watch: https://www.hrw.org/feature/2021/06/25/dismantling-free-society/hong-kong-one-year-after-national-security-law

Human Rights Watch. (2022, 1 27). *Beijing Olympics begin amid atrocity crimes.* Retrieved from Human Rights Watch: https://www.hrw.org/news/2022/01/27/beijing-olympics-begin-amid-atrocity-crimes

Human Rights Watch. (2022). *China.* Retrieved from Human Rights Watch: https://www.hrw.org/world-report/2022/country-chapters/china-and-tibet#12ffb1

II, W. F. (2023). *Public Choice.* Retrieved from EconLib: https://www.econlib.org/library/Enc/PublicChoice.html

Illmer, A. (2021, April 4). *China is 'trampling on Hong Kong's democracy'.* Retrieved from BBC: https://www.bbc.com/news/world-asia-china-56585731

Information Office of the State Council of the Peo. (2005, December 12). *China's peaceful development road.* Retrieved from Permanent Mission of the People's Republic of China to the United Nations Office at Geneva and other International Organizations in Switzerland: https://web.archive.org/web/20220119044848/https://www.fmprc.gov.cn/ce/cegv/eng/zywjyjh/t227733.htm

International, A. (1998). Economic, social, and cultural rights: Questions and answers. New York City, New York , USA.

International, A. (2022). *1989 Tiananmen Square protests.* Retrieved from Amnesty International: https://www.amnesty.org.uk/china-1989-tiananmen-square-protests-demonstration-massacre

Ip, G. (2021, August 06). Why is China targeting its own internet companies? (M. M. Carino, Interviewer)

Isidore, C. (2018, March 5). *Who likes tariffs? generally speaking, it's not the same people who like Trump.* Retrieved from CNN Business: https://money.cnn.com/2018/03/05/news/economy/trump-steel-aluminum-tariffs-support/index.html

J.Y. (2018, September 5). *What is Falun Gong?* Retrieved from The Economist: https://www.economist.com/the-economist-explains/2018/09/05/what-is-falun-gong

Jalil, Z. A. (2022, May 31). *China sends 30 warplanes into Taiwan air defence zone.* Retrieved from BBC: https://www.bbc.com/news/world-asia-61642217

James, L. (2021, May 1). *Beyond Xinjiang: Xi Jinping's Ethnic Crackdown.* Retrieved from The Diplomat: https://thediplomat.com/2021/04/beyond-xinjiang-xi-jinpings-ethnic-crackdown/

Jia, C. (2022, July 28). *Human rights used as political tool, say experts.* Retrieved from China Daily: http://www.chinadaily.com.cn/a/202207/28/WS62e1e6f6a310fd2b29e6edac.html

Jia, S. S. (2023). Sun Yat sen, Liang Qichao: Friends, foes and nationalism. Atlanta , Georgia , USA.

Jian, C. (2006). The Tibetan Rebellion of 1959 and China's changing relations with India and the Soviet Union. *Journal of Cold War Studies*, 54-101.

Johnson, D. O. (2021, December 13). Pacific Century: Wang Huning: The World's Most Dangerous Thinker? (M. R. Auslin, Interviewer)

Johnson, I. (2021, August 24). *How will China deal with the Taliban?* Retrieved from Council on Foreign Relations: https://www.cfr.org/in-brief/china-afghanistan-deal-with-taliban

Johnson, I. (2022, May 27). *Biden's grand China strategy: eloquent but inadequate.* Retrieved from Council on Foreign Relations: https://www.cfr.org/in-brief/biden-china-blinken-speech-policy-grand-strategy

Jones, L., & Hameiri, S. (2020, August 19). *Debunking the myth of 'debt-trap diplomacy'.* Retrieved from Chatham House: https://www.chathamhouse.org/2020/08/debunking-myth-debt-trap-diplomacy/1-introduction

Jordan, Z. (2017, December 14). *Does Xi Jinping thought teally matter?* Retrieved from The Diplomat: https://thediplomat.com/2017/12/does-xi-jinping-thought-really-matter/

Kaufman, A. A. (2011, March 10). Testimony before the U.S.-China Economic and Security Review Commission Hearing on "China"s Narratives Regarding National Security Policy": The "Century of Humiliation" and China's National Narratives. Washington, DC, USA.

Kelly, D. (2023). *Back to 'hide and bide'?* Retrieved from Lowy Institute: https://interactives.lowyinstitute.org/features/china-rules-based-order/articles/hide-and-bide/

Kempe, F. (2022, June 19). *President Xi's damage control focuses on Europe and the Chinese economy.* Retrieved from Atlantic Council: https://www.atlanticcouncil.org/content-series/inflection-points/president-xi-damage-control-focuses-on-europe-chinese-economy/

Kessler, A. (2022, March 27). *Ukraine's asymmetric war*. Retrieved from The Wall Street Journal: https://www.wsj.com/articles/ukraine-asymmetric-war-technology-starlink-mariupol-theater-collapse-russia-explosives-internet-drones-weapons-11648400672

Kirchner, R., & Bone, S. (2013, March 13). *China's lost decade*. Retrieved from DW: https://www.dw.com/en/looking-back-at-chinas-lost-decade/a-16667956

Kleven, A. (2019, May 6). *Belt and Road: colonialism with Chinese characteristics*. Retrieved from The Interpreter: https://www.lowyinstitute.org/the-interpreter/belt-road-colonialism-chinese-characteristics

Knowlton, B. (2003, December 10). *Bush warns Taiwan to keep status quo: China welcomes U.S. stance*. Retrieved from The New York Times: https://www.nytimes.com/2003/12/10/news/bush-warns-taiwan-to-keep-status-quo-china-welcomes-us-stance.html

Kobayashi, S., Baobo, J., & Sano, J. (1999, September). The "Three Reforms" in China: Progress and outlook. *RIM*.

Korab-Karpowicz, W. J. (2017). *Political realism in international relations*. Retrieved from Stanford Encyclopedia of Philosophy: https://plato.stanford.edu/entries/realism-intl-relations/

Kratz, M. &. (2021, January 4). *China's belt and road: Down but not out*. Retrieved from Rhodium Group: https://rhg.com/research/bri-down-out/

Kristof, N. (2013, January 16). *Looking for a jump start in China*. Retrieved from New York Times: https://www.nytimes.com/2013/01/06/opinion/sunday/kristof-looking-for-a-jump-start-in-china.html

Kuang, W. (2021, July 4). *How China's patriotic education became one of the 'longest successful propaganda campaigns'*. Retrieved from ABC News: https://www.abc.net.au/news/2021-07-05/ccp-patriotic-education-young-people-in-australia/100260298

Kuo, K. (2019, February 18). *Kuora: Explaining China's Warlord Period, which splintered the country*. Retrieved from The China Project: https://thechinaproject.com/2019/02/18/kuora-explaining-chinas-warlord-period-which-splintered-the-country/

Kuo, L. (2019, August 28). *Chinese liberal thinktank forced to close after being declared illegal*. Retrieved from The Guardian: https://www.theguardian.com/world/2019/aug/28/chinese-liberal-thinktank-forced-to-close-after-being-declared-illegal

Kuo, L. (2020, October 19). *China becomes first major economy to recover from Covid-19 pandemic*. Retrieved from The Guardian: https://www.theguardian.com/business/2020/oct/19/china-becomes-first-major-economy-to-recover-from-covid-19-pandemic

Kupchan, C. A. (2022, February 24). *Why Putin's War With Ukraine Is a Miscalculation.* Retrieved from Council on Foreign Relations: https://www.cfr.org/in-brief/why-putins-war-ukraine-miscalculation

Kurlantzick, J. (2019, December 19). *Taiwan's presidential election: What to know.* Retrieved from Council on Foreign Relations: https://www.cfr.org/in-brief/taiwans-presidential-election-what-know

Kusa, I. (2022, June 21). *China's strategic calculations in the Russia-Ukraine war.* Retrieved from Wilson Center: https://www.wilsoncenter.org/blog-post/chinas-strategic-calculations-russia-ukraine-war

Lama, J. Y. (2021, May). *The Seventeen Point Agreement: Seventy years of China's occupation of Tibet.* Retrieved from Origins: https://origins.osu.edu/milestones/seventeen-point-agreement-seventy-years-china-s-occupation-tibet?language_content_entity=en

Lau, M. (2022, August 11). *Beijing removes pledge not to station military personnel in Taiwan and offer of 'high degree of autonomy' in new reunification paper.* Retrieved from South China Morning Post: https://www.scmp.com/news/china/politics/article/3188454/beijing-removes-pledge-not-station-military-personnel-taiwan

Lee, J. (2014, March 28). *Expressing the Chinese Dream.* Retrieved from The Diplomat: https://thediplomat.com/2014/03/expressing-the-chinese-dream/

Leffler, M. (2019, December 2). *China isn't the Soviet Union. Confusing the two Is dangerous.* Retrieved from The Atlantic: https://www.theatlantic.com/ideas/archive/2019/12/cold-war-china-purely-optional/601969/

Legal Information Institute. (2023). *Separation of powers.* Retrieved from Legal Information Institute: https://www.law.cornell.edu/wex/separation_of_powers

Leibold, J. (2016). Interethnic conflict in the PRC: Xinjiang and Tibet as exceptions? In B. Hillman, & G. Tuttle, *Ethnic conflict and protest in Tibet and Xinjiang: Unrest in China's west* (pp. 223-250). New York: Columbia University Press.

Lendon, B., & Bae, G. (2022, May 3). *North Korea launches ballistic missile, Japan and South Korea say.* Retrieved from CNN: https://www.cnn.com/2022/05/03/asia/north-korea-missile-launch-intl-hnk-ml/index.html

Leuchtenburg, W. E. (2022). *Frankling D Roosevelt: Foreign Affairs.* Retrieved from Miller Center: https://millercenter.org/president/fdroosevelt/foreign-affairs

Levesque, G. (2021, June 30). (J. Rausch, Interviewer)

Li, C. (2012, November 2012). *The Powerful Factions Among China's Rulers.* Retrieved from Brookings: https://www.brookings.edu/articles/the-powerful-factions-among-chinas-rulers/

Li, J. (2021, July 26). *China is extending its regulatory storm from tech to education*. Retrieved from Quartz: https://qz.com/2037818/china-is-extending-its-regulatory-storm-from-tech-to-education

Li, X., & Brodsgaard, K. E. (2013). SOE reform in China: Past, present and future. *The Copenhagen Journal of Asian Studies*, 54-78.

Liao, H.-c. (2021, March 31). An Interpretation of Xi's Taiwan policy—and Taiwan's response. *Indo-Pacific Perspective*, pp. 25-29.

Lieberthal, K. G. (2011, December 21). *The American pivot to Asia*. Retrieved from Brookings: https://www.brookings.edu/articles/the-american-pivot-to-asia/

Liu, A., & Yang, E. (2022, November 8). *A Seat at the Table: The Risks of Complacent Data Privacy Governance*. Retrieved from American Institute for Economic Research: https://www.aier.org/article/a-seat-at-the-table-the-risks-of-complacent-data-privacy-governance/

Liu, O. (2022, July 16). *Patriotic Education Centre to launch classes for Hong Kong students from September.* Retrieved from South China Morning Post: https://www.scmp.com/news/hong-kong/education/article/3185545/patriotic-education-centre-launch-classes-hong-kong

Lloyd-Damnjanovic, A. (2018). *A preliminary study of PRC political influence and interference activities in American higher education.* Washington, DC: Wislon Center.

Lockett, H. (2022, June 11). *How Xi Jinping is reshaping China's capital markets.* Retrieved from Financial Times: https://www.ft.com/content/d5b81ea0-5955-414c-b2eb-886dfed4dffe

Long, Q., Hwang , C.-m., Chingman, & Chan, E. (2021, July 1). *China's leader ramps up rhetoric of national power on Party centenary.* Retrieved from Radio Free Asia: https://www.rfa.org/english/news/china/ccp-100th-xi-07012021100119.html

Lu, S. (2022, May 23). *Didi says It will proceed with delisting from NYSE.* Retrieved from The Wall Street Journal: https://www.wsj.com/articles/didi-says-it-will-proceed-with-delisting-from-nyse-11653310564

Ma, J. (2021, May 14). *China's Communist Party and the military: who the army reports to and what's changed under Xi Jinping.* Retrieved from South China Morning Post: https://www.scmp.com/news/china/military/article/3133210/why-chinas-communist-party-maintains-tight-grip-military

Ma, J. (2021, June 30). *From Mao Zedong to Xi Jinping: how China's Communist Party leaders have shaped its ideology.* Retrieved from South China Morning Post: https://www.scmp.com/news/china/politics/article/3139347/mao-xi-how-chinas-communist-party-leaders-have-shaped-its

Ma, J. (2021, April 6). *Is China in danger of losing control of its rising nationalism?* Retrieved from South China Morning Post: https://www.scmp.com/news/china/politics/article/3128482/china-danger-losing-control-its-rising-nationalism

Ma, M. S. (2021, December 07). China's Power: Up for Debate 2021 - Debate 2. (B. Lin, Interviewer)

MacArthur, D. (1950, June 14). Memorandum on Formosa, by General of the Army Douglas MacArthur, Commander in Chief, Far East, and Supreme Commander, Allied Powers, Japan. Tokyo, Japan.

Maclaren, J. (2020, Janaury 25). *With Its new aircraft carrier, Is China now a blue water navy?* Retrieved from The Diplomat: https://thediplomat.com/2020/01/with-its-new-aircraft-carrier-is-china-now-a-blue-water-navy/

Madhani, A., & Long, C. (2021, November 16). *Biden, Xi try to tamp down tension in long virtual meeting*. Retrieved from AP News: https://apnews.com/article/biden-xi-meeting-e6013378e03727b85a8f59f71fe61f4a

Magnarella, P. J. (2004). COMMUNIST CHINESE AND "ASIAN VALUES" CRITIQUES OF UNIVERSAL HUMAN RIGHTS. *Journal of Third World Studies* , 179-192.

Mai, J. (2021, October 19). *China promotes its most sanctioned official to Tibetan Communist Party chief.* Retrieved from South China Morning Post: https://www.scmp.com/news/china/politics/article/3152821/china-promotes-its-most-sanctioned-official-tibetan-party-chief

Maizland, L. (2021, May 19). *China's fight against climate change and environmental degradation*. Retrieved from Council on Foreign Relations: https://www.cfr.org/backgrounder/china-climate-change-policies-environmental-degradation

Maizland, L. (2022, September 22). *China's repression of uyghurs in xinjiang*. Retrieved from Council on Foreign Relations: https://www.cfr.org/backgrounder/china-xinjiang-uyghurs-muslims-repression-genocide-human-rights

Maizland, L. (2022, May 19). *Hong Kong's freedoms: What China promised and how it's cracking down.* Retrieved from Council on Foreign Relations: https://www.cfr.org/backgrounder/hong-kong-freedoms-democracy-protests-china-crackdown

Maizland, L. (2022, August 3). *Why China-Taiwan relations are so tense*. Retrieved from Council on Foreign Relations: https://www.cfr.org/backgrounder/china-taiwan-relations-tension-us-policy-biden

Makichuk, D. (2019, 29 November). *China building a powerful blue water navy*. Retrieved from Asia Times: https://asiatimes.com/2019/11/does-china-need-more-aircraft-carriers/

Martin, P. (2022, October 22). Understanding Chinese wolf warrior diplomacy. (J. Nawrotkiewicz, Interviewer) Retrieved from https://www.nbr.org/publication/understanding-chinese-wolf-warrior-diplomacy/: https://www.nbr.org/publication/understanding-chinese-wolf-warrior-diplomacy/

Maryland, U. o. (2022). *The People's Republic of China: II*. Retrieved from http://

www.chaos.umd.edu/history/prc2.html

Massari, P. (2021, November 15). *China in Africa: Exporting authoritarianism?* Retrieved from Harvard University Graduate School of Arts and Sciences: https://gsas.harvard.edu/news/stories/china-africa-exporting-authoritarianism

Mastro, O. S. (2022, August 10). *China's huge exercises around Taiwan were a rehearsal, not a signal, says Oriana Skylar Mastro*. Retrieved from The Economist: https://www.economist.com/by-invitation/2022/08/10/chinas-huge-exercises-around-taiwan-were-a-rehearsal-not-a-signal-says-oriana-skylar-mastro

McBride, J., & Chatzky, A. (2019, May 13). *https://www.cfr.org/backgrounder/made-china-2025-threat-global-trade#chapter-title-0-5*. Retrieved from Council on Foreign Relations: https://www.cfr.org/backgrounder/made-china-2025-threat-global-trade#chapter-title-0-5

Mearsheimer, J. (2005, November 18). *The Rise of China Will Not Be Peaceful at All*. Retrieved from The Australian: https://www.mearsheimer.com/wp-content/uploads/2019/06/The-Australian-November-18-2005.pdf

Mearsheimer, J. (2016, September). *Can China rise.* Retrieved from The National Interest: http://www.eastlaw.net/wp-content/uploads/2016/09/Can-China-Rise-Peacefully_-_-The-National-Interest.pdf

Meiser, J. (2018, February 18). *Introducing Liberalism in International Relations Theory*. Retrieved from E-International Relations: https://www.e-ir.info/2018/02/18/introducing-liberalism-in-international-relations-theory/

Mendhell, E. (2021, December 6). *What Is China Evergrande, and why is its crisis worrying markets?* Retrieved from The Wall Street Journal: https://www.wsj.com/articles/evergrande-china-crisis-11632330764

Menzel, U. (2021, December 17). *The rise of China and the future world order*. Retrieved from Geopolitical Intelligence Services: https://www.gisreportsonline.com/r/china-world-order/

Ministry of Foreign Affairs (China). (2003, November 19). *The Hong Kong Special Administrative Region*. Retrieved from Consulate General of the People's Republic of China in Auckland: https://web.archive.org/web/20220825170908/https://www.mfa.gov.cn/ce/cgak/eng/zt/zggk/xzqh/t44047.htm

Ministry of Foreign Affairs (China). (2004). *China's independent foreign policy of peace*. Retrieved from Ministry of Foreign Affairs: https://web.archive.org/web/20220301234217/https://www.mfa.gov.cn/ce/cegv//eng/zgbd/zgwjzc/t85889.htm

Ministry of Foreign Affairs (China). (2015, March 28). *China continues to promote win-win cooperation*. Retrieved from 2015 Boao Forum for Asia: https://web.archive.org/web/20220813111524/https://www.mfa.gov.cn/ce/ceug//eng/zt/t1249604.htm

Ministry of Foreign Affairs (China). (2021, March 9). *"Patriots governing Hong Kong" will safeguardthe implementation of "One Country, Two Systems"*. Retrieved from Embassy of the People's Republic of China in the Republic of South Africa: https://web.archive.org/web/20220702233306/https://www.mfa.gov.cn/ce/cezanew/eng/sgxw/t1859538.htm

Ministry of Foreign Affairs (China). (2022). *Human rights in China*. Retrieved from Embassy of the People's Republic of China in Lithuania: https://web.archive.org/web/20220804125748/https://www.fmprc.gov.cn/ce/celt/eng/zt/zfbps/t125236.htm

Ministry of Foreign Affairs (China). (n.d.). *White Paper--The Progress of Human Rights in China.* Retrieved from Chinese Embassy of the People's Republic of China in the United States of America: https://web.archive.org/web/20220309110758/https://www.mfa.gov.cn/ce/ceus/eng/zt/ppflg/t36621.htm

Mitter, R. (2021, June 17). Nationalism, legitimacy, and the future of the CCP. (J. Blanchette, Interviewer)

Mitter, R., & Johnson, E. (2021). *What the West gets wrong about China*. Retrieved from Harvard Business Review: https://hbr.org/2021/05/what-the-west-gets-wrong-about-china

Miura, Y. (2022). The Reality of "Common Prosperity" Advocated by the Xi Jinping Administration. *Pacific Business and Industries.*

Moravcsik, A. (1997). Taking Preferences Seriously: A Liberal Theory of International Politics. *International Organization*, 513–53.

Moreno-Tejada, J. (2020, November 6). *Moral Economy*. Retrieved from Global South Studies: https://globalsouthstudies.as.virginia.edu/key-concepts/moral-economy

Moritsugu, K. (2021, March 24). *China bashes US over racism, inequality, pandemic response*. Retrieved from AP News: https://apnews.com/article/pandemics-race-and-ethnicity-health-disparities-beijing-health-0aff37842b094560cb043c0800796e21

Morrison, J. S., Kennedy, S., & Huang, Y. (2022, June 27). *China's zero-covid: What should the West do?* Retrieved from CSIS: https://www.csis.org/analysis/chinas-zero-covid-what-should-west-do

Morton, H. (2007). Who gets what, when and how? Housing in the Soviet Union. *Soviet Studies* , 235-259 .

Mullen, A. (2021, June 1). *China's 1-child policy: what was it and what impact did it have?* Retrieved from South China Morning Post: https://www.scmp.com/economy/china-economy/article/3135510/chinas-one-child-policy-what-was-it-and-what-impact-did-it

Mullen, A. (2021, June 1). *China's 1-child policy: what was it and what impact did it have?* Retrieved from South China Morning Post: https://www.scmp.com/economy/china-economy/article/3135510/chinas-one-child-policy-what-was-it-and-what-impact-did-it

Myers, S. L. (2021, July 28). *China offers the Taliban a warm welcome while urging peace talks.* Retrieved from The New York Times: https://www.nytimes.com/2021/07/28/world/asia/china-taliban-afghanistan.html

New York Times. (2021, November 11). *China's Xi Jinping remakes the Communist Party's history in his image.* Retrieved from New York Times: https://www.nytimes.com/live/2021/11/11/world/china-xi-jinping-cpc

New York Times. (1959, April 3). *Dalai Lama enters India and asks for sanctuary.* Retrieved from New York Times: https://archive.nytimes.com/www.nytimes.com/library/world/asia/040359tibet-special.html

News, B. (2020, January 23). *China wants activists out of it's war on pollution.* Retrieved from Bloomberg News: https://www.bloomberg.com/features/2020-china-wuhan-pollution/#xj4y7vzkg

News, B. (2021, September 7). *Xi's 'Common Prosperity' drive triggers a rare debate in China.* Retrieved from Bloomberg News: https://www.bloomberg.com/news/articles/2021-09-07/xi-s-common-prosperity-drive-triggers-a-rare-debate-in-china#xj4y7vzkg

News, B. (2022, May 23). *China Triples Solar Investments as Clean Energy Push Accelerates.* Retrieved from Bloomberg: 22-05-23/china-triples-solar-investments-as-clean-energy-push-accelerates?leadSource=uverify%20 wall

Nicolaou, A., Barker, A., & Shepherd, C. (2021, April 23). *China and Hollywood: the end of the affair.* Retrieved from Financial Times: https://www.ft.com/content/8e8d38d6-65c1-4b2c-9da6-37977a7b9b3d

Nikkei Asia. (2019, December 16). *China exports AI surveillance tech to over 60 countries: report.* Retrieved from Nikkei Asia: https://asia.nikkei.com/Business/China-tech/China-exports-AI-surveillance-tech-to-over-60-countries-report

North, D., Wallis, J., & Weingast, B. (2009). *Violence and Social Orders.* Cambridge: Cambridge University Press.

Nye Jr., J. S. (2012, January 18). *Why China Is weak on soft power.* Retrieved from The New York Times: https://www.nytimes.com/2012/01/18/opinion/why-china-is-weak-on-soft-power.html?_r=1

Omara, D. (2016, October 28). *U.S. role on global stage bigger and stronger than ever, Kerry says in Chicago.* Retrieved from Medill Reports Chicago: https://news.medill.northwestern.edu/chicago/americas-role-on-global-stage-bigger-and-stronger-than-ever-kerry/

Oswald, R. (2021, February 23). *China likely to attack Taiwan within five years, panel told*. Retrieved from Roll Call: https://rollcall.com/2021/02/23/china-likely-to-attack-taiwan-within-five-years-panel-told/

Oud, M. (2023). *Rule of Law*. Retrieved from Decoding China: https://decodingchina.eu/rule-of-law/

Out, M. (2023). *Human Rights / 人权*. Retrieved from Decoding China: https://decodingchina.eu/human-rights/

Overholt, W. H. (2019). *Hong Kong: The rise and fall of "One Country, Two Systems"*. Boston: Harvard Ash Center for Democratic Governance and Innovation.

Paal, D. H. (2018, November 09). *China, U.S. Heading for 'Increasing Confrontation'*. Retrieved from Carnegie Endowment for Peace: https://carnegieendowment.org/2018/11/09/china-u.s.-heading-for-increasing-confrontation-pub-77688

Page, J. (2015, September 20). *Why China Is turning back to Confucius*. Retrieved from The Wall Street Journal: https://www.wsj.com/articles/why-china-is-turning-back-to-confucius-1442754000

Pai, H.-T. (2022, November 22). *Who's who in the new era of Xi Jinping's China*. Retrieved from Australian Strategic Policy Institute: https://www.aspistrategist.org.au/whos-who-in-the-new-era-of-xi-jinpings-china/

Palmer, J. (2020, February 3). *Chinese officials can't help lying about the Wuhan virus*. Retrieved from Foreign Policy: https://foreignpolicy.com/2020/02/03/wuhan-coronavirus-coverup-lies-chinese-officials-xi-jinping/

Parks, B. (2022, June 7). Banking On Beijing: The aims and impacts Of china's overseas development program. (L. Diamond, Interviewer)

Patalano, A. (2021, August 11). *Why is a British carrier strike group heading to the Indo-Pacific?* Retrieved from War on the Rocks: https://warontherocks.com/2021/08/why-is-a-british-carrier-strike-group-heading-to-the-indo-pacific/

Peach, S. (2021, March 20). *Why did Alibaba's Jack Ma disappear for three months?* Retrieved from BBC: https://www.bbc.com/news/technology-56448688

Petis, M. (2021, October 15). *Will China's Common Prosperity upgrade Dual Circulation?* Retrieved from Carnegie Endowment for International Peace: https://carnegieendowment.org/chinafinancialmarkets/85571

Phillips, T. (2016, May 10). *The Cultural Revolution: all you need to know about China's political convulsion*. Retrieved from The Guardian: https://www.theguardian.com/world/2016/may/11/the-cultural-revolution-50-years-on-all-you-need-to-know-about-chinas-political-convulsion

Pietrucha, M. (2022, May 18). *Amateur Hour Part I: The Chinese invasion of Taiwan*. Retrieved from War on the Rocks: https://warontherocks.com/2022/05/amateur-hour-part-i-the-chinese-invasion-of-taiwan/

Piketty, T., Yang, L., & Zucman, G. (2019, April 1). *Income inequality is growing fast in China and making it look more like the US.* Retrieved from London School of Economics Blog: https://blogs.lse.ac.uk/businessreview/2019/04/01/income-inequality-is-growing-fast-in-china-and-making-it-look-more-like-the-us/

Pillsbury, M. (2015). *The Hundred-Year Marathon.* Henry Holt and Co.

Plante, T. (1999). U.S. Marines in the boxer rebellion. *Genealogy Notes.*

Poling, G. B., Natalegawa , A., & Tran Hudes, S. (2021). *The unlikely, indispensable U.S.-Vietnam partnership.* Washington, DC: Center for Strategic and International Studies .

Pompeo, M. (2020, July 23). Secretary of State. Washington, DC, USA.

Popkin, S. (1979). *The rational peasant the political economy of rural society in Vietnam.* University of California Press.

Poudel, S. S. (2022, June 9). *Nepal is caught between the US and China on Tibetan refugee issue.* Retrieved from The Diplomat: https://thediplomat.com/2022/06/nepal-is-caught-between-the-us-and-china-on-tibetan-refugee-issue/#:~:text=According%20to%20Human%20Rights%20Watch,neighborhoods%20on%20politically%20sensitive%20dates.

PTI. (2021, December 24). *2021: A year of record trade amid frozen India-China ties over Ladakh chill.* Retrieved from The Economic Times: https://economictimes.indiatimes.com/news/economy/foreign-trade/india-plans-to-cut-gold-import-duty-to-arrest-smuggling/articleshow/97249579.cms

Qi, L. (2022, June 3). *China is haunted by its One-Child Policy as It tries to encourage couples to conceive.* Retrieved from The Wall Street Journal: https://www.wsj.com/articles/china-is-haunted-by-its-one-child-policy-as-it-tries-to-encourage-couples-to-conceive-11641205807

Qu, T., & Cao, A. (2022, January 6). *China tech crackdown: fresh antitrust fines on Alibaba and Tencent signal continued scrutiny in 2022.* Retrieved from South China Morning Post: https://www.scmp.com/tech/big-tech/article/3162387/china-tech-crackdown-fresh-antitrust-fines-alibaba-and-tencent-signal

Ramli, D. (2021, September 8). *Ray Dalio defends investing in China, saying its opportunities can't be ignored.* Retrieved from Fortune: https://fortune.com/2021/09/08/ray-dalio-defends-china-investment-future-prospects-crackdown/

Reagan Foundation. (2023). *The Second American Reveolution: Reagnomics.* Retrieved from Ronald Regan Presidential Foundation & Institute: https://www.reaganfoundation.org/ronald-reagan/the-presidency/economic-policy/

Regilme Jr, S. S., & Hodzi, O. (2021). Comparing US and Chinese foreign aid in the era of rising powers. *Italian Journal of International Affairs*, 114-131.

Reiter, D. (2019, May 02). *Democratic Peace Theory.* Retrieved from Oxford Bibliographies: https://www.oxfordbibliographies.com/display/document/obo-9780199756223/obo-9780199756223-0014.xml

Ren, S. (2022, May 2). *China's 'Common Prosperity' drive morphs Into common poverty*. Retrieved from Bloomberg News: https://www.bloomberg.com/opinion/articles/2022-10-02/china-s-common-prosperity-drive-morphs-into-common-poverty-after-crackdowns

Reuters. (2017, January 16). *China's top judge warns courts on judicial independence*. Retrieved from Reuters: https://www.reuters.com/article/us-china-policy-law/chinas-top-judge-warns-courts-on-judicial-independence-idUSKBN1500OF

Reuters. (2018, March 4). *China says lifting term limits is about protecting authority of party*. Retrieved from Reuters: https://www.reuters.com/article/us-china-parliament-politics/china-says-lifting-term-limits-is-about-protecting-authority-of-party-idUSKBN1GG0CR

Reuters. (2021, December 20). *China to tighten antitrust legal enforcement - new antitrust bureau head*. Retrieved from Reuters: https://www.reuters.com/world/china/china-tighten-antitrust-legal-enforcement-new-antitrust-bureau-head-2021-12-19/

Reuters. (2022, March 4). *China's parliment can justify rubber stamp*. Retrieved from Reuters: https://www.reuters.com/breakingviews/chinas-parliament-can-justify-new-rubber-stamp-2022-03-04/

Rinke, A. (2021, November 17). *Germany may have been naive on China at first, Merkel says*. Retrieved from Reuters: https://www.reuters.com/world/europe/exclusive-germany-may-have-been-naive-china-first-merkel-says-2021-11-17/

Roberts, D. (2021, December 16). *What is "Common Prosperity" and how will it change China and its relationship with the world?* Retrieved from Atlantic Council: https://www.atlanticcouncil.org/in-depth-research-reports/issue-brief/common-prosperity/

Roberts, D. T. (2021, April 14). *How much support does the Chinese Communist Party really have?* Retrieved from Atlantic Council: https://www.atlanticcouncil.org/blogs/new-atlanticist/how-much-support-does-the-chinese-communist-party-really-have/

Rogin, J. (2022, August 11). *What China's overreaction to Pelosi's Taiwan visit really tells us*. Retrieved from The Washington Post: https://www.washingtonpost.com/opinions/2022/08/11/china-reaction-pelosi-visit-taiwan-reunification/

Romer, P. (2019, April 22). Paul Romer on Growth, Cities, and the State of Economics. (R. Roberts, Interviewer)

Ross, R. S. (2000). The 1995-96 Taiwan Strait confrontation: Coercion, credibility, and the use of force. *International Security*, 87-123.

Roy, D. (2022, April 12). *China's growing influence in Latin America*. Retrieved from Council on Foreign Relations: https://www.cfr.org/backgrounder/china-influence-latin-america-argentina-brazil-venezuela-security-energy-bri

Rozelle, S. (2022, June 7). Professor. (I. Mazzocco, Interviewer)

Ruan, L. Y. (2105, September 30). *The Chinese Communist Party and legitimacy.* Retrieved from The Diplomat: https://thediplomat.com/2015/09/the-chinese-communist-party-and-legitimacy/

Rudd, K. (2018, March 3). Prime Minister. (T. Harshaw, Interviewer)

Rudd, K. (2022, May 11). Prime Minister. (J. Bishop, Interviewer)

Rudd, K. (2022). *The avoidable war.* Public Affairs.

Ruwitch, J. (2018, March 16). *Timeline - The rise of Chinese leader Xi Jinping.* Retrieved from Reuters: https://www.reuters.com/article/us-china-parliament-xi-timeline/timeline-the-rise-of-chinese-leader-xi-jinping-idUSKCN1GS0ZA

Saich, T. (2015). *The National People's Congress: functions and membership.* Boston: Harvard Kennedy School.

Schram, S. R. (1971). Mao Tse-tung and the Theory of the Permanent Revolution, 1958-69. *China Quarterly* , 221-244.

Schull, A. (2022, March 10). *Putin has become so isolated during the pandemic that he no longer meets friends for 'drinks and barbecues,' a Russian journalist said.* Retrieved from Yahoo News: https://news.yahoo.com/putin-become-isolated-during-pandemic-031030994.html

Scissors, D. (2013, December 11). *The Importance of Chinese Subsidies.* Retrieved from American Enterprise Institute: https://www.aei.org/research-products/testimony/the-importance-of-chinese-subsidies/

SCMP. (2002, July 22). *Crossing the river by feeling the stones.* Retrieved from South China Morning Post: https://www.scmp.com/article/385907/crossing-river-feeling-stones

Scott, J. (1977). *The moral economy of the peasant: rebellion and subsistence in Southeast Asia.* New Haven: Yale University Press.

Sen, S., & Martin, P. (2022, May 17). *US seeks to wean India From Russia weapons with arms-aid package.* Retrieved from Bloomberg: https://www.bloomberg.com/news/articles/2022-05-17/us-seeks-to-wean-india-from-russia-weapons-with-arms-aid-package

Shapiro, J. (2015, March 9). *Supporting the status quo in the Asia-Pacific: An interview with General Vincent Brooks.* Retrieved from Brookings: https://www.brookings.edu/blog/order-from-chaos/2015/03/09/supporting-the-status-quo-in-the-asia-pacific-an-interview-with-general-vincent-brooks/

Sharwood, S. (2022, April 6). *China rolls out bots to enforce 'temporary closed-off management' of Shanghai.* Retrieved from The Register: https://www.theregister.com/2022/04/06/shanghai_lockdown_robots/

Shih, C.-y. (1998). A postcolonial reading of the state question in China. *Journal of Contemporary China* , 125-139.

Shullman, D. O. (2019, January 22). *Protect the Party: China's growing influence in the developing world.* Retrieved from Brookings: https://www.brookings.edu/articles/protect-the-party-chinas-growing-influence-in-the-developing-world/

Simalcik, M. (2016, December 25). *Confucianism in Chinese Foreign Policy: A Strategic-Cultural Analysis of the South China Sea Dispute.* Retrieved from SSRN: https://papers.ssrn.com/sol3/papers.cfm?abstract_id=2908834

Simmons , R., Thomas, D. W., & Yonk, R. (2010/2011). Bootleggers, baptists, and political entrepreneurs. *The Independent Review.*

Singapore, E. o. (2015, September 29). *Working together to forge a new partnership of win-win cooperation and create a community of shared future for mankind.* Retrieved from Ministry of Foreign Affairs (China): https://web.archive.org/web/20220506110818/https://www.mfa.gov.cn/ce/cesg/eng/jrzg/t1305051.htm

SIPRI. (2022, March 14). *SIPRI arms transfers database.* Retrieved from Stockholm International Peace Research Institute: https://www.sipri.org/databases/armstransfers

Skidmore, Z. (2022, January 27). *Will China continue its ban of Australian coal?* Retrieved from Mining Technology: https://www.mining-technology.com/features/australian-coal-china-ban/

Snyder, S. (2022, May 11). *China-South Korea relations under South Korea's new Yoon administration: The challenge of defining 'mutual respect'.* Retrieved from Forbes: https://www.forbes.com/sites/scottasnyder/2022/05/11/china-south-korea-relations-under-south-koreas-new-yoon-administration-the-challenge-of-defining-mutual-respect/?sh=6aaf6e2445cd

Somin, I. (2016, August 3). *Remembering the biggest mass murder in the history of the world.* Retrieved from Washington Post: https://www.washingtonpost.com/news/volokh-conspiracy/wp/2016/08/03/giving-historys-greatest-mass-murderer-his-due/

Song, Y. (2011, August 25). *Chronology of mass killings during the Chinese Cultural Revolution (1966-1976).* Retrieved from Mass Violence and Resistance - research network: https://www.sciencespo.fr/mass-violence-war-massacre-resistance/en/document/chronology-mass-killings-during-chinese-cultural-revolution-1966-1976.html

Songtian, L. (2009, September 8). How to achieve Win-Win Cooperation. Malawi.

Soon, W. (2022, March 23). *China's e-commerce giant JD.com is reportedly laying off at least 400 workers, adding to massive layoffs seen at other major Chinese tech firms like Alibaba and Tencent.* Retrieved from Insider: https://www.businessinsider.com/jdcom-said-to-ax-400-alibaba-tencent-might-fire-thousands-2022-3#:~:text=China's%20e%2Dcommerce%20giant%20JD,firms%20like%20Alibaba%20and%20Tencent&text=A%20bookmark%20An%20envelope.,ability%20to%20send%20an%20email.

Spegele, B. (2011, March 4). *National People's Congress: not just a rubber stamp session.* Retrieved from Wallstreet Journal: https://www.wsj.com/articles/BL-CJB-13428

St Louis Federal Reserve. (2023). *The Fed and the dual mandate*. Retrieved from St Louis Federal Reserve: https://www.stlouisfed.org/in-plain-english/the-fed-and-the-dual-mandate#:~:text=The%20Federal%20Reserve%20System%20has,other%20words%2C%20conducting%20monetary%20policy.

Standaert, M. (2021, March 24). *Despite pledges to cut emissions, China goes on a coal spree*. Retrieved from Yale Environment 360: https://e360.yale.edu/features/despite-pledges-to-cut-emissions-china-goes-on-a-coal-spree

State Council (China). (2015, May 8). *Notice of the State Council on printing and distributing "Made in China 2025"*. Retrieved from Gov.cn: Notice of the State Council on Printing and Distributing "Made in China 2025"

State Department (US). (2020, May). *Military-civil fusion and the People's Republic of China*. Retrieved from US State Department: https://www.state.gov/wp-content/uploads/2020/05/What-is-MCF-One-Pager.pdf

State Department (US). (2021, November 10). *U.S.-China Joint Glasgow Declaration on Enhancing Climate Action in the 2020s*. Retrieved from US Department of State: https://www.state.gov/u-s-china-joint-glasgow-declaration-on-enhancing-climate-action-in-the-2020s/

State Department (US). (2022, May 2). *People's Republic of China efforts to amplify the Kremlin's voice on Ukraine*. Retrieved from US Department of State: https://www.state.gov/disarming-disinformation/prc-efforts-to-amplify-the-kremlins-voice-on-ukraine/

State Department (US). (2023). *Bandung Conference (Asian-African Conference), 1955*. Retrieved from Office of the Historian: https://history.state.gov/milestones/1953-1960/bandung-conf

Steele , L. G., & Lynch , S. M. (2014). The pursuit of happiness in China: Individualism, collectivism, and subjective well-being during China's economic and social transformation. *Soc Indic Res.*

Strangio, S. (2021, August 6). *ASEAN grants United Kingdom 'Dialogue Partner' status*. Retrieved from The Diplomat: https://thediplomat.com/2021/08/asean-grants-united-kingdom-dialogue-partner-status/

Sun, L. (2022, April 26). *China's Hainan free-trade port tipped to deepen Asean ties, but island must 'brave' uncertainty*. Retrieved from South China Morning Post: https://www.scmp.com/economy/china-economy/article/3175452/chinas-hainan-free-trade-port-tipped-deepen-asean-ties-island

Sun, Y. (2015, September 21). *China's 3 desires: More influence, more Respect, and more Space*. Retrieved from Stimson Center: https://www.stimson.org/2015/chinas-3-desires-more-influence-more-respect-and-more-space/

Sweeney, P. (2022, March 3). *China's parliament can justify new rubber stamp*. Retrieved from Reuters: https://www.reuters.com/breakingviews/chinas-parliament-can-justify-new-rubber-stamp-2022-03-04/

Takala, R. (2021, July 23). *Jim Cramer Says Chinese regime is gunning for american investors: 'This is Stalinist'.* Retrieved from Mediate: https://www.mediaite.com/news/jim-cramer-says-chinese-regime-is-gunning-for-american-investors-this-is-stalinist/

Tan, C. (2018, March 14). *China spending puts domestic security ahead of defense.* Retrieved from Nikkei Asia: https://asia.nikkei.com/Spotlight/China-People-s-Congress-2018/China-spending-puts-domestic-security-ahead-of-defense

Tang, F. (2020, November 19). *What is China's dual circulation economic strategy and why is it important?* Retrieved from South China Morning Post: https://www.scmp.com/economy/china-economy/article/3110184/what-chinas-dual-circulation-economic-strategy-and-why-it

Tang, F. (2022, January 23). *China's wealth inequality has worsened in pandemic, highlighting 'alarming' global trend, Oxfam finds.* Retrieved from South China Morning Post: https://www.scmp.com/economy/china-economy/article/3164291/chinas-wealth-inequality-has-worsened-pandemic-highlighting

Tennant, C. (2022, August 27). *China's salami-slicing divide and conquer tactics in India are a warning of its growing aggression everywhere.* Retrieved from INews: https://inews.co.uk/news/world/china-salami-slicing-divide-conquer-tactics-india-aggression-1817547

Tharoor, I. (2020, October 7). *What the US Election Means in China.* Retrieved from Washington Post.

The Business Standard. (2021, July 23). *China threatens Japan with nuclear war over intervention in Taiwan.* Retrieved from The Business Standard: https://www.business-standard.com/article/international/china-threatens-japan-with-nuclear-war-over-intervention-in-taiwan-121072300030_1.html

The Economist. (2020, November 19). *Why commercial ties between Taiwan and China are beginning to fray.* Retrieved from The Economist: https://www.economist.com/business/2020/11/19/why-commercial-ties-between-taiwan-and-china-are-beginning-to-fray

The White House. (2006, April 20). *President Bush meets with President Hu of the People's Republic of China.* Retrieved from The White House: https://georgewbush-whitehouse.archives.gov/news/releases/2006/04/20060420-1.html

The White House. (2021). *Indopacific Strategy of the United States.* Washington, DC: The White House.

The White House. (2022, April 5). *FACT SHEET: Implementation of the Australia – United Kingdom – United States partnership (AUKUS).* Retrieved from The White House: https://www.whitehouse.gov/briefing-room/statements-releases/2022/04/05/

fact-sheet-implementation-of-the-australia-united-kingdom-united-states-partnership-aukus/

The-Chinese-People's-Political-Consultative-Conference. (2021, August 26). *Roles and functions of Chinese People's Political Consultative Conference.* Retrieved from The Chinese People's Political Consultative Conference: http://en.cppcc.gov.cn/overview.html

The-Economist. (2022, August 18). *The creative ways Chinese activists protest pollution.* Retrieved from The Economist: https://www.economist.com/china/2022/08/18/the-creative-ways-chinese-activists-protest-pollution

The-Royal-Swedish-Academy-of-Sciences. (1986, October 16). *Press release.* Retrieved from NobelPrize.org: https://www.nobelprize.org/prizes/economic-sciences/1986/press-release/

Thompson, E. (1971). The moral economy of the English crowd in the eighteenth century. *Past & Present,* 76-136.

Thu, H. L. (2022, April 22). *Japan's crucial role in Southeast Asia amid the Ukraine War.* Retrieved from Center for Strategic and International Studies: https://www.csis.org/analysis/japans-crucial-role-southeast-asia-amid-ukraine-war

Tibetan Government in Exile. (2023). *Brief introduction to Tibetan Government In-Exile.* Retrieved from The Office of Tibet-Pretoria: https://www.officeoftibet.com/index.php/2014-08-21-17-03-06/brief-introduction-to-tibetan-government-in-exile

Tilly, C. (2006). How and Why History Matters. In *The Oxford Handbook of Contextual Political Analysis.,* 417-437.

Times, G. (2021, August 21). *CHINA / POLITICS Xi Jinping thought added into curriculum: Ministry of Education.* Retrieved from Global Times: https://www.globaltimes.cn/page/202108/1232364.shtml

Ting, F. (2021, July 7). *Chinese social media giant WeChat shuts LGBT accounts.* Retrieved from Associated Press: https://apnews.com/article/media-social-media-technology-e4d565c04b5683be1263a2d90befe494

Torode, G., & Mai, N. (2018, March 3). *PAC MARCH 3, 201811:14 PMUPDATED 5 YEARS AGO Vietnam seeks to pacify China as landmark U.S. carrier visit signals warming ties.* Retrieved from Reuters: https://www.reuters.com/article/us-usa-vietnam-carrier/vietnam-seeks-to-pacify-china-as-landmark-u-s-carrier-visit-signals-warming-ties-idUSKCN1GG03W

Torrey, Z. (2017, October 10). *The human costs of controlling Xinjiang.* Retrieved from The Diplomat: https://thediplomat.com/2017/10/the-human-costs-of-controlling-xinjiang/

Tran, H. (2021, April 21). *Is the US-China strategic competition a cold war?* Retrieved from Atlantic Council: https://www.atlanticcouncil.org/blogs/new-atlanticist/is-the-us-china-strategic-competition-a-cold-war/

Treasury Department (US). (2023). *Chinese military companies sanctions.* Retrieved from US Department of Treasury: https://home.treasury.gov/policy-issues/financial-sanctions/sanctions-programs-and-country-information/chinese-military-companies-sanctions

Treaty of Shimonoseki. (1895, April 17). Shimonseki , Japan .

Trichet, J.-C. (2008, February 25). President. Frankfurt, Germany.

Tsang, S. (2021, December 02). Professor. (N. Luchsinger, Interviewer)

Tsang, S., & Cheung, O. (2021, March 2). *Uninterrupted rise: China's global strategy according to Xi Jinping thought.* Retrieved from The Asan Forum: https://theasanforum.org/uninterrupted-rise-chinas-global-strategy-according-to-xi-jinping-thought/

Turner, M. S. (2007). *Chinese Economic Coercion Against Taiwan: A Tricky Weapon to Use.* Santa Monica: Rand Corporation .

U.S.-China Economic and Security Review Commission. (2022, December 9). *China's position on Russia's invasion of Ukraine.* Retrieved from U.S.-China Economic and Security Review Commission: https://www.uscc.gov/research/chinas-position-russias-invasion-ukraine

Ullman, H. (2022, February 18). *Reality check #10: China will not invade Taiwan.* Retrieved from Atlantic Council: https://www.atlanticcouncil.org/content-series/reality-check/reality-check-10-china-will-not-invade-taiwan/

United Nations. (1966, December 16). International Covenant on Civil and Political Rights. New York City, New York, USA.

United Nations. (1966, December 16). International Covenant on Economic, Social and Cultural Rights. New York City, New York , USA.

United States Trade Representative. (2023). *The People's Republic of China.* Retrieved from Office of United States Trade Representative: https://ustr.gov/countries-regions/china-mongolia-taiwan/peoples-republic-china

United States Trade Representative. (2023). *The People's Republic of China.* Retrieved from Office of the US Trade Representative: https://ustr.gov/countries-regions/china-mongolia-taiwan/peoples-republic-china

University of Washington. (2023). *Essay: The Boxer Rebellion.* Retrieved from University Library (University of Washington): https://content.lib.washington.edu/chandlessweb/boxer.html#:~:text=This%20settlement%20allowed%20Austria%2C%20France,as%20%22spheres%20of%20influence%22.

University, O. (2106, September 12). *China's infrastructure investments 'threaten its economic growth'.* Retrieved from Oxford University: https://www.ox.ac.uk/news/2016-09-12-chinas-infrastructure-investments-threaten-its-economic-growth

US Mission China. (2021, November 17). *China remains the top sender of international students to the United States in 2020/2021*. Retrieved from U.S. Embassy & Consulates in China: https://china.usembassy-china.org.cn/china-remains-the-top-sender-of-international-students-to-the-united-states-in-2020-2021/#:~:text=According%20to%20the%20Open%20Doors,students%20in%20the%20United%20States.

USC Shoa Foundation. (2023). *Nanjing Massacre*. Retrieved from USC Shoah Foundation: https://sfi.usc.edu/collections/nanjing-massacre

US-Chamber-of-Commerce. (2022, February 16). *U.S. antitrust legislative proposals: A global perspective*. Retrieved from US Chamber of Commerce: https://www.uschamber.com/finance/antitrust/u-s-antitrust-legislative-proposals-a-global-perspective

US-China-Business-Council. (2023, January 23). *Chinese government*. Retrieved from US- China Business Council: https://www.uschina.org/resources/chinese-government

Vahabi, M. (2016). A positive theory of the predatory state. Public Choice, 153-175.

Victor, D. G. (2021, October 28). *Rebuilding US-Chinese cooperation on climate change: The science and technology opportunity*. Retrieved from Brookings: https://www.brookings.edu/blog/planetpolicy/2021/10/28/rebuilding-us-chinese-cooperation-on-climate-change-the-science-and-technology-opportunity/

Walker, C. (2018). What is "Sharp Power". *Journal of Democracy*, 9-23.

Walker, C. (2019, May 16). China's foreign influence and sharp power srategy to shape and influence democratic institutions. Washington, DC, USA.

Wang, A. (2022, June 15). *Sanctioned hardline former Xinjiang chief Chen Quanguo moves to rural affairs role for 'last job before retirement'*. Retrieved from South China Morning Post: https://www.scmp.com/news/china/politics/article/3181820/sanctioned-hardline-former-xinjiang-chief-chen-quanguo-moves

Wang, C. (2018, December). *CWIHP working paper 88*. Retrieved from Wilson Center: https://www.wilsoncenter.org/publication/the-chinese-communist-partys-relationship-the-khmer-rouge-the-1970s-ideological-victory

Wang, D. (2013). U.S.-China Trade, 1971–2012: Insights into the U.S.-China Relationship. *The Asia Pacific Journal*.

Wang, V., & Qian, I. (2022, May 7). *Shanghai residents in lockdown criticize China's 'zero Covid' strategy*. Retrieved from The New York Times: https://www.nytimes.com/2022/04/07/world/asia/shanghai-china-covid-protests.html

Wang, Y. (2020, September 1). *In China, the 'Great Firewall' Is changing a generation*. Retrieved from Politico: https://www.politico.com/news/magazine/2020/09/01/china-great-firewall-generation-405385

Wang, Y., & Minzer, C. (2015). The rise of the Chinese security state. *The China Quarterly* , 339-359.

Wang, Z. (2008). National humiliation, history education, and the politics of historical memory: Patriotic education campaign in China. *International Studies Quarterly*, 783-806.

Watanabe, S. (2021, November 3). *China's tutoring crackdown puts over 3 million jobs at risk*. Retrieved from Nikkei: https://asia.nikkei.com/Business/Education/China-s-tutoring-crackdown-puts-over-3-million-jobs-at-risk#:~:text=DALIAN%2C%20China%20%2D%2D%20China's%20drive,the%20sector%2C%20one%20analysis%20shows.

Wedeman, A. (2021, May 27). *Flies into tigers: The dynamics of corruption in China*. Retrieved from China Research Center: https://www.chinacenter.net/2021/china_currents/20-1/flies-into-tigers-the-dynamics-of-corruption-in-china/

Wees, G. v. (2020, December 1). *Has Taiwan always been part of China?* Retrieved from The Diplomat: https://thediplomat.com/2020/12/has-taiwan-always-been-part-of-china/

Wei , D., Low , D., & Hau , T. (2021). *China's Wild Summer of Stock Market Shocks*. Retrieved from Bloomberg Quint: https://www.bqprime.com/markets/china-s-wild-summer-of-stock-market-shocks-a-timeline

Weise, K., & Mozur, P. (2021, October 14). *LinkedIn to shut down service in China, citing 'challenging' environment*. Retrieved from The New York Times: https://www.nytimes.com/2021/10/14/technology/linkedin-china-microsoft.html

Wescott, B. (2021, July 25). *Xi Jinping set out to save the Communist Party. But critics say he made himself its biggest threat*. Retrieved from CNN: https://www.cnn.com/2021/07/25/china/xi-jinping-ccp-100-party-intl-hnk/index.html

Wilson Center. (2023). *Chinese foreign policy database*. Retrieved from Wilson Center: https://digitalarchive.wilsoncenter.org/theme/chinese-foreign-policy-database/timeline?year=1957

Wilson, J. (2021, November 9). *Australia shows the world what decoupling from China looks like*. Retrieved from Foreign Policy: https://foreignpolicy.com/2021/11/09/australia-china-decoupling-trade-sanctions-coronavirus-geopolitics/

Womack, B. (2017). International crises and China's rise: comparing the 2008 global financial crisis and the 2017 global political crisis. *The Chinese Journal of International Politics*, 383–401.

Wong, C. (2011). The fiscal stimulus programme and public governance issues in china. *OECD Journal on Budgeting*.

Wong, E. (2016, June 13). *Nearly 14,000 companies in China violate pollution rules*. Retrieved from The New York Times: https://www.nytimes.com/2017/06/13/world/asia/china-companies-air-pollution-paris-agreement.html

World Atlas. (2023). *Countries bordering the highest number Of other countries.* Retrieved from World Atlas: https://www.worldatlas.com/articles/countries-bordering-the-highest-number-of-other-countries.html

World Peace Foundation. (2016, December 14). *China: The cultural revolution.* Retrieved from Mass Atrocity Endings: https://sites.tufts.edu/atrocityendings/2016/12/14/china-the-cultural-revolution/

World Uyghur Congress. (2022). *East Turkistan.* Retrieved from World Uyghur Congress: https://www.uyghurcongress.org/en/east-turkestan-2/

Wright, L. (2022, May 31). *Rethinking China's economic future.* Retrieved from Rhodium Group: https://rhg.com/research/rethinking-chinas-economic-future/

Wu, G. (2022). *China's Common Prosperity program: Causes, challenge, and implications.* Asia Society Policy Insitute .

Wu, S. (2020, November 26). *China wields patriotic education to tame Hong Kong's rebellious youth.* Retrieved from Reuters: https://www.reuters.com/article/us-hongkong-security-education-insight/china-wields-patriotic-education-to-tame-hong-kongs-rebellious-youth-idUSKBN2861GE

Wu, W. (2019, Ocotber 30). *How Africa is breaking China's neo-colonial shackles.* Retrieved from The Interpreter: https://www.lowyinstitute.org/the-interpreter/how-africa-breaking-china-s-neo-colonial-shackles

Xi , J. (2021, July 1). Speech by Xi Jinping at a ceremony marking the centenary of the Communist Party of China. Beijing , China.

Xi, J. (2021, July 1). Full text of Xi Jinping's speech on the CCP's 100th anniversary. Beijing , China.

Xiaoshan, X. (2021, April 15). *Beijing revises 'correct' version of Party history ahead of centenary.* Retrieved from Radio Free Asia: https://www.rfa.org/english/news/china/history-04152021091451.html

Xie, S. Y. (2022, April 3). *Xi Jinping's 'Common Prosperity' was everywhere, but China backed off.* Retrieved from The Wall Street Journal: https://www.wsj.com/articles/xi-jinpings-common-prosperity-was-everywhere-but-china-backed-off-11648978380

Xin, Z. (2020, September 17). *China's Xi Jinping calls for loyalty from private sector as Beijing readies for battle with US.* Retrieved from South China Morning Post: https://www.scmp.com/economy/china-economy/article/3101942/chinas-xi-jinping-calls-loyalty-private-sector-beijing

Xinhua. (2008, August 8). *Beijing Olympics opening features four inventions of ancient China.* Retrieved from China.org: http://www.china.org.cn/olympic/2008-08/08/content_16167587.htm

Xinhua. (2013, December 24). *China promotes core socialist values.* Retrieved from China Daily USA: http://usa.chinadaily.com.cn/china/2013-12/24/content_17192145.htm

Xinhua. (2015, May 26). *Full text: China's mlitary strategy*. Retrieved from China.org: http://www.china.org.cn/china/2015-05/26/content_35661433_5.htm

Xinhua. (2017, October 24). *19th CCP Congress*. Retrieved from Xinhua News: http://www.xinhuanet.com/english/2017-10/24/c_136702025.htm

Xinhua. (2021, October 9). *Xi Focus: Xi says Taiwan question will be resolved as national rejuvenation becomes reality*. Retrieved from Xinhua: http://www.news.cn/english/2021-10/09/c_1310233813.htm

Xinhua. (2021, July 2). *Xi rallies Party for "unstoppable" pursuit to national rejuvenation as CPC celebrates centenary*. Retrieved from The National People's Congress of the People's Republic of China: http://www.npc.gov.cn/englishnpc/c23934/202107/6ff93d39da7548fbae37cbed01184c34.shtml

Xu, V. X. (2019, October 1). *China's youth are trapped in the cult of nationalism*. Retrieved from Foreign Policy: https://foreignpolicy.com/2019/10/01/chinas-angry-young-nationalists/

Xue, Y. (2021, October 22). *China's economic sanctions made Australia more confident*. Retrieved from The Interpreter: https://www.lowyinstitute.org/the-interpreter/china-s-economic-sanctions-made-australia-more-confident

Yang, D. (2020, March 10). *Wuhan officials tried to cover up covid-19*. Retrieved from Washington Post: https://www.washingtonpost.com/politics/2020/03/10/wuhan-officials-tried-cover-up-covid-19-sent-it-careening-outward/

Yang, E. (2021, March 28). *China attempts to silence western companies on Xinjiang*. Retrieved from American Institute for Economic Research: https://www.aier.org/article/china-attempts-to-silence-western-companies-on-xinjiang/

Yang, E. (2021, May 03). *China Unleashes Financial Tech Crackdown*. Retrieved from American Institute for Economic Research: https://www.aier.org/article/china-unleashes-financial-tech-crackdown/

Yang, E. (2021, April 21). *Taiwan: The new geopolitical and economic flash point*. Retrieved from American Institute for Economic Research: https://www.aier.org/article/taiwan-the-new-geopolitical-and-economic-flash-point/

Yang, E. (2021, September 3). *What can we lose to China by isolating Afghanistan?*. Retrieved from American Institute For Economic Research: https://www.aier.org/article/what-can-we-lose-to-china-by-isolating-afghanistan/

Yang, E. (2021, January 2021). *Where is Jack Ma?* Retrieved from American Institute for Economic Research: https://www.aier.org/article/where-is-jack-ma/

Yang, E. (2022, February 18). *Why China's aggression In Asia Is backfiring*. Retrieved from American Institute for Economic Research: https://www.aier.org/article/why-chinas-aggression-in-asia-is-backfiring/

Yang, Y. (2021, June 18). *How China is targeting Big Tech*. Retrieved from Financial Times: https://www.ft.com/content/baad4a14-efac-4601-8ce4-406d5fd8f2a7

Yang, Z. (2022, June 18). *Now China wants to censor online comments.* Retrieved from MIT Technology Review: https://www.technologyreview.com/2022/06/18/1054452/china-censors-social-media-comments/

Ye, N. (2020, September). *The 1911 Revolution and China's "Internationalist Nationalism":.* Retrieved from Yale Review of International Studies: http://yris.yira.org/global-issue/4210

Yeo, M. (2020, June 1). *China's missile and space tech is creating a defensive bubble difficult to penetrate.* Retrieved from Defense News: https://www.defensenews.com/global/asia-pacific/2020/06/01/chinas-missile-and-space-tech-is-creating-a-defensive-bubble-difficult-to-penetrate/

Yergin , D., & Stanislaw, J. (1998). *Deng Xiaoping.* Retrieved from Commanding Heights: https://www.pbs.org/wgbh/commandingheights/shared/minitext/prof_dengxiaoping.html

Yufan, H., & Zhihai, Z. (1990). China's decision to enter the Korean War: History revisited. *The China Quarterly*, 94-115.

Zhai, K., & Chun , H. (2021, June 29). *China's effort to tame 'Wolf Warrior' diplomats Is stymied by nationalism.* Retrieved from Wall Street Journal: https://www.wsj.com/articles/china-wants-howling-diplomats-to-quiet-down-but-nationalism-gets-in-the-way-11624962559

Zhao, D. (2009). The Mandate of Heaven and Performance Legitimation in Historical and Contemporary China. *American Behavioral Scientist*, 53(3), 416-433.

Zhang, J., & Vortherms, S. (2021, August 10). *Unstoppable force meets an immovable object: U.S.-China supply chains in the age of decoupling.* Retrieved from Wilson Center: https://www.wilsoncenter.org/blog-post/unstoppable-force-meets-immovable-object-us-china-supply-chains-age-decoupling

Zhang, P. (2021, October 26). *China's largest private education company cuts services for youngsters amid tutoring reforms.* Retrieved from South China Morning Post: https://www.scmp.com/news/people-culture/social-welfare/article/3153716/chinas-largest-private-education-company-cuts

Zhang, Z. (2021, September 9). *"996" is ruled illegal: understanding China's changing labor system.* Retrieved from China Briefing: https://www.china-briefing.com/news/996-is-ruled-illegal-understanding-chinas-changing-labor-system/#:~:text=%E2%80%9C996%E2%80%9D%20is%20Ruled%20Illegal%3A%20Understanding%20China's%20Changing%20Labor%20System,-September%209%2C%202021&text=China's%20top%

Zhao, S. (1998). A state-led nationalism: The Patriotic Education Campaign in Post-Tiananmen China. *Communist and Post-Communist Studies* , 287-302.

Zhen, S. K. (2017). Eminent domain in the United States and China: Comparing the practice across countries. *Inquiries Journal.*

Zheng, S. (2021, August 10). *China-US trade war: American retailers claim tariffs on Chinese goods hurt business during pandemic.* Retrieved from South China Morning Post: https://www.scmp.com/news/china/diplomacy/article/3144489/china-us-trade-war-american-retailers-claim-tariffs-chinese

Zhong, R. (2021, April 9). *China fines Alibaba $2.8 billion in landmark antitrust case.* Retrieved from New York Times: https://www.nytimes.com/2021/04/09/technology/china-alibaba-monopoly-fine.html

Zhou, C. (2019, Augut 24). *Why Macau hasn't been swept up by Hong Kong's pro-democracy protests.* Retrieved from ABC News: https://www.abc.net.au/news/2019-08-25/why-macau-hasnt-been-swept-up-by-hong-kong-protests/11432804

Zhou, C. (2021, April 27). *Xi Jinping tries to reassure China's private firms of their place in nation's economic development.* Retrieved from South China Morning Post: https://www.scmp.com/economy/china-economy/article/3131307/xi-jinping-tries-reassure-chinas-private-firms-their-place

Zhou, H. (2012). Internal Rebellions and External Threats: A Model of Government Organizational Forms in Ancient China. *Southern Economic Journal*, 78(4), 1120-1141.

Zhu, J., Yang, Y., & Yew, L. (2022, March 16). *Reeling from China's crackdown, Alibaba and Tencent readying big job cuts-sources.* Retrieved from Reuters: https://www.reuters.com/technology/reeling-chinas-crackdown-alibaba-tencent-readying-big-job-cuts-sources-2022-03-16/

Zhu, M. (2021, April 03). *Jury still out on China's legal reform and judicial independence.* Retrieved from South China Morning Post: https://www.scmp.com/economy/article/3128422/jury-still-out-chinas-legal-reform-and-judicial-independence

Zibang, X. (2022, June 21). *China buys $7.5 billion of Russian energy with crude oil at record.* Retrieved from Business Standard: https://www.business-standard.com/article/international/china-buys-7-5-billion-of-russian-energy-with-crude-oil-at-record-122062100024_1.html#:~:text=China's%20total%20imports%20from%20Russia,amount%20of%20a%20year%20ago.

About the Authors

Ryan M. Yonk is Senior Research Faculty at the American Institute for Economic Research. He holds a PhD from Georgia State University and a MS and BS from Utah State University. Prior to joining AIER he held academic positions at North Dakota State University, Utah State University, and Southern Utah University, and was one of the founders of the Strata Policy. He is the (co) author or editor of numerous books including *Green V. Green*, *Nature Unbound: Bureaucracy vs. the Environment*, *The Reality of American Energy*, and *Politics and Quality of Life: The Role of Well-Being in Political Outcomes*. He has also (co) authored numerous articles in academic journals including *Public Choice*, *The Independent Review*, *Applied Research in Quality of Life*, and the *Journal of Private Enterprise*. His research explores how policy can be better crafted to achieve greater individual autonomy and prosperity.

Ethan Yang is an Adjunct Research Fellow at the American Institute for Economic Research. He will receive his Juris Doctorate from Antonin Scalia Law School-George Mason University and obtained his BA from Trinity College in Hartford, Connecticut. While at Trinity, Ethan co-founded the Mark Twain Center for the Study of Human Freedom. His research focuses on Chinese political economy, foreign relations, technology policy, and antitrust law. Alongside his work at AIER, Ethan has held research positions at organizations such as the Cato Institute, Federal Trade Commission - Office of International Affairs, United States Senate, and BowerGroupAsia. He was also a Google Public Policy Fellow in 2023 where his work centered on domestic and international digital platform regulation.

INDEX

Made in the USA
Middletown, DE
28 May 2024

54805055R00136